Gothic Architecture

Louis Grodecki

Gothic Architecture

Contributions by Anne Prache and Roland Recht

Electa/RIZZOLI
NEW YORK

Produced under the supervision
of Carlo Pirovano, Editorial Director
of Electa Editrice

Design:
Diego Birelli

Layout:
Arturo Anzani

Photographs:
Bruno Balestrini

Drawings:
Studio Enzo di Grazia and Studio Lodolo-Süss

Translated from the French by
I. Mark Paris

ISBN 0-8478-0473-9
LC 82-62751
Printed in Italy

TABLE OF CONTENTS

Chapter I:
DEFINITIONS AND THEORIES/
HISTORICAL AND PHYSICAL CIRCUMSTANCES

DEFINITIONS AND THEORIES

The concept of Gothic art or architecture is unclear in that, unlike Carolingian art, for instance, it does not correspond to a well-defined historical or geographical locus; the formal, technical, and iconographical features most often associated with it are by no means invariable. In the final analysis, the term *Gothic* is a conventional label that art historians, yielding to tradition, have generally accepted, but whose meaning nonetheless varies according to interpretation. Italian writers in both the fifteenth century (Filarete, Manetti) and the sixteenth century (notably Vasari) used it to qualify western European art and architecture as a barbaric prelude to the Renaissance. From their point of view, the so-called *maniera tedesca* or *maniera dei Goti* was antithetical to those sound traditions of antiquity that reasserted themselves in the fifteenth and sixteenth centuries. Therefore, as proposed and unanimously accepted in the seventeenth century, the term was a pejorative one, used reproachingly to explain both ethnically and historically an alien interruption (cf. the invasions of the Early Middle Ages). Witness the reference in Molière's poem *La Gloire du Val de Grâce* (1669) to "... fade goût des ornements gothiques, Ces monstres odieux des siècles ignorants, Que de la barbarie ont produit les torrents..." ["... the insipid taste of Gothic ornamentation, these odious monstruosities of an ignorant age, produced by the torrents of barbarism..."]. The first movement to reevaluate medieval art began in the eighteenth century; such critics as Père Laugier, William Gilpin, and August Wilhelm Schlegel gave the term *Gothic* a positive, even laudatory connotation. However, the term met with some resistance in the nineteenth and twentieth centuries. For instance, a large number of German writers after Johann Wolfgang von Goethe considered this style the embodiment of Germanic genius, calling it *deutsche Architektur*; a smaller number of French writers, such as Camille Enlart, proposed instead the label *architecture française*. The latter group based their assertions on a passage from the chronicle of Burchard von Halle (c. 1280) that states that the Church of Bad Wimpfen (choir built 1269-74) was constructed "*opere francigeno*" ("in the French style"). For the time being, it appears that these nationalistic disputes have subsided and that the term *Gothic* has been universally accepted.

In general, those who attempt to define *Gothic* no longer refer to the nomadic civilizations—Franks, Teutons, and "Goths"—that invaded the West during the Early Middle Ages, even though certain authors (most recently, Hans Sedlmayr) still detect an "anti-Mediterranean" strain inimical to Greco-Roman civilization. This post-Romantic concept received blunt and naïve support in the early 1900s from such critics as Wilhelm Worringer.

In any case, present-day definitions of *Gothic* are based for the most part on technical, formal, and spatial observations, as well as on historical and ideological data.

The Componential Approach

Since the pioneer eighteenth-century studies on Gothic architecture, some critics have attempted to describe the Gothic style in terms of a certain number of characteristic distinguishing features. The first of these typical forms is the pointed arch, often given the name *ogive* (today this term is used to designate not the pointed arch but a rib that stretches diagonally across a vault). Originally a very ancient Eastern motif, the pointed design was introduced in the West during the eleventh century, not counting its earlier appearance in Muslim structures in Spain and Sicily. Its constant use throughout a period of several centuries, in decorative tracery as well as in arches, even gave rise to the now-abandoned term *ogival architecture*. Another essential component, according to this analytical approach, is vaulting supported by conspicuous intersecting arches. A less ubiquitous, but certainly no less typical feature is the flying buttress, an element that contributes importantly to church exteriors in certain countries. Eventually, historians accumulated a fairly large number of these singular forms, forms unknown either to Classical antiquity or to early medieval art. They include piers with bundles of engaged colonnettes, pinnacles (used to give additional weight to a buttress, often crowned with a small spire), gables, multifoil rose windows, and openings divided into multiple lancet-shaped sections. Various combinations of these forms have been singled out and used to distinguish national or regional aspects of Gothic architecture or to define its evolutionary stages. Thus, such designations as Rayonnant, Flamboyant, and, in England, Perpendicular Style have emerged from the observation of such isolated elements as window tracery, pier moldings, and the like.

Paul Frankl has called this conception of Gothic architecture "componential"; his idea had already appeared in the mid-nineteenth-century works of Arcisse de Caumont, Robert Willis, and Franz Mertens. Its principal merits—self-evidence and the kind of analysis indispensable to archaeologists—made it an attractive approach for many other writers as well. The evolution of each formal element, if accurately observed and described, would help the historian to arrive at precise chronologies, to judge relationships between edifices, to perceive influences, and, to a certain extent, to account for historical or geographical peculiarities.

The major shortcoming of this method or definition is that it does not yield the kind of synthesis that subordinates all formal elements according to the principles of coherence, convergence, or unity. It scarcely touches such general phenomena as absolute or relative dimensions, proportions, and systems of form or structure; moreover, it barely allows for a consideration of the wider problem of the historical or spiritual meaning of the total effect. In addition, this concept has led to serious—at times absurd—errors, which occur even in very recent studies. For example, if the pointed arch is considered an essential determining feature, then those structures whose principal contours consist of round arches—as, for

*1. Method of construction
of Gothic vaults, following
Viollet-le-Duc.*

2. A. Scheme of the interlacing of vault ribs.

1. Examples of French ribbing (left) and English ribbing
(right). Perspective and projection examples in the plans for
interlacing and binding the ribs in the Cathedrals of:
2. Exeter
3. Norwich
4. Peterborough.

*B. Schemes for covering cross-vaults with
projections of vaults.*

1. Pelplin (Poland): Cistercian Church
2. Braniewo (Poland): Parish Church
3. Wroclaw (Poland): Sandkirche
4. Burghausen (West Germany): Sankt Jakob
5. Prague: Choir of the Cathedral
6. Schwäbisch Gmünd: Heiligkreuzkirche
7. Annaberg (East Germany): Annenkirche.

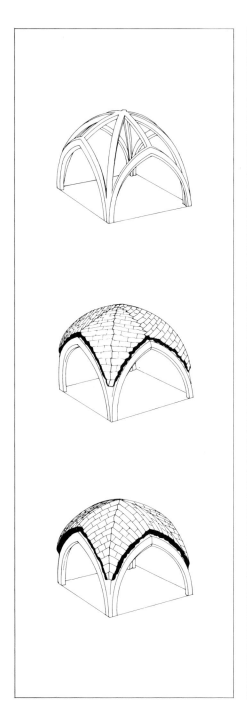

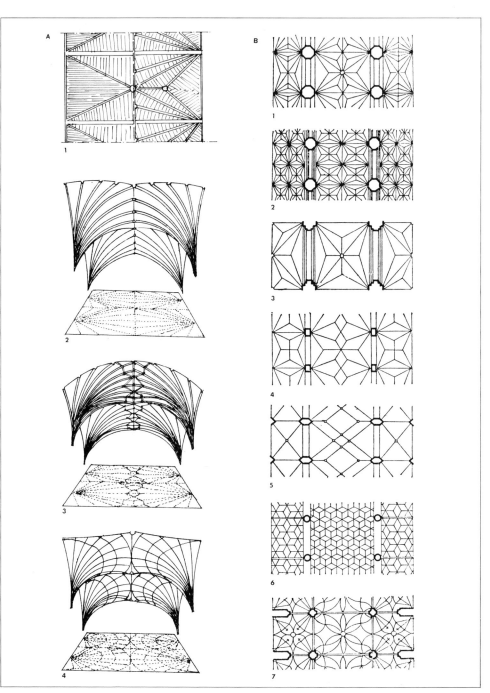

3. Structures of a Gothic nave,
following Viollet-le-Duc: Amiens,
Cathedral and Saint-Denis,
Abbey Church.

example, the façade of Laon Cathedral—must be excluded from the Gothic category. But if one considers the use of cross-ribbed vaulting a key element, then buildings dating from the twelfth century and even from the eleventh, such as the transept of Durham Cathedral, must be included.

The Structural Approach

About the middle of the nineteenth century, a period marked by the restoration of ancient monuments and the construction of Neo-Gothic edifices (the nave of Cologne Cathedral, Sainte-Clothilde in Paris), speculation about medieval architecture turned toward more technical considerations. Although a certain amount of credit is due to scholars in Germany (Johannes Wetter, Mertens) and England (Willis), the most eminent advocate of this critical perspective was the French architect Eugène Viollet-le-Duc. His lead was taken up by numerous archaeologists, historians, and architects right down to the present day, including Jules Quicherat, Auguste Choisy, and Marcel Aubert. "Everything is a function of structure," wrote Viollet-le-Duc, "the gallery, the triforium passage, the pinnacle, and the gable; no Gothic architectural form is the result of flights of fancy." This structural functionalism can best be illustrated by examining the vault and its system of support. Based on a logical system of diagonal arches (so-called ogives) and arches that enclose the vault field (transverse and wall arches), the thrust exerted by the groin vault is shifted from the walls to specific points on supporting masses. The formerly massive walls could now be reduced in thickness or replaced with windows. As a result of the curvature of the vaults and arches, the weight of the roofing is thrown out as localized oblique thrusts, which Gothic architects counterbalanced either by opposing thrusts (flying buttresses) or by calculated vertical pressures (pinnacles). This system is a dynamic one, as opposed to the static solutions of ancient architecture. Indeed, one might even call this system elastic. Since its constituent elements play diverse structural roles, thereby achieving a certain mutual independence, it can withstand and adjust to shifts in masonry resulting from sinking or buckling. The Gothic structural system thus allowed for a lightening of mass and afforded greater ease of vertical construction; the overall result was a clear distribution of components. Of course, this approach may also be applied to investigate the ongoing development of other structural solutions and the forms they engendered.

This seemingly scientific approach has been frequently contested. For instance, the presence of pointed arches or of diagonal arches under the roofing might be considered only preliminary pre-Gothic experiments. In addition, Georg Dehio and Mertens note that a substantial number of civil, military, and even religious edifices (i.e. nonvaulted churches) exist that are considered Gothic but that do not conform to this system. These

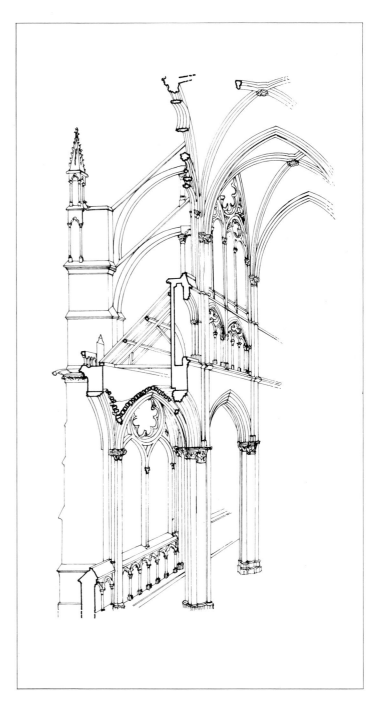

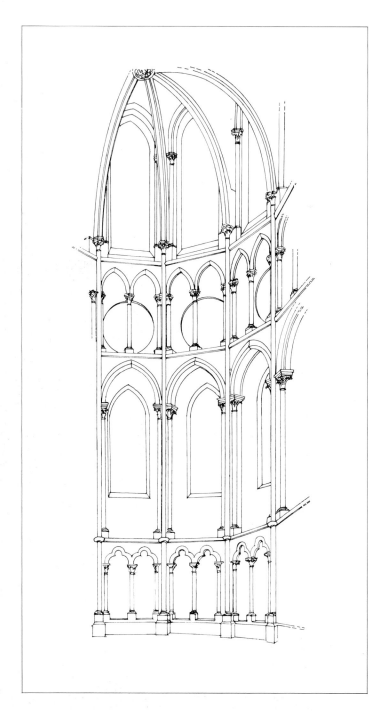

are structures whose builders were, for economic, technical, or aesthetic reasons, unable or unwilling to fully realize the style and who were satisfied with a kind of simplified Gothic. Pol Abraham and A. Kingsley-Porter contend that the presumed importance of the diagonal arch's supporting role is, in fact, often illusory and that the principles of dynamism and elasticity have been proved false by modern scientific analysis of medieval masonry. In any event, the ideas of Viollet-le-Duc are still used in the reinforcement and restoration of Gothic monuments; they have even nourished the development of modern versions of skeletal construction that feature rigorously localized thrusts. Not surprisingly, technicians always find the structural approach interesting. However, this functional definition hardly satisfies art historians. They not only feel that, in general, material structure alone can never adequately define a style, but also they believe that the formal traits of this particular style have little to do with material structure and that this proposed definition actually conflicts with historical fact.

The Spatial Approach

During the last quarter of the nineteenth century, the trend in archaeological and art historical studies toward establishing closer links with the human sciences gave rise to a new methodology. According to this concept (first proposed in Germany), every work of art—the architectural monument in particular—is a portion of space, both in the theoretical/geometric and in the experimental/physiological (i.e. visual or tactile) sense of the word. A building is a spatial structure, a creation with space, or, to use the expression of Henri Focillon, an "interpretation of space." Space is defined by its dimensions, its proportions, its division or unity, its location, its limits, and its visibleness.

A great deal of attention has been given to the problem of the proportions of interior spaces, and rightly so. Accustomed as they were to seventeenth- and eighteenth-century Baroque and Neoclassical architecture, nineteenth-century critics found it shocking, admirable, or simply noteworthy that buildings from the 1200s and 1300s—especially the naves of such large churches as the cathedrals of Beauvais, Cologne, and York—were erected "vertically" of high and narrow proportions and were much longer than they were wide. Furthermore, these proportions are accentuated by the linear arrangement of the piers and colonnettes that support the vaulting. As early as the eighteenth century (Goethe), this space was considered fantastic or "sublime." More recently, such archaeologists as Dehio, Walter Ueberwasser, Frankl, and Maria Velte have seriously endeavored to rediscover the Gothic "system of proportions." To this end various tools have been pressed into service: building measurements; speculation about old documents; drawings of major projects (the cathedrals of Vienna and Strasbourg, for example); references in texts pertaining to construction, such as the famous minutes of the

technical reports (1391-1400) about Milan Cathedral; and indications given by medieval philosophical treatises, such as those of Saint Thomas Aquinas. Hans R. Hahnloser's close examination of the thirteenth-century manuscript of Villard de Honnecourt and Robert Branner's study of the drawings of Reims Cathedral both show that the quest for geometric proportions was indeed a constant preoccupation in the Middle Ages. Several of these systems, though innovative, were based on the equilateral triangle, the square, the circle, and parts of the circle; they were not destined to be retained by the Renaissance.

An even more characteristic feature of Gothic architecture is the division of interior space in edifices both large and small, civil and ecclesiastical alike. As they travel along walls or piers, the ribs of oblong, square, or trapezoidal vaults conspicuously delineate distinct portions of space. These spatial cells, in turn, are juxtaposed lengthwise in a transverse, oblique, or semicircular manner. Whether the cells are equal or, as is often the case, different in size, this spatial disposition constituted a wholly original formal and structural system unknown to antiquity or to the Early Middle Ages. Some scholars have emphasized the mathematical or geometric nature of this arrangement. Frankl, for instance, sees this as a creation by division, as opposed to Romanesque architecture's creation by addition; but Viollet-le-Duc, along with August Schmarsow and Wilhelm Pinder, agree upon the term *articulated architecture*. Regardless of the label one finally chooses, the phenomenon in question remains the same: a system based on the combination of visually and logically distinct parts, whose simplified version may be found in unvaulted Gothic halls and buildings.

However, the converse of the partition theory of Gothic space is Focillon's and Jean Bony's notion of spatial unification, the creation of an interior void that is visionary in nature. The multiple interaction of longitudinal, transverse, oblique, and vertical perspectives; the sheer number of elements in play; the superposition of interior levels; and the gradual reduction in supporting masses within the edifice—all of these features, according to this approach, contribute to the visual impression that the actual dimensions of the building have been increased.

One of the most obvious and frequently studied aspects of Gothic space is the graphic or linear quality of its component boundaries. That is, the colonnettes and moldings extend the ribs of the vaulting, dress the piers, divide and subdivide the surfaces of interior partitions, and accentuate the structural divisions of exterior surfaces. The contours of the vertical, horizontal, or oblique moldings are thus designed to multiply the strokes of a profuse—at times overwhelming—script. Is this feature determined by the structural system, as Viollet-le-Duc believed? Should we, together with Abraham, interpret it as a surface phenomenon that expresses structural functions? Perhaps, as Erwin Panofsky claims, it corresponds to a general artistic mode shared by painting and sculpture, according to which the space and depth of the real world are conceived, imagined, and represented as the physical counterparts of the spiritual world. The development of this linearity might have indeed been favored by the tendency of medieval architectural design to reduce space to plane surfaces. Whatever its ultimate justification may be, several writers have underscored the importance of this characteristic in the discussion of Gothic design. Ernst Gall uses it to explain the origins of the style; Werner Gross, its evolution; Dagobert Frey, its last flowering at the end of the Middle Ages.

The boundaries of interior space and exterior volumes—walls and partitions—have been carefully examined as well. Hans Jantzen has proposed a series of observations to be interpreted according to what he called the "principle of diaphanousness." For example, the walls of Gothic churches were often furnished with passages (galleries, triforia, other thoroughfares at window level) whose visible far ends create the impression that the wall surface has been doubled. Just as widespread was the application of a blind arcade to a wall. In addition, the piers separating side aisles from nave are no longer perceived as chunks of wall, but as independent volumes or bodies that stand out from the aisle wall. As for the exterior, one can similarly analyze the flying buttresses, their supports, or any other protruding abutment. All of these surround the actual walls with volumes that are materially and visually separate from them. Generally speaking, the perception of spatial boundaries is imprecise; and the complexity of the decorative sculpture—it too "stands out" from the wall—compounds that of the wall space.

An even more obvious and ubiquitous tendency is the lightening and opening up of the walls. Gradually, translucent partitions filled with stained-glass windows replaced the pierced continuous walls of Romanesque architecture. The mural surface was reduced to a very small proportion and, in fact, virtually eliminated. Viollet-le-Duc, Max Dvořak, Aubert, and Focillon all consider this dematerialization one of the most typical facets of Gothic architectonics. Was this simply the logical and fortunate outgrowth of a structural system pushed to its furthest technical limits? Or did the desire to allow more light into the building come first, thus forcing the architects to seek the necessary structural solution? The author has pointed out elsewhere that, in any case, the overall effect of the largest openings is spectacularly enhanced by the customary presence of extremely colorful stained-glass windows. The thinning down of the wall remains one of the most significant features of Gothic architecture, despite the fact that this trend did not assert itself everywhere with equal force.

Of all possible ways, it is probably the investigation of the problem of light as form and symbol that leads to the most valid definitions of Gothic space. There were many solutions less extreme and ideal than the translucent or luminescent wall. One might, for instance, place larger

6. *Example of the method of construction of a Gothic vault.*

7. *Problem of the measurements of Gothic cathedrals; sections of the Cathedral of Cologne.*

8. *The problem of equal rhythm in classical French Gothic style.*

Comparison in the same scale of the arrangement of the parts of the nave of the Cathedrals of:
1. Noyon
2. Laon
3. Paris
4. Chartres
5. Reims
6. Amiens.

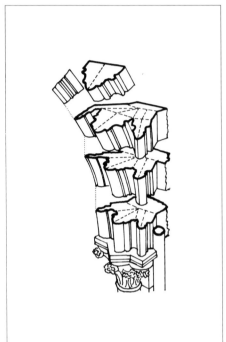

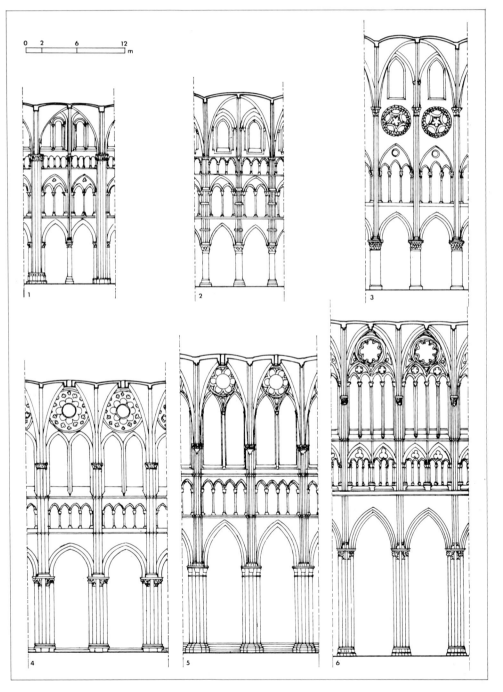

numbers of windows at the upper levels of the structure or in such key areas as the choir and the arms of the transept. It should be understood that Gothic space is not merely an enclosed volume to be geometrically defined. It is a function of light; it is transfigured by light. In fact, this concept is stated unequivocally in medieval texts to which the builders of these churches had access. All formal and most structural approaches to Gothic architecture were superseded by the definition (proposed by Otto von Simson, Panofsky, and Sedlmayr) that utilizes the notion of "light-space" to interpret the medieval church as the material realization of spiritual ideas, religious or philosophical. Purely formal, spatial, and structural analyses all appear to be inadequate tools in the search for a precise delineation of this architectural style.

Historical and Iconographical Definitions

Because most important Gothic monuments were intended for religious use, it is quite natural that Gothic architecture in general should be interpreted or even defined in the context of religious meaning. The theological, didactic, liturgical, and mystical texts of medieval writers constantly refer to the significance of the physical church. In their view, it is literally the House of God, the dwelling place of his mystical person, or the material manifestation of such spiritual phenomena as the community of the faithful or the Church of the Elect. Sedlmayr points out that it was even considered the temporal image of Paradise, of the New Jerusalem. Although this symbolic level was already operative in the primitive Christian basilica, it received a much clearer and better coordinated formal expression in the Gothic church. The vertical and horizontal sweep of twelfth-, thirteenth-, and fourteenth-century cathedrals, together with the flood of light—symbol of the grace of God— allowed to pass through immense, fantastic openings in the walls, expresses better that at any other time the mystical potential of Christian architecture. The author has noted elsewhere that the multicolored, luminescent stained-glass windows were compared to the precious stones said to encrust the walls of the New Jerusalem, and that the numerous towers and pinnacles evoke similar structures that appear in the visions of Saint John. Since the cathedral is the image of the Christian universe, a cosmic symbolism imposes an arrangement of iconographical elements (sculptures, paintings, and windows) that conforms with mystical or didactic cycles (Emile Mâle). Let us note that these are not hasty interpretations, inspired by lyrical admiration. If Gothic architecture is proposed not as a structure or spatial field but as an illustration of religious thought, one can certainly base this valid, though complex, definition on the fact that the traditional symbols and allusions of Christian liturgy do indeed carry truly universal meanings (Joseph Sauer and Sedlmayr).

A different set of interpretations springs from medieval theology and philosophy. The mystical current of thought during the Middle Ages inspired a coherent aesthetics whose notions of material and immaterial, of ugly and beautiful, were spiritualized and revealed in the immaterialization of the edifice (terminology of Dvořak and Edouard de Bruyne). Moreover, Dehio and especially Panofsky have related the essence of Gothic architectural design to the current of medieval Scholastic logic. Specifically, arrangement of parts to the whole through hierarchical subdivision is seen to characterize both the architect's approach and the format of the theological *Summa*. The birth and evolution of Gothic, therefore, follow those of Scholastic thought, from Peter Abelard to Albertus Magnus; the principles of Scholastic dialectic appear to be borne out in architectural design. There is, in fact, little to prevent one from applying the tenets of logical thought contemporaneous with these buildings in order to explain the functional or decorative role of their elements.

Political and sociological considerations have also been brought into play. Gothic art is sometimes viewed as the expression of the feudal age. On the other hand, it has also been interpreted as the harbinger of modern civilization, its architecture paralleling the advent of new social structures. To be sure, feudal organization itself was being contested by the middle of the twelfth century; in certain countries, it was even entering a period of decline. Nevertheless, a certain schema of social hierarchy, of external forms, did subsist and shape attitudes up to and beyond the end of the Middle Ages. The ostentatious nobility of civil and military architecture in general—the châteaux of lords and bishops in particular—was often imbued with knightly ideals. Nor did religious architecture prove to be immune to this kind of pomp as soon as political motives entered into the organization of the decor (witness the extraordinary sumptuousness of projects sponsored by kings and nobles). In any case, even if political connotations obtain in certain French cathedrals, or in the Sainte-Chapelle in Paris, they still cannot be deemed a decisive factor (G. Bandmann). Viollet-le-Duc maintained instead that the blossoming of the Gothic style was a consequence of the liberalization of the cities and of the building professions. Allowing for the fact that the role of thirteenth-century communities in Italy or in the North (Strasbourg, Lübeck) did, in fact, expand and frequently predominate by the end of the Middle Ages, this remains nonetheless an external circumstance. What must be stressed is the manner in which social transformations (mendicant orders, parishes, etc.) brought about changes in Gothic architecture. We will consider this topic at a later point.

The most striking aspect of this brief résumé is that the prolific efforts on the part of art historians, spanning more than a hundred years, have resulted in a cumulative array of analytical approaches, each of which has its particular merits. Some are helpful in guiding research, others facilitate works of restoration, and still others help one better to understand the prodigious richness of Gothic architectural form. Although these methods open up various perspectives on the nature of Gothic, none

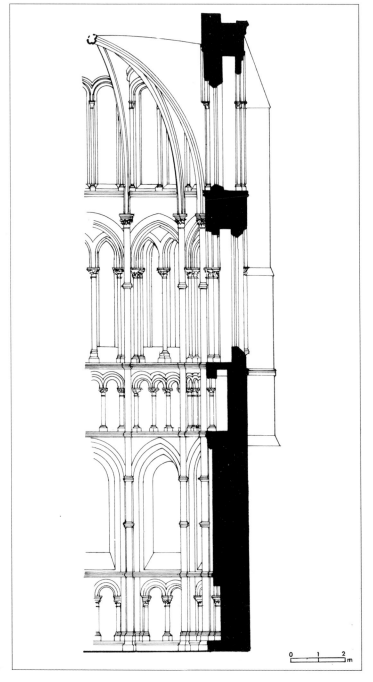

9. Elevation of a part of the choir and of the transept of the Cathedral of Noyon.

of them give it a firm, rigorous definition. Political and social factors sometimes induce diverse local variations; many of these lose their validity as the definition of Gothic undergoes successive stages of development. But there are two other determining factors in the history of this style that Frankl has dubbed the exemplary *Werdenstil*. The first is what Focillon called *la vie des formes*: the idea of Gothic is subjected to continual metamorphosis due to old traditions, new influences, and formal innovations determined by the internal dialectic of historical evolution. The second is man himself—the creator who, in a single stroke, can alter the course of history.

Historical and Physical Circumstances

The geographical expansion of Gothic architecture reflects the spread of Roman Catholicism throughout Europe. From the time of the last unsuccessful efforts to achieve Christian unity in the eleventh century, the Eastern Church bore the cultural and artistic stamp of the Byzantine tradition. Although the boundary between these influences roughly cuts north to south through central Europe, one must also take into account the effect of missions and other temporary Western encroachments in the East: the Holy Land and the islands of Cyprus and Rhodes were all exposed to Gothic art. The conquests resulting from the First, Second, and Third Crusades (1097-98, 1148-50, and 1204, respectively) permitted the establishment of Latin kingdoms and Venetian colonies that were to last until the end of the Middle Ages. In general, the Gothic domain encompassed the following regions: the British Isles, Scandinavia, the Netherlands, and France, together with the Holy Roman Empire and its political or cultural dependencies (Bohemia, Poland, Hungary, and the Baltic areas Christianized by military orders). In the Mediterranean basin, the domain of Gothic included the Iberian peninsula, Italy, the eastern shore of the Adriatic, and the former Roman colonies in Greece and Asia Minor. For purposes of art history, we may exclude the later efforts to implant the Gothic style in the Portuguese and Spanish colonies of America and Africa.

The widely diverse climates and geographical/geological characteristics of these countries and territories, along with their varying economic, political, and social rhythms, sometimes produced different building techniques. Indeed, these regional *tempi* during the so-called Gothic period (c. 1150-1450 and, in some areas, up to and beyond the end of the sixteenth century) were divergent in the extreme. For instance, medieval European population statistics, so far as we can analyze them, reveal incredible disparities. While northern France in the twelfth and thirteenth centuries was studded with parish churches, rich abbeys, and local strongholds of the nobility, building activity in countries marked by more highly developed urban concentrations was limited to a few important cities. Furthermore, countries farther north were less gravely affected by

10. Le Mans, Cathedral, vaults.

the harsh demographic and economic depression of the mid-fourteenth century than were France and Italy. Therefore, the historian must investigate building conditions peculiar to individual countries, even individual monuments.

Gross economic imbalances resulted from the fact that great concentrations of wealth, at first limited to a few nobles and to rich, powerful monasteries, soon spread to Italian, Catalonian, and Hanseatic bankers. On both the international and local scales, the permanent chaos of medieval economy prior to the fifteenth century complicates the evaluation of its role in the development of architecture. As Roberto López points out, paradoxical situations were by no means uncommon. Whereas small cities such as Amiens possess immense, luxurious structures, great economic capitals such as Cologne, for all their ambition, were unable to finance such projects. Only by the 1400s had the disastrous economic effects of the preceding century been eradicated, and the cities and regions now grown quite wealthy—Flanders, Normandy, the cities of Tuscany, and southern Rhenish Germany—entered into architectural competition. It is only at this point that the economic forces involved in Gothic art can be clearly perceived.

It is just as difficult to get a precise idea of the impact of social and political history. The incredible tangle of international conflicts, not to mention the even greater number of civil wars, makes an easy determination of the effect of such events almost impossible. Yet, this is precisely what historians have been trying to do since the mid-1800s. Generally speaking, great historical movements either facilitate or obstruct contacts, favor expansion or retrenchment, and explain periods of crisis or prosperity. During the formation and initial successes of Gothic architecture (c. 1150-1250), two preeminent political facts overshadowed western European history. The first was the organizational struggle for the Empire and supremacy in the West, brought about by the Hohenstaufens and their old investiture disputes. The second was the Norman Conquest in 1066 and the subsequent territorial and political interpenetration of France and England. Of course, one should also mention the Reconquest of Spain and the consolidation of the states in the Iberian peninsula, as well as the Byzantine conflict arising from the establishment of Western power at Constantinople in 1204.

It is very tempting to link the movement of influential Anglo-Norman art before 1150 to the vicissitudes of Anglo-French relations. L. Olschki, for instance, sees nascent French Gothic as a "royal" phenomenon that coincided with the efforts of Louis VI and Louis VII to consolidate monarchical authority. Likewise, one may wish to equate architecture in the Anjou and Maine regions with the Plantagenet Empire of Henry II of England and Eleanor of Aquitaine. It is also feasible to attribute to the southern orientation of the Hohenstaufens the magnificent blossoming of Late Romanesque (*Spätromanisch*) in the Rhineland and in the Holy

Roman Empire, with its Lombard and Italian elements and its borrowings from Sicilian Byzantine art. If this is indeed the case, such a political presence might explain the failure of Gothic initiatives to penetrate Italy and the Empire. Finally, one may justify the Gothic incursion into the Iberian peninsula by referring to the fact that, during the last third of the twelfth century, politics in the south of France were oriented toward Spain.

The thirteenth century brought an end to the dream of a pan-European *imperium*. There was a shift in the Western balance of power, especially after the deaths of Frederick II (1250) and his son Conrad IV (1254). Political anarchy reigned in Germany, thereby opening her frontiers to any and all artistic currents. For the time being, the Treaty of Paris in 1259 settled the Anglo-French conflict, and after the successes of Philip II and Louis VIII in southern France, the French monarchy entered upon an era of undisputed economic expansion and heightened prestige. This was the so-called Century of Saint Louis, an epoch that extended French hegemony from Spain to the short-lived Sicilian kingdom of Charles d'Anjou. Even the papacy succumbed: it was transferred to Avignon. French art in general, and Gothic art in particular, spread rapidly through the West and even won out in such resistant areas as the Rhineland. However, beginning in the late 1200s, national reactions against this hegemony began to develop in Catalonia, Aragon, Tuscany, and England. As a result, regional variants of French Gothic began to appear everywhere (Gross and K. Gerstenberg).

Due to political, economic, and demographic factors, the international balance was again disrupted in the second quarter of the fourteenth century. An interminable war between France and England (1338-1453) gradually ruined the economies of the two countries, slowing or putting a halt to construction. The population of Europe was considerably reduced by the Black Death of 1347-51 and by other epidemics and famines. In addition, from the twelfth century on, pressures exerted by Asian peoples (Tartars, Turks, etc.) took the form of destructive raids in central and eastern Europe; and this movement prompted migrations, the founding of new cities, and the development of defensive architecture. Thus, the tendency toward greater international contact was, to a certain extent, counterbalanced by the slowdown in building and the dispersion of influences. If a genuine artistic internationalism did take root in Europe prior to 1400, architecture—except for the so-called Flamboyant Style—had little to do with it.

During this same period (1380-1420), a new order of political events and a new socio-cultural situation were taking shape in western Europe. The feudal system, now reduced to a purely superficial phenomenon, bowed to the authority of monarchs and princes: concentration of power became the political order of the day. In the face of this authority, free cities and aristocratic republics (as in Italy) arose that had at their disposal considerable financial resources. Consider, for example, the defeat of the Grand Duchy of Burgundy—one of the most ambitious political enterprises of the century—at the hands of municipal militias during the Battle of Grandson. The expansion of the Holy Roman Empire, directed since 1440 by the new and powerful Austria of the Hapsburgs, could be disturbed only by interference from the free cities within the Empire itself. Despite the continuing menace of the Turks—they had vanquished the last Byzantine pockets of resistance and now occupied a portion of southeastern Europe—the West prospered, expanded, and showed itself ripe for colonial adventures in Africa and America. During these years, building activity flourished. Work on long-abandoned sites was now begun anew, and nobles competed with each other to erect sumptuous private or religious structures. The newly enlarged, affluent merchant and industrial cities of Flanders, Germany, and Catalonia established new parishes and erected municipal buildings. In fact, so prolific was fifteenth-century Gothic architecture that a satisfactory history of its development has yet to be written. Apart from certain exceptional cases—the completion of Milan Cathedral, and the construction of Pienza Cathedral by a Germanophile pope—Italy proceeded to separate herself from the Gothic world in pursuit of a new artistic and humanistic ideal.

However, Gothic was not completely overwhelmed by the rapid, triumphant intrusion of the Italian Renaissance, even if various decorative elements or general designs were occasionally subject to Italianate influence (e.g. in the northern Alps or the Iberian peninsula). The new movements of European politics, dominated by the rise of the Hapsburgs and the nascent power of Spain, often met with resistance from firmly established national traditions. In England, for instance, Gothic left its mark on nonecclesiastical architecture as late as the seventeenth century. Certain masterpieces of Gothic art in Spain and Portugal (such as Belém in Portugal) date from the sixteenth century. Only the pressures of the Counter-Reformation and Jesuit expansion would be sufficiently powerful to impose Italian models on French and English religious architecture.

It appears that the multiple, contradictory political and economic forces of the Middle Ages favored the tendency to break up lines of homogeneous evolution, to diversify environments, and to particularize structures. Yet, a common Gothic art—with variations, to be sure—did manage to emerge in the West. In fact, one conceives of European unity more readily in terms of architecture than of historical events. Focillon wrote: "The most significant documents about the Middle Ages are its edifices." Needless to say, this unity owed its continuity and coherence to the religious movement that inspired the greatest and most remarkable of these edifices. Although the Church encountered innumerable crises during the Gothic period—schisms, heresies, internal struggles, and con-

flicts with civilian power—nothing could crack its profound unity, its internationalism. This spirit was rooted not only in the countless contacts among clergymen, linked already by a common language and a common evangelistic purpose, but also in the dense network of parallel or supplementary institutions. Two factors stand out in particular: the centralized organization of the Roman Church, and the religious orders, which were almost always international in scope.

The Romanesque era, the so-called age of monasticism, is sometimes contrasted to the Gothic era, the age of cathedrals. This, however, is a false antithesis: the role of religious orders did not diminish with the advent of Gothic art. As a matter of fact, the chief promoters of Gothic in the twelfth century were the Benedictines in Normandy, England, and France. Certain English cathedrals, such as Durham, are Benedictine projects; in France, Saint-Denis Vézelay, and Saint-Remi at Reims are all Benedictine abbey churches. Although the order attained the peak of its financial and political power in the 1100s, it continued to enjoy a wealthy status throughout the Middle Ages. Some of its more impressive constructions or reconstructions in France include Saint-Nicaise at Reims, Saint-Ouen at Rouen, Saint-Robert at La Chaise-Dieu, and the choir of Mont-Saint-Michel; in England, Westminster Abbey, Tynemouth, and the reconstructed Benedictine cathedral at Canterbury. Benedictine efforts continued into the fifteenth and sixteenth centuries, with such projects as Saint-Jacques at Liège and Sankt Ulrich at Regensburg.

From the time of their founding, the Cistercians were likewise associated with the expansion of Gothic architecture. Inaugurated in Burgundy at the beginning of the twelfth century as a result of the reform of the Benedictine rule, this new order underwent prodigious growth. Between 1112 and 1152, 343 Cistercian monasteries were founded; by the end of the Middle Ages, nearly 750 Cistercian monasteries for men—and 750 for women—were scattered throughout western Christendom. Architecturally speaking, although the Cistercians first utilized Romanesque design to reflect their spirit of poverty, the monks soon became the principal disseminators of Gothic architecture as far east as Poland and as far to the southeast as Hungary. Moreover, they began to incorporate more elaborate and luxurious elements into their buildings during the thirteenth century.

Less widespread—but no less significant—was the influence of the Carthusians and the Premonstratensians. Established in 1084 by Saint Bruno at La Grande Chartreuse, near Grenoble, the Carthusian rule required a spirit of contemplation and an ideal of austerity. It flourished in virtually every Christian area, especially in Germany, France, Italy, and Spain. By the end of the medieval era, their vast monastic structures, often raised near cities (Paris, Nuremberg, Dijon, Pavia), numbered about 200; many of them were set up by such nobles as the duke of Burgundy (Champmol, near Dijon) and the Visconti (Pavia).

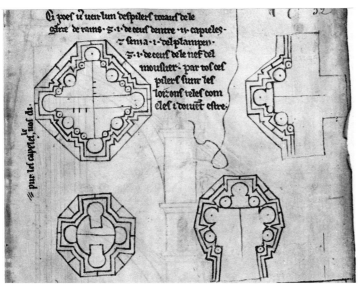

13. Plans of pillars and other designs. From the Notebook of Villard de Honnecourt, Fr. 19093, f. 32. Paris, Bibliothèque Nationale.

Of all the active religious orders, none did more to transform thirteenth- and fourteenth-century art than the mendicant orders—the Dominicans and the Franciscans. After an initial period of activity under the direction of Saint Dominic, the Dominican order was officially founded in 1215. In 1221, there were 60 Dominican convents; by 1359, there were 612, not counting the more than 350 convents for women. The Dominican vows focused on action through speech: directing the conscience of the people through preaching and teaching. The Dominicans quickly became teachers at schools and universities; at the University of Paris, medieval Scholasticism reached its zenith under the influence of Albertus Magnus and Saint Thomas Aquinas. Moreover, as prime opponents of heresy, they waged Inquisition-like battles against such groups as the Cathari at the time of the crusade against the Albigensians. In order to maintain contact with the people, the Dominicans built their churches and convents in cities. In general, their architectural style is sober, but occasionally marked by vast and grandiose dimensions designed to accommodate large crowds. Since it was they who imparted new vigor to medieval religious and moral thought, it was only natural that, beginning in 1250, their architecture became imprinted with the stamp of that vitality.

Contemporaries of the Dominicans, the Franciscans (rule accepted by the Holy See in 1222) not only had a similar organization consisting of national provinces directed by a central authority, but also they sought to work directly with the faithful. Nourished on the mystical thought of Saint Francis of Assisi, the order was originally vowed to poverty, charitable assistance, and social action, but it soon compromised these principles. As for their architecture, the minor friars, male and female orders alike, built their structures in cities, not counting the admirable mother church at Assisi. In fact, a kind of competition arose between them and the Dominicans, as illustrated in the study by F. Antel of the situation in Tuscany at the beginning of the fifteenth century. One notes that Franciscan convents were usually of more modest dimensions and less richly decorated than those of the Dominicans. However, from the fourteenth century on, the immense success of Franciscan thought, especially in Italy, attracted memberships and donations that eventually caused its architectural efforts to belie the former vow of poverty (for example, Santa Croce in Florence). In any event, they, like the Dominicans, constituted a great propagating force in the expansion of Gothic architecture, especially toward Eastern countries.

Lastly, we must not omit the military orders that emerged at the time of the reconquest of the Holy Land, from the late 1000s to the early 1100s—Knights Templars (Poor Knights of Christ), Knights Hospitalers (Order of the Hospital of Saint John of Jerusalem), and others. They constructed castles, or commanderies, both in the Holy Land and on sites that marked stations along the pilgrimage route to Jerusalem. Although the subsequent Muslim reconquest from the midtwelfth century through the thirteenth forced them out of the East, they subsisted in Europe until 1309, making no significant contributions to architectural development. On the other hand, the Teutonic Knights and the *Schwertbrüder*, created in the Holy Land and transplanted during the struggle against the pagan Baltic peoples (1225-26), spread Gothic art through Pomerania, eastern Prussia, and the Baltic region (castle at Malbork, Riga, Tallinn). Despite the fact that these organizations were strongly tinged with a Germanic spirit, they played the same internationalizing Christian role as the mendicant orders.

Aside from religious orders, the diocesan clergy, in spite of their aristocratically exclusive membership, were open to and even obliged to maintain international channels of communication. Delegated to councils, synods, and papal or royal diplomatic missions, or sent to fulfill duties at Rome, Avignon, or in foreign lands, medieval bishops were the great travelers of their day. Italian and Spanish prelates were elected bishops in France or Germany; French and Spanish bishops, in turn, became popes. Through family alliances, the aristocratic organization of cathedral canons also favored these far-flung contacts.

With the help of certain documents, D. Knoop and G.P. Jones, P. du Colombier, J. Gimpel, and other scholars have tried to get an idea of the actual conditions surrounding the construction of Gothic edifices. If the initiative depended on religious authorities (bishops or abbots) or on political or municipal sources (as in Florence), then the financial and technical road was an uneven and intricate one indeed. In the case of endeavors sponsored by kings or other nobles—such as Caernarvon Castle, Château-Gaillard, and the Sainte-Chapelle in Paris—work could proceed very rapidly. Thanks to the practically limitless financial resources of the nobility and the pool of forced labor they were empowered to assemble, such projects could be completed in only three to five years (L.F. Salzmann). Even bishops and canons, however, were unable to underwrite singlehandedly the elevation of such truly immense structures as cathedrals, although they did submit a part of the revenue drawn from the wealth of their dioceses. While other moneymaking activities—fairs, markets, processions of relics, and outright soliciting—did help somewhat, these were at best uncertain sources of revenue. The few Gothic cathedrals or abbeys that were erected in a single twenty-five-or-thirty-year effort, such as Chartres or Royaumont, were exceptions to the rule. Most of them, albeit begun amidst enthusiasm and a ready flow of money, experienced difficulties that resulted in slowdowns or stoppages. In 1232, a conflict between the city of Reims and its archbishop interfered with the construction of the Cathedral for several years. At Beauvais, a serious accident and its subsequent repair caused the work on the choir of the Cathedral to be drawn out over a century. When the

great economic and political depression of the fourteenth century arrived—in France, a direct consequence of the Hundred Years War—many projects ceased altogether, not to be resumed until the fifteenth, sixteenth, or, in the case of Cologne Cathedral, the nineteenth century. Parish churches and monasteries (e.g. La Trinité at Vendôme) were affected just as seriously as the major monuments.

Beginning with the mid-1100s, the costs of construction increased dramatically. For example, Aubert and Simson have estimated that, between 1140 and 1144, the Abbot Suger spent approximately 1000 *livres* on the choir of his abbey at Saint-Denis, but the fifty-year campaign to build the nave and transept and to modify the choir (1231-82) cost 80,000 *livres*. This inflation, so to speak, probably resulted from the ever-increasing cost of builders—masons, carpenters, and sculptors—whose talents became specialized in proportion to the increasing complexity of construction and decoration. But the main expenditures were always divided between the extraction of stone from the quarry, its transportation to the building site, and the cost of constantly replacing stonecutters' tools. If the work was under the auspices of the quarries, the sandpits, or the forests that provided the wood for scaffolding and frameworks; or if unspecialized laborers provided voluntary or free (that is, forced) transport services—the cost of construction could be considerably reduced. A number of texts concerning the organization and bookkeeping of such projects as Saint-Urbain at Troyes, Vale Abbey, and Caernarvon Castle survive. Together with investigations (P. Deschamps and Teresa Frisch), these sources help us arrive at a more informed appreciation of the financial and technical aspects of construction.

It is especially the English texts that reveal the role of the actual creators: the architects, the engineers, the so-called masters (John Harvey's term). One often hears the ill-considered assertion that opposes the great individual master architects of the Renaissance, such as Brunelleschi or Michelozzo, to the anonymous builders of medieval architecture, who created the so-called collective work of an entire people. In point of fact, we know a good many Gothic architects by name, beginning with Guillaume de Sens, who worked at Canterbury between 1174 and 1178. Some were rich, celebrated architects to kings and recognized as international experts. Pierre de Montreuil, whom his epitaph designates *doctor lathomorum*, directed several important Parisian projects, including Saint-Denis and the Cathedral of Notre-Dame, all the while buying quarries and selling plots of land. In the second half of the century, Jean Deschamps was put in charge of simultaneous works located as far apart as Clermont-Ferrand, Limoges, Rodez, and Narbonne. Raymond du Temple and Guy de Dammartin were masters of great renown, associated especially with works for royalty and the nobility. In England Walter of Hereford was master mason of the thirteenth-century royal works at Vale Abbey and Caernarvon Castle; Henry Yevele worked on

Westminster Abbey and other London buildings in the 1300s; and William of Wykeham, the master of Winchester Cathedral, also worked at Windsor Castle and at Westminster Abbey. Many well-known German masters, notably members of the Parler family—Heinrich, Peter, and Wentzel—were active during the fourteenth century and their buildings may be found at Cologne, Schwäbisch Gmünd, Prague, and Vienna. These architects are more than just names in an official record book. In some cases we have access to information about their lives, personalities, careers, and artistic styles. For example, the life and style of Pierre de Montreuil have been fully discussed by Branner and the present writer; his personality has, in turn, been contrasted with those of both known masters (such as Robert de Luzarches) and anonymous ones (Branner's Master of Saint-Denis). According to P. Booz and O. Kletzl, the style of the Parlers represents a phase of southern German and Bohemian Gothic just as surely as the Florentine style of 1300 can be defined in terms of Arnolfo di Cambio. Hopefully, this kind of research will continue and will ultimately yield a history of Gothic architecture as fully elaborated as that of fifteenth-century Italy.

One of the most hotly debated questions has been the organization of medieval masons and architects. To what extent did corporate structure, so strictly regulated from the thirteenth century on, manage to influence architecture? The social rank and mobility of the great medieval architects indicate that they successfully avoided corporate regulation. However, through such texts as the Parisian *Livre des métiers* of Étienne Boileau (1258), we know that masonic corporate statutes did exist. Elsewhere, labor forces, assembled to work on great religious buildings or nobles' castles throughout a set period of time, would group together in lodges. One such lodge is mentioned in a text from Amiens dating from 1220. Beginning in the late 1200s, permanent associations affiliated with major endeavors appeared at Strasbourg and York; these, in turn, provided the impetus for the creation of quasi-secret lodges in the Holy Roman Empire and in England during the fifteenth century (Frankl, Knoop and Jones). We have access to the statutes of the great lodges of Vienna and Strasbourg. They exerted authority over mason, master mason, and architect alike. Reaching its apogee in the sixteenth and seventeenth centuries, this activity was more characteristic of the declining years of the Gothic style than its period of ascendancy. In addition, the Freemason movement that spread from England during the 1600s and 1700s tried to identify itself with the medieval associations.

What role did these fraternities play within the architectural profession itself? The great enterprises at Cologne, Strasbourg, and Vienna have disclosed compilations of plans and technical/theoretical drawings that reveal a kind of collective architectural legacy, to be passed on from generation to generation. Books containing models or instructions—that of Villard de Honnecourt dates from the second quarter of the thirteenth century—undoubtedly had a similar goal in mind. Indeed, such texts as the *Livre des pinâcles* (1486) of Roriczer were veritable manuals of architecture.

These documents also indicate that the medieval master was a truly multifaceted individual. Not only was he technician and engineer, but also he was responsible for sketches of moldings, for decorative elements, and even for sculptures and paintings. Upon close observation of those important thirteenth- and fourteenth-century structures that were gradually built under the successive regimes of several masters, one can see that certain styles of general contour or ornamentation correspond to individual master builders. For instance, Kletzl and Karl Svoboda point out that a distinctive Parlerian style of sculpture is to be found in those buildings whose construction was directed by members of the Parler family.

All of this proves, better than does the synthetic approach to medieval history, that Gothic architecture had always been intimately connected with sculpture, painting, and the other arts. In order to account for the common evolution of the arts during the Middle Ages, many have accepted the principle that all artistic activity during this era was dominated by architecture. The primacy of architecture is said to extend over sculpture, stained-glass painting, and precious objects to the illuminated manuscript, which often accurately reproduces contemporary architectural features (e.g. the *Psautier de Saint Louis* at the Bibliothèque Nationale in Paris). However, this theory needs to be corrected. Gothic architecture—especially at the end of the Middle Ages—owes a great deal to sources not directly linked to its own forms: the designs of rose windows and of traceries, the decorative borders of paintings, and the baldachins and bases of statues and paintings. Fantastic animal forms, typical of the gargoyled waterspouts and crockets of gabled pinnacles, are just as prolific in illuminated manuscripts as in architecture. In other words, the profuse ornamentation of Flamboyant art does not derive from architectural tradition; it was borrowed instead from contemporary tastes, as revealed in precious metalwork and in the ornamental fancies of illuminated manuscripts. It is only in the context of this overall evolution of form that Gothic architecture can be properly discussed and fully understood.

ORIGINS

It was in the Île-de-France, at the end of the first half of the twelfth century, that Gothic architecture first emerged as a coherent style: the Cathedral of Sens (1130-62) and the Abbey Church of Saint-Denis (c. 1130-40 and 1140-44) are the two preeminent examples of this early stage of development. Other, less decisively Gothic efforts of the same period are to be found in Normandy and England, as well as in western France. The events leading up to the formation of Gothic architecture, however, long antedate its ultimate appearance as a clearly identifiable form.

Certain of its characteristic elements are of Eastern origin. First widely used in Sassanid art, the pointed arch was adopted by Islamic art, which, in turn, utilized it as a key feature from the seventh century on. Such Muslim structures as the Great Mosque at Kairouan, Tunisia, and the Great Mosque (now the Cathedral) at Córdoba, Spain, offer ample evidence of its popularity, as do certain Sicilian buildings constructed by the Christians after the Norman reconquest in 1059. Quite naturally, the pointed arch may be found in Romanesque art both in Italy (Cathedral of Modena) and in Burgundy, in which latter region it was quickly incorporated into such celebrated Romanesque edifices as Paray-le-Monial, Saint-Lazare at Autun, and the monumental transept of Cluny. However, the responsibility for extending this elementary contour to Notre-Dame in Paris or to the Cathedral of Noyon lies chiefly with Gothic architects.

Even more crucial is the history of the cross-ribbed vault, whose successive structural and plastic modifications led to Saint-Denis and Sens. Although ribs were occasionally applied under vaulting by ancient Roman architects—most notably at the Villa Sette Bassi in Campania—these do not seem to have been the models, even in Lombardy, for the first such vaults in the West. On the other hand, ribbed vaults became a sophisticated component of the architecture of Sassanid Mesopotamia and Islamic Iran (the Mosque of Shah Abbas I at Esfahan). In the great eleventh-century North African and Moorish mosques, the patterns of ribbing that decorate the tower halls and the domed mihrabs (a mihrab is a niche that houses the Koran) are spectacularly complex. Dating from the year 1000, the small Mosque of Bib-al-Mardum at Toledo may be considered the consummate product of this period of art. Only much later and more rarely did Gothic counterparts of the Islamic ribbed vault even begin to approximate the ornamental richness of Muslim architecture. During the twelfth century, several structures in France and Spain (e.g. the Hospital of Saint-Blaise in the Pyrenees) did follow the Muslim example, but remained for the most part Romanesque. Efforts more characteristic of the first real Western experiments with ribbing are the buildings in Armenia and Georgia studied by Jurgis Baltrušaitis. From the tenth to the thirteenth century (dates uncertain), the buildings of this region displayed such features as ribbed domes (Ani, Nicorzminda), diagonal arches on a square field (Ani), and arches perpendicular to the walls (Horomos Vank). The role of these arches is unquestionably structural, not decorative. However, at times they do not support the vault directly: their extrados shoulder masonry that, in turn, supports level roofing. Precisely the same structural arrangements, as well as strikingly similar formal solutions, may be found at Casale Monferrato in northern Italy; in the Tour Guinette at Étampes, near Paris; and in the lower hall of a tower in the Cathedral of Bayeux (c. 1080). At the time of this construction, there were numerous economic and political contacts between Armenia and western Europe; and a certain group of ribbed vaults in the West—for instance, at San Nazaro Sesia and at Lodi Vecchio in Lombardy and at Saint-Aubin at Angers in France—may possibly be traced to these Eastern models.

However, it is by way of one of the most vigorous and clearly defined architectural styles of the eleventh and twelfth centuries—Anglo-Norman art—that the plastic and structural experiments leading to French Gothic can be most readily perceived. In these countries, the appearance of diagonally arched vaulting did not precede but rather followed the elaboration of a formal system of supports and walls. Here, too, Anglo-Norman design roughly outlined later Gothic solutions to the problem of buttressing. We may safely assume that it was the organization of walls and supports that prompted ribbed coverings, not the use of ribbed vaults that led to the design of the supports. Once the relationship of the roofing and the division of interior space, as well as the attendant considerations of articulation and lighting, were fully established and developed, Gothic architecture was born. The first examples of cross-ribbed vaulting appeared almost simultaneously in England and Normandy: in England, Durham (choir side aisle, 1093-1100; north arm of the transept, before 1104; choir, before 1110), Winchester, Peterborough, and Gloucester; in Normandy, the choir and transept of Lessay (c. 1100), Duclair, Saint-Paul at Rouen, and perhaps the chapter house at Jumièges (before 1110). Whether square or rectangular, these vaults are placed on very thick walls; but, contrary to more archaic designs, the ribs are amply molded with single or double convex as well as angular contours. The subsequent addition of sculptured geometric ornamentation to the moldings (Bristol, choir of Durham, the chapter house of Saint-Georges-de-Boscherville) attests to a desire not only for decoration, but also for harmonization of these elements with the piers and wall supports. The years between 1120 and 1130 ushered in a new phase in the history of the Norman vault. Large edifices that had been initially designed without vaulting (Saint-Étienne and Sainte-Trinité, both at Caen) now received either sexpartite vaults enclosing two bay fields or, as at Sainte-Trinité at Caen and the church at Barnières, false sexpartite vaults with the middle transverse rib supporting walls (as in Armenian examples). However, these Norman ex-

15. Toledo, Mosque of Bib-al-
Mardum, ribbed vault.
16. Moissac, Saint-Pierre, vault
of the bell tower.

periments with vaulting came to a halt after the mid-1100s, as they precluded a lightening of the walls. In early-twelfth-century England, more traditional habits persisted, resulting in such unvaulted churches as Ely and Southwell, among others. In a sense, the efforts of architects in the Vexin, Valois, and Île-de-France regions took up where the Anglo-Norman experiments left off.

French projects in this direction, often modest and involving buildings of only secondary importance, can be dated between 1125 and 1135. Unfortunately, the most important structure in this group, the late-eleventh-century Saint-Lucien at Beauvais, is no longer extant. Of the remaining edifices—the churches at Rhuis, Acy-en-Multien, Cambronne, Morienval, and Saint-Étienne at Beauvais—only the last two are noteworthy. Both of these churches feature lightened vaults contoured in a single or double convex profile, as well as thinner walls. At Morienval, the vaulting covers curved, trapezoidal bays radiating around an ambulatory. In subsequent years, the ambulatories at Sens and Saint-Denis were to profit not only from this lightening of the vaulting and its supports, but also from the new possibilities of adapting this system to innovative ribbed roofing. It would, however, be erroneous to consider the French experiments as completely divorced from the Norman system. Norman architects did participate in French construction both in the Vexin region (Saint-Germer-de-Fly at Saint-Germer, c. 1140-45) and in the region of Paris (the narthex of Saint-Denis, dedicated in 1140).

Other projects, paralleling those described above, were in progress during the first half of the twelfth century. In the Maine, Anjou, and Poitou regions—an area then under Anglo-Norman political influence and, after 1152, an essential part of the Plantagenet English domain—an original and very beautiful style was to emerge from this activity. It will be discussed at a later point. Despite some experimentation with vaulting, Romanesque forms in Lombardy and the Holy Roman Empire remained essentially unaltered: witness Sant'Ambrogio in Milan (Lombardy), Murbach (Alsace), and the transept of Speyer Cathedral (Palatinate). We must therefore conclude that the technology of the ribbed vault was not necessarily the great driving force behind the development of Gothic. In fact, of all the tendencies we have been enumerating, the only fully successful formal and technical relationship occurred between the Anglo-Norman state and the Kingdom of France. Two features of Norman Romanesque architecture were to play a part in the birth of Gothic: on the structural level, the use of wall buttresses and flying buttresses; on the level of spatial configuration, the double-shell or "thick" wall at the window level, whose passageways would help provide a model for the triforium.

Transverse arches (perpendicular to the upper level of the lateral walls and hidden under the gallery roofing) appeared about 1100 in the choir at Durham and at Cérisy-la-Forêt. Since there was certainly no need to give additional reinforcement to the already thick walls, one may wonder about the function of these arches. They seem to have been invented to facilitate roofing and the erection of "wallbuttresses" indented with a passageway opening. This effect was obtained at Sainte-Trinité at Caen and the nave at Durham and was to be used by Gothic architects in Saint-Germer-de-Fly at Saint-Germer and in the Cathedral of Laon. As this device was later refined and applied, its function became clearer. In the second half of the twelfth century, architects also buttressed the upper stories of the church by means of galleries, already used in the eleventh century, either groin-vaulted (Jumièges after 1040) or round-arched (Gloucester in the late 1000s and the reconstructed gallery of Saint-Étienne at Caen). This is not, however, an exclusively Norman design.

More significant is the role of the so-called thick wall. Invented as a convenient means to reach the windows, this passage, literally carved out of the wall mass, first appeared about 1040-50 in the transepts of Bernay and Jumièges. Not only does it afford the wall increased solidity, but also it creates a remarkable hollowed-out effect (Jantzen's "diaphanousness") that is heightened when the bays facing the nave are furnished with partitioning colonnettes. Its use in the great eleventh-century "model" churches—the abbey churches of Saint-Étienne and Sainte-Trinité at Caen and the cathedrals of Saint Albans, Durham, and Winchester—influenced the design of Lessay and of Saint-Georges-de-Boscherville and, after 1100, became a customary Norman device. As for England, the double-shell wall established a mode of construction and elevation that was to characterize almost all important churches until the fourteenth century. (We will elaborate on the English style later.) Termed the *mur dédoublé* in France, this window-level passageway inspired admirable creations (Noyon), generated a distinct Burgundian style in the thirteenth century, and gave an effect of lightness and plastic richness to Gothic art in general (Bony, Gall).

Gall has shown that it was Normandy that nurtured the formal system that Gothic was to develop and adopt as one of its dominant traits: namely, the principle of the graphic (that is, linear) nature of the support system and of the plasticity of the wall divisions. The abbey churches of Saint-Étienne at Caen (1060-77) and of Jumièges are the most representative monuments in Norman Romanesque art. In fact, it would not be incorrect to contrast this style to the Romanesque of southern France or the Holy Roman Empire. Since 1030, the Loire region had furnished the model for the arrangement of four half columns engaged in a pier. In Norman Romanesque, however, the pier mass is dressed with eight engaged half colonnettes over a dosseret, thereby creating a clearly linear effect. The engaged half columns facing the central nave strongly articulate the supports as they travel up to the windows or even to the summit of the walls. The resulting rhythm created by such a configuration of vertical supports is found not only in England (Peterborough), but also in all

typical Norman structures after 1100 (the churches at Cérisy-la-Forêt, Lessay, and Saint-Georges-de-Boscherville). Moreover, the elevation of this vigorously outlined wall consists of several stories, each clearly delineated by a molded fillet: double-rolled arcade; the gallery arches; and finally, the level at which windows appear behind a passage cut from the wall, open to the interior through several small decorative arches. Even before the advent of cross-ribbed vaulting in the 1120s, this conspicuous mural structure already provided the first model for Gothic diaphanousness, for the spatial script written by colonnettes and the angles of the dosserets. One is even led to believe that sexpartite cross-ribbed vaults must have emerged from the structure of this type of elevation. As both spatial structure and formal script, this principle was fully utilized in the first Gothic buildings. According to Sedlmayr, of all two- or three-story Romanesque elevations, only this one opened the way for the birth of Gothic; that is, it alone successfully broke with the old-fashioned contours of Romanesque murality, according to which pilasters or engaged colonnettes were passively applied to walls. The heavy, massive elevations of the Auvergne; the ponderous mural elevation of the great Salic structures, such as the nave at Speyer; and, despite the generous plasticity of their supporting masses, the low elevations at Cluny—none of these led to the same formal definition that Norman Romanesque ultimately provided the nascent Gothic style.

SENS AND SAINT-DENIS

All historians agree today that Abbot Suger's Saint-Denis (c. 1130-40 and 1140-44) and Henri Sanglier's Cathedral of Sens (c. 1130-64) stand out as the best examples of buildings whose elements clearly attest to the development of Norman Romanesque features into a new Gothic style. Now, this metamorphosis was not brought about solely by the systematic use of the structural technique of cross-ribbed vaulting. One must look instead to the new ordering of interior space, now accented by freestanding or engaged supports, as well as the shifting of emphasis from structural massiveness to an appreciation of the organizational and modeling capacities of light. Although modifications over the years prevent our observing these structures as they were first built, we can still legitimately recreate the original plan. As Francis Salet points out, Sens is clearly the older of the two. Its general layout—there is an ambulatory, but no transept—reproduces those of the great Romanesque edifices. The supports (compound piers alternating with twin double columns) articulate double bays that create a rhythm reminiscent of the great Norman alternations (Jumièges). Its three-story elevation (high pointed arcade, openings above vaulting, and windows) derives not from Burgundy, but from the triple divisions of Normandy and England. In addition, the sexpartite vaulting of the central nave is probably of Norman origin. In the ambulatory, which is the oldest section of the church, a certain reticence

20. Saint-Denis, Abbey Church, narthex.

may be observed in the curved, oblong bays—harking back to Morienval—for whose vaults cross-ribbing had not been planned. The presence of wall ribs belies a Burgundian influence. Neither the admirable plasticity nor the strongly alternating rhythm of the nave (about 49 feet wide) negates the linear quality achieved both by the colonnettes engaged in piers and walls and by the coherent grouping of pointed arches at the level of the false gallery. The upper wall is relatively thin and, therefore, does not follow the Norman model. Was it originally reinforced by exterior flying buttresses? The answer is unknown, for the eighteenth-century improvements to the original windows forever altered the upper level. In general, Sens was to exert considerable influence, in spite of certain archaic features: it helped spread the idea of a transept reduced in size or altogether eliminated, the sexpartite vault, alternating interior rhythm, and the three-story elevation.

Saint-Denis is more complex and more innovative. There is a conspicuous difference between the narthex (1140) and the ambulatory enclosing the choir (all that remains of the structure consecrated in 1144). Sheltering three upper halls, the narthex—or antenave—is a descendant of the pre-Romanesque or Ottonian western mass or *Westwerk*. The single remaining tower of the originally two-towered façade follows the Romanesque models developed in Normandy. In both stylistic and iconographical terms, the three carved portals assert for the first time a sculpture that is unequivocally no longer Romanesque. Especially revealing are two structural details of the westwork interior: heavy and generously molded cross-ribbing that delineates oblong and square vault fields, and supports composed of multiple projecting colonnettes positioned precisely under the volutes of the archivolts or the springings of the ribs. All of these elements conspire to create a linearity that both profits from and surpasses the Anglo-Norman experiments. In fact, certain details of molding or decoration, such as the serrated transverse ribs, prove that a master architect in the Norman tradition was summoned here to create a revolutionary work of art.

A different spirit breathes in the apse of Saint-Denis, begun one month after the completion of the narthex. Here there is no desire for monumentality. Incorporated in the double ambulatory of this exceptionally subtle and refined section are seven radiating and two rectangular chapels (only one of the latter survives). The main elevation of the choir disappeared as a result of reconstruction in the thirteenth century. Moreover, the transept and nave must have barely been started when the builder of the church, Abbot Suger, died in 1151. Consequently, any restoration of the original plan remains hypothetical. We can nevertheless assume that side aisles were envisioned for the nave and that, like Sens, the choir consisted of three stories, with apertures beneath the clerestory level throwing light to the ambulatory vaulting. Each radiating chapel is lit by two large windows whose archivolts merge with the wall ribs of the vaults; the five-part vaults, in turn, extend to cover both the chapels and the outer ambulatory, thereby articulating compartments whose extreme lightness is augmented by the ambulatory's slender columns. As at Morienval and Saint-Étienne at Beauvais, the ribs are molded in the so-called French profile, a simple convex curve. The floral decoration reinforces the clear departure from Norman art. Perhaps the most striking aspect of this structure is the astounding amount of light, far more abundant here than in most twelfth-century Gothic edifices. Simson, Panofsky, and S. McK. Crosby have attempted to explain its importance, using a text written by Abbot Suger himself. He marvels at the continuous light (*lux continua*) provided by the windows, illuminating the entire building with the marvelous brilliance of stained glass, "lifting the mind from the material to the spiritual." Thus, Saint-Denis lives up to all the proposed definitions of Gothic art; it satisfies formal/structural as well as aesthetic/symbolic criteria. In any case, it must be kept in mind that this abbey church was built by the chief advisor to Louis VI and Louis VII for the purpose of more closely uniting his monastery to the French monarchy. The construction of Saint-Denis was by no means innocent of feudalistic political motives.

A structure as extraordinarily precocious as Saint-Denis did not directly spawn any projects worthy of its innovative design. To appreciate its unique architectural status, one need only compare it to contemporary or slightly later Parisian churches—Saint-Martin-des-Champs, awkward in layout and vaulting, or Saint-Germain-des-Prés (choir begun 1150-55, dedicated 1163). Allowing for its very lovely sculpted decoration and its carefully turned molding, the apse of Saint-Germain still falls short of the luminous, clearly drawn volumes of Saint-Denis. Does the Saint-Germain elevation, with its false gallery over clerestory windows, derive from Sens or the lost elevation at Saint-Denis? We do not know. But one important element does stand out at Saint-Germain: the flying buttresses, added either during construction or shortly thereafter and reconstructed in the seventeenth century. It is safe to assume (as does K.J. Conant) that they originated from those built in 1145-50 for the Sens and Saint-Denis prototypes. As a matter of fact, several minor and relatively unimpressive churches did timidly base themselves on the Saint-Denis plan, among them Saint-Maclou at Pontoise and Saint-Ouen-le-Vieux at Rouen. Many believe that Suger's abbey was the kernel from which sprang the four-storied elevation of Early Gothic architecture. In our opinion, although it is possible that the nave—never built—was to have had a four-tiered configuration, it is just as likely that this invention originated elsewhere.

EARLY GOTHIC ARCHITECTURE IN THE ÎLE-DE-FRANCE AND NORTHERN FRANCE

During the second half of the twelfth century, there was an incredible amount of building activity in the regions north of the Loire between

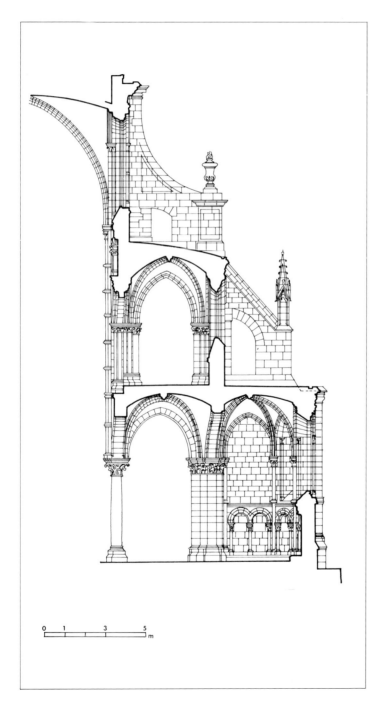

Burgundy and Normandy. It is as if the newly adopted methods of construction had prompted the partial or total replacement of the older, more simple churches in this area. In those sections of France where vaulting had been standard procedure from the late 1000s—Burgundy as well as southern, western, and central regions—the need to reconstruct was less pressing. The number of urban or rural churches rebuilt according to the new procedures is so prodigious that we must focus our attention on only the truly significant episcopal, abbatial, and collegiate structures. Even among these, not all have survived, and many of them were modified during or after the thirteenth century. Most serious is the loss of the Cathedral of Arras (1160-1200), the Cathedral of Cambrai (1148-67), and the Abbey Church of Notre-Dame-la-Grande at Valenciennes (after 1171). We have selected four cathedrals that adequately define this architectural style: Senlis, Noyon, Laon, and Notre-Dame at Paris.

Their plans reveal that the choir underwent considerable development: it is surrounded by an ambulatory (in Paris, a double ambulatory) that extends, with the exception of Paris, into adjoining radiating chapels similar to those at Saint-Denis. The lengthening of the choir to the west was in response to the increased number of canonic chapters. As for the transept, it may be absent (Senlis), patterned after Sens, or greatly reduced in size (Paris). However, other developments in the transept area, drawn from older models, compensate for this and enhance the beauty of the edifice. These include the addition of surrounding side aisles (Laon, based on the Romanesque models of Saint-Remi at Reims and pilgrimage churches) and the rounding of the transept arms (Noyon). This very beautiful arrangement, which groups three semicircular naves around the crossing, already existed at Cambrai, Valenciennes, and Saint-Lucien at Beauvais. Lacking ambulatories in the transept arms, the Noyon arrangement is even simpler than those of certain buildings that, although no longer extant, can be studied today through later examples—namely, the south transept arm of Soissons (after 1180) and the Cathedral of Tournai. (The transept of the latter was added after 1150-60 to a thoroughly Romanesque, but highly original nave.) The rounded-transept design was undoubtedly based on a very ancient idea, one to which Romanesque art in the Holy Roman Empire was to remain faithful from the eleventh century (Sankt Maria im Kapitol at Cologne) until well into the twelfth. Following the Sens model, the alternating rhythm of the piers at Senlis and Noyon responds to the unequal springings of the sexpartite vaults. However, such a pattern is virtually absent at both Notre-Dame at Paris and at Laon. In the former, the only alternation is that of the piers separating the double side aisles; in the latter, it is observable only in the easternmost bay of the nave. Thus, it appears that the builders of Paris and Laon (not to mention numerous minor churches in the region) rejected alternating rhythm in favor of uniformity: cylindrical piers in

single file, reminiscent of Romanesque, Carolingian, or Early Christian alignments. Only the colonnettes, which vary regularly in number as they extend the unequal springings of the sexpartite vaults, mark a kind of cadence along the side walls of the nave. Except for Senlis, the elevations are four-storied: groundlevel arcade; vaulted gallery; an intermediate level of blind arches, arcades, or rose windows; and clerestory, with one or two windows to each vault field. This configuration was very typical of Early Gothic architecture (for instance, Saint-Remi at Reims, Montierender, and Mouzon in Champagne); but it was not without precedent. The English precursors (Tewkesbury) are less clearly delineated than the Cathedral of Tournai, whose nave—undoubtedly constructed before the end of the first half of the twelfth century—had already proclaimed this superposition, albeit in a Romanesque manner. Another example, obviously Gothic but rather clumsily so, is Saint-Germer-de-Fly at Saint-Germer (c. 1140-45). Furthermore, one cannot exclude the hypothesis (previously mentioned) that the twelfth-century nave of Saint-Denis was the seed of the four-story pattern. In any event, what counts is not so much the source of this multiple elevation as its stylistic significance, for, shortly before 1200, it was to be summarily abandoned, as if High Gothic wanted nothing more to do with it (Meaux, Rouen, Bourges). This can be explained by practical reasons. Since the vaulted galleries had to be covered with a single-pitch roof, the clerestory windows had to be placed above. Consequently, there was a band of wall space corresponding to the height of this roofing, which could be filled with blind arches (choir at Noyon), superposed apertures (rose windows at Paris, rectangular windows at Saint-Germer), or a continuous passageway (the triforia at Noyon and Laon). The stacking of these tiers—each with its own rhythm and scale, each clearly separated from the other by molded strips (especially at Laon and in the choir of Noyon)—creates a formal effect of horizontal spatial division that perfectly matches that of the bays juxtaposed to the elevation. In addition, this multiplication of levels may be seen as a response to the ever-increasing height of the churches (at Paris, about 112 feet to the vault imposts), and it augments the effect by a kind of vertical perspective. Unfortunately, the lengthening of the windows of Notre-Dame at Paris during the thirteenth century severely damaged the rich impression created by this type of church.

We should mention here a technical and formal problem of paramount importance: namely, the equilibrium of buildings vaulted at ever higher levels. It is sometimes said that Early Gothic architecture was ignorant of, or, at best, unfamiliar with the flying buttress. At the end of the twelfth century, it was this element of abutment that engendered a new stylistic phase (especially at Chartres) by eliminating the gallery, unifying the elevation, and raising the height of the roofing to about 135 feet. But can we be quite sure that the flying buttress was born only as late as 1190? If we agree that, from 1180-85, the nave of Notre-Dame at Paris was supported by flying buttresses with intermediate piers (according to the universally accepted reconstruction of Viollet-le-Duc), and if we take into account the plastic perfection of the system conceived in 1195 for the nave of Chartres, then we ought to inquire about the kinds of experiments that predated these projects. Now, we will not go as far as the hypothesis of Conant, who believes that fully developed flying buttresses were present at Cluny (c. 1130), the Cathedral of Sens, and the Saint-Denis of Suger (before 1150). All the same, we must ask ourselves whether the subsequent decades between 1150 and 1170 saw the gradual replacement of the wall-buttress technique of Saint-Germer-de-Fly at Saint-Germer and of the choir of the Cathedral of Laon by the endeavors at Saint-Germer-des-Prés (Paris), the apse of the Abbey Church at Saint-Leu-d'Esserent, and Notre-Dame at Paris.

All of these observations indicate that the evolution of Early Gothic art, albeit generally coherent, does reveal diverse phases and tendencies. Following a period of great, decisive, experimental production—notably the Cathedral of Sens, Saint-Denis, and Saint-Germer-de-Fly (apse c. 1140-50)—there was a new phase of construction between 1150 and 1160. This includes the cathedrals of Senlis (1155-91) and Noyon (c. 1150/55-85, completion of the apse and transept), the choir of Saint-Germain-des-Prés (1155-62), and small related buildings in the Oise Valley north of Paris. A second phase includes structures begun about 1160 or thereafter: the Cathedral of Laon (c. 1160-1210?), Notre-Dame at Paris (1163?-82, apse; 1180-1200, nave), the transept of the Cathedral of Soissons (after c. 1180), and numerous related edifices, notably Saint-Leu-d'Esserent (c. 1165-90) and the Collegiate Church of Mantes (façade begun before 1175). A new period—Classical or High Gothic—commenced toward 1195; it was dominated by the Cathedral of Chartres, the Abbey Church of Braine, and the Cathedral of Bourges.

Senlis, Noyon, Laon, and Paris

Senlis is the smallest and least well preserved of these four cathedrals; its original effect was altered when its entire upper level was rebuilt during the sixteenth century. In the restoration of Aubert, it shows striking similarities to Sens: no transept (the present one dates from the thirteenth and fourteenth centuries), strongly marked alternating supports, and a three-story elevation. More significant is the gallery. Like the one at Saint-Germer-de-Fly, it is entirely vaulted with crossed ribs. Within a rather limited space, the ambulatory and chapels reveal a dense network of colonnettes and convex ribs in the Saint-Denis manner. Thanks to its highly elaborate linearity and a fairly abundant amount of light in its lower levels, this building marks a stage in the evolution of Gothic that surpasses Sens.

Noyon, despite extensive restoration after World War I, is not only better preserved, but also more complex and much more accomplished

(Charles Seymour, Jr.). With its rounded transept arms, the plan of Noyon belongs to the traditional northern group. The strongly alternating cadence of the supports in the central nave responds well to the sexpartite vaulting overhead. As for the elevation, the effect of diaphanousness is especially well realized in the gallery, which is amply lighted through its own windows and which opens up to the central area by two pointed arches grouped beneath a relieving arch. In the apse, the gallery is topped by a blind arcade; in the nave, by a triforium passage. A truly singular arrangement is to be found in the transept: ground-level blind arcades, a low gallery, a tall gallery, and the upper windows. This should be interpreted, not as the uncertain product of a hesitant master, but as a testimony to his respect for the scale of the elevation, his concern for providing better lighting for the ends of the transept by means of additional windows, and his desire to create a richer double-shell effect by arcades, apertures, and colonnettes. At the clerestory level, the passage is carried to the exterior by the window recesses. The principle of the double-shell wall is utilized even more perfectly in the nave (probably built after 1170; western bays, at the beginning of the thirteenth century); it may be considered a Gothic interpretation of Bony's *mur épais*.

The subtlety of spatial, structural, linear, and divisional effects qualifies Noyon as one of the great Gothic masterpieces, whose powerful influence was to be felt at Laon as well as in Champagne. However, at Laon, a more monumental and systematic architectural idea directed the determination of the plan and general solutions (Hanna Adenauer, Bony). At some point after 1205, the original choir (relatively short, without ambulatory) was replaced by the greatly lengthened present-day choir, accompanied by a rectilinear apse perforated with very tall windows and a large rose window. This is one of the most successful arrangements in Gothic art of the early thirteenth century. Attention is especially focused on the transept, which is completely encircled with side aisles that are, in turn, crowned with galleries. As a result, there are two huge platforms at the extremities of the transept arms, over which are placed windows and large rose windows. Following the Romanesque model—and especially the Norman style—a lantern (i.e. a tower) atop the roof draws all of the interior volumes to a central point. As the nave extends to the west, the lines of its simple cylindrical piers create a steady rhythm. The similarities between Laon and Noyon are obvious: the same subdivision of levels, in the same proportions; and the use of the double-shell wall in the two double-tiered chapels of the transept. Even though the alternation of supports is now gone, the clear, linear quality of the bay articulation has been preserved, thanks to the use of adjoining colonnettes punctuated by bands in relief. What emerges is a more systematic and rigorous spirit that seeks to preserve a unified effect. Moreover, the contributions of elements foreign to strictly French tradition augment the exceptional

25. Laon, Cathedral, plan.
26. Laon, Cathedral, exterior.

27. Laon, Cathedral, nave.

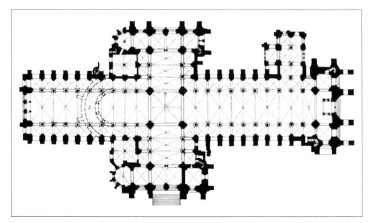

architectural value of Laon. The lantern not only lends an upward sweep to the concert of interior volumes, but also it serves as a focal point of the exterior masses—a pair of towers at each extremity of the transept, together with two façade towers. Evidently, the model for this configuration is the Cathedral of Tournai, whose central complex of five towers—more densely arranged than those at Laon—is in itself a development of a Germanic architectonic solution. Although dating from only the thirteenth century, the towers, like the façade, restate the formal characteristics of the Laon style: namely, clearly delineated stories, and the highlights of the masonried surfaces accentuated by deep apertures. The completely hollowed-out upper levels of the towers, with profusely colonnetted, canopied niches at their corners, translate the traits of Gothic diaphanousness, structural lightness, and repetitive rhythm into truly fantastic compositions. Villard de Honnecourt marveled at these towers, judged them to be without peer, and drew them in 1230. We should now briefly consider the question of the rose windows at Laon. Those of the transept are made up of several juxtaposed multifoils; the one in the façade is subdivided by mullions (slender dividing bars). Except for its late appearance in Rhenish art after 1200, the circular window was rarely used in Romanesque architecture and never figured as an essential element of illumination. The first partitioned, decorated rose windows appeared more or less simultaneously in Italy (San Zeno at Verona, in Tuscany) and—perhaps as a result of Italian influence—in France. At Saint-Denis and Saint-Étienne at Beauvais, it was as much an exterior embellishment as a functional element geared to interior effect. Toward 1180-90, the two transept rose windows at Laon were to stand out as components of capital importance in the disposition of interior lighting. This marked only the first step in a marvelous evolution: the role of the rose window was to remain strong in thirteenth-century art, weakening only in the fourteenth century. On the iconographical level, the rose window attracted the most beautiful themes and the richest symbols known to the Gothic church.

The influence of Laon was prodigious. It overshadowed all Gothic art in the northern region of France for several decades. Prior to the great structures at Orbais and the Cathedral of Reims, the art of Champagne depended heavily on Laon. Its influence extended to Lorraine, the Rhineland, and even to Limburg an der Lahn, well into the thirteenth century. In fact, that formidable creation of the second Gothic phase—the Cathedral of Chartres—is tied more closely to Laon than to Paris.

Many consider Notre-Dame at Paris (begun a few years after Laon) to be the final and most accomplished masterpiece of Early Gothic architecture. To be sure, the formal and, in particular, technical aspects of the structure of Notre-Dame occasionally surpass the harmonious order of Laon. The plan of Paris is certainly more ambitious, as patently indicated

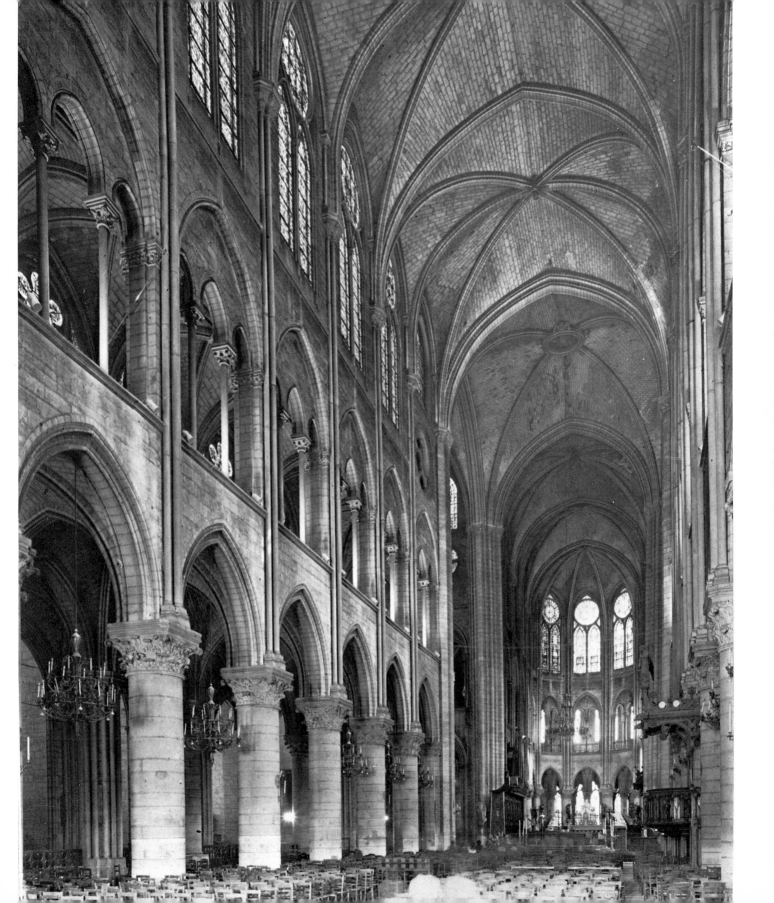

by the double side aisles and double ambulatory. Although the growth of the choir is immense, its nonprojecting transept does not parallel the monumental arrangement at Laon. Notre-Dame's four-story elevation, modified beginning in 1225, lacks a triforium: in its place are rose-shaped oculi (roundels) that project light to the roof. Originally, the clerestory windows were no larger than those at Noyon and Laon, but they afforded less light, as the church was appreciably taller (about 116 feet to the vault imposts). The very large and well-lighted gallery opens to the central nave through triple-arched openings. As at Laon, the ground level is punctuated with single rows of simple cylindrical piers. In spatial terms, the subdivision of bays—of the spatial cells—is now more complex by virtue of the increased number of bays in the side aisles. The principal shortcoming of the Notre-Dame plan is the fact that there is inadequate light in the middle and lower sections. Quite simply, the farther a surface is from the light source, the less light it receives.

As far as we can determine, the structural operations at Notre-Dame were the object of great interest. The cathedral was built according to the "thin-wall" principle; the shallowness of the window recesses and of the gallery arcade make this thinness noticeable at every level. Although the vaulted gallery could prop up the building at mid-elevation, the springings of the gallery vaults could not be braced by exterior piers above the supports separating the two ambulatories or the two side aisles. Thus, wall piers under the roof framework were needed. Given the height of the edifice, this method was deemed insufficient, and the builders turned to flying buttresses as a final solution. During restoration, Viollet-le-Duc proposed a series of statements and hypotheses that have since become generally accepted: there were no flying buttresses in the choir (completed before 1182), but they did exist in the nave area (1180-1200). Moreover, these were quite sophisticated, with intermediate abutments built above the piers of the first side aisle, and outer abutments above the piers of the second side aisle, while a lower second row linked the exterior wall of the gallery to the outer abutment. Since, beginning in 1230, these were entirely reconstructed and altered, nothing can be proposed with any real certainty. Yet, there are old (albeit redecorated) abutments surrounding the apse: these could only have been supports for flying buttresses. This is quite probable, given the fact that Saint-Germain-des-Prés had been furnished with flying buttresses during or shortly after construction (1160). At Saint-Leu-d'Esserent, the oldest flying buttresses probably date from 1180. At Saint-Remi at Reims, in Champagne, and especially in large structures designed shortly after 1190, this device was soon to evolve into nearly definitive forms. It is very likely that Paris was a pioneer testing ground for this development. In addition, there is another area where the master of Notre-Dame displayed his genius at technical creation: the diagonally arched bays of the ambulatory vaulting are replaced by an arrangement of triangular sections that divide the

33. Châlons-sur-Marne, Notre-Dame-en-Vaux, choir and transept.

space in a regular manner. This device was to be immediately exploited in Champagne and later at Bourges. Together with Aubert, we must emphasize that the influence of Notre-Dame was negative. Its four-story elevation, its numerous but low side aisles, and its complex division of poorly illuminated space could only result in creations that departed from or even opposed their plans. Be that as it may, Notre-Dame was the model for a great many structures of lesser dimensions and importance in the diocese of Paris and its vicinity during the last third of the twelfth century.

The most noteworthy of these is unquestionably the Collegiate Church of Mantes, begun about 1170 at the western end. Although reduced in plan—with no transept, single side aisles, and only three stories—the church at Mantes nevertheless reproduces the gallery, type of support, and vaulting found at Paris. The gallery lighting system features the oculi characteristic of Notre-Dame. Other similarities are that the rhythm of the sexpartite vaulting is not carried through to the nave arcade, and that the molding of the column capitals features carved decoration. Additional examples include, among others, the churches at Montreuil-sous-Bois, Gonesse, and Larchant, as well as the curious church at Chars, at the edge of the Vexin, where one discovers a miniature reproduction of the four-story Paris elevation mixed with certain archaic Norman features.

THE EXPANSION OF EARLY GOTHIC IN FRANCE

For geographical, political, and economic reasons, Champagne was the French province most readily influenced by the creation of Gothic architecture. Beginning about 1160-65, imitations (albeit often modest) of the Île-de-France endeavors began to appear in the Brie region, which was divided between *domaine royal* (crown lands) and the counts of Champagne. One of the oldest and most remarkable of these structures is Saint-Quiriace in the town of Provins, a commercial center of the utmost importance and one of the most populous cities of twelfth-century France. Only the choir of this church stands out as peculiar to this area: its unusual plan comprises three bays preceding the apsidal semicircle, each half of which is vaulted in eight ogival sections. The three-story elevation is adapted from Sens. Much more noteworthy are Notre-Dame-en-Vaux at Châlons-sur-Marne and the apse of the famous Abbey Church of Saint-Remi at Reims. Notre-Dame at Châlons is not a homogeneous structure. A choir with three radiating chapels was built about 1180-90 between two towers and against a transept, both dating from the mid-1100s; it is quite similar to the choir at Saint-Remi, which was begun in 1170 by Pierre de Celle and completed before 1200. As at Laon and Noyon, these are four-story elevations resting on circular supports, with vaulted gallery and triforium passage. Their beautiful distinguishing trait is that the increased number of windows—three to each bay (two or three at Châlons)—almost entirely eliminates the wall surface and allows very abundant light to filter into the interior. Moreover, slender colonnettes link the divisions of the triforium to those of the windows, resulting in a more conspicuous linear continuity between levels. Another singular feature is the plan and vaulting of the ambulatory: here the idea of triangular bays (like those at Paris) is combined with quadripartite vaulting. Flanking the chapel entrances are very elegant columns that receive the springings of the numerous vault ribs, thereby creating a semicircular ambulatory colonnade that enhances the overall effect of lightness and transparency. In addition, double flying buttresses, supported by protruding, highly elongated piers, not only give effective support to an extremely lightened surface, but also surround the choir with a kind of "cage" composed of independent elements. This is one of the fundamental effects of Gothic art. In general, the edifices of Champagne, and Saint-Remi in particular, represent the final technical and formal improvements of Early Gothic architecture in all its spatial and linear subtlety and delicacy. Only one other structure (geographically related) can be compared to the Champagne churches: the south transept arm at Soissons. Begun 1175-80, it is attached to the side of an early-thirteenth-century Gothic cathedral, but the striking disparity between the two sections is due not so much to mere chronological distance as to the sudden aesthetic changes that occurred about 1200. The south arm of the transept features a four-story elevation; the Champagne "colonnade," shifted to the inside of the semicircle; a chapel with an upper story (as at Laon), its plastic qualities reminiscent of the chapels at Reims; light flooding through groups of three windows; clear, yet subtle divisions; and imaginatively elegant decoration. One might almost label this architecture Mannerist, for it attained the utmost in stylistic refinement.

In Burgundy, the situation was quite different. From southern Champagne to the Lyonnais, from Sens to Geneva, Romanesque architecture had reached a very high level of plastic and technical development in the twelfth century. Buildings in this area were covered either with barrel vaulting (often pointed) on transverse arches or with groin vaulting (Vézelay) embellished with classical pilasters or columns engaged in walls and piers. Since this style was already coherent in every respect, it did not immediately lend itself to formal renewal. One of the largest and most sumptuous abbey churches in Christendom, the one at Cluny—the so-called Cluny III, begun in 1088—served as a model for an entire period of Burgundian Romanesque art, until superseded by the Cathedral of Langres (begun c. 1160). Even the nearly simultaneous adoption of cross-ribbed vaulting at Cluny (c. 1140?) and in the narthex at Vézelay in no way affected the Romanesque spirit of their spatial volumes. Wilhelm Schlink has recently selected Langres, a contemporary of Laon and Noyon, as a perfect example of this tendency. Despite the systematic use of cross-ribbed vaults in the transept and nave, the spatial configuration of Langres hardly approaches the Gothic. Its three-storied walls conflict

35. Pontigny, Abbey Church,
interior.

36. Vézelay, Sainte-Madeleine,
interior of the choir.

with the linear division of the bays and cancel out the diaphanous or hollowed-out effect.

There was, it is true, a second tendency that had its origins and initial expansion in Burgundy—Cistercian architecture. This style presents a problem, international in scope, that we will examine later in this chapter. In the meantime, we will mention that the Cistercians adopted cross-ribbed vaulting in the nave of the Abbey Church of Pontigny (1150-55). The use of longitudinal (i.e. wall) ribs, the wall divisions, and the pronounced spatial divisions all contribute to this structure's technical perfection. However, its lack of galleries or triforium, its bare walls, and its deliberately stripped appearance oppose it diametrically to the Gothic trend in the Île-de-France. Only in the choir of Pontigny (after 1186) do new tendencies appear; but its enriched form, foreign to Cistercian traditions, was, in any case, not to play a major role in the expansion of French Gothic.

It is only toward 1170 that real French Gothic took shape in Burgundy, brought about by the development of the two-story type, as in the nave of Notre-Dame at Montréal (a village near Vézelay), and by the imitation of the Sens and Noyon models. The choir of Sainte-Madeleine at Vézelay (after 1185) is the masterpiece of this trend. A vaulted gallery over an ambulatory produces a three-story elevation; its equilibrium is maintained by wall buttresses and flying buttresses, the latter added in the course of construction. In spite of certain clearly archaic or awkward traits, the graceful piers and the free movement of air and light throughout the interior create an overall effect of studied, accomplished beauty. At a certain level, the partitions between the radiating chapels are hollowed out. Finally, the prolific use of colonnettes bedded against the grain of the chapel and ambulatory walls results in an almost overabundant linear expression. In a very short space of time, the choir at Vézelay would be imitated in Spain (the Cathedral of Ávila). But in Burgundy, this was, so to speak, a monument without a future, for Gothic architecture in this region was to take a new direction in the thirteenth century. Three cathedrals of the Rhone area should be included in the Early Gothic style of Burgundy: Geneva (begun c. 1160, completed only after 1265 following modification), Lausanne (begun 1160), and Lyons (begun after 1165). Here Gothic solutions are indeed in evidence: gallery at the clerestory level (Lausanne interior, Lyons exterior) echoing the double-shell technique; use of a triforium passage like the one at Laon; three-story elevation; and long colonnettes creating a linearity that ensures well-articulated bays. Yet, the volumes remain massive; the proportions have barely been slenderized. During the thirteenth century, other French contributions influenced the plans of these cathedrals and partially erased the twelfth-century forms.

Normandy presents us with yet a different case. It was here that the structure, even the general design of Gothic had received its initial in-

spiration. Yet, Normandy did not develop the style on its own. The great churches of the late eleventh and early twelfth centuries, such as Saint-Georges-de-Boscherville, were completed or modified; and nothing important was initiated after 1130 (Montivillers and Saint-Omer at Villers are unvaulted). It was only by way of French influence that changes in form occurred toward 1170-75. We will see that the same situation existed in England. Only three edifices in Normandy are of special interest: the Abbey Church of La Trinité at Fécamp (after 1168), the Cathedral of Lisieux, and, toward 1200, the choir of Saint-Étienne at Caen. One of the most glorious Benedictine abbeys in France, Fécamp conforms to the traditional church type, with gallery and passageway at the clerestory level. But there was also an attempt to utilize coherently Gothic vaulting, accompanied by narrow, high, strongly delineated volumes in the French manner. However, the ponderous supports and thick walls isolate this building from the trend toward diaphanousness and hollowness. The Cathedral of Lisieux was begun at the nave and built before 1185, except for the upper level. Its cylindrical piers, false bedding, and general outlines clearly mark it as a descendant of the Laon model, though reduced in size and number of stories. For all its charm and beauty, it still lacks originality. The full potential and high quality of Gothic innovations as applied to Norman architecture were realized only in the choir of Saint-Étienne at Caen, begun about 1200 (1202?). It has three stories; an unvaulted gallery that opens generously to the nave through double arches crowned with perforated tympani; single or double clerestory windows behind a fine arcature that not only embellishes the mural passageway, but also integrates it with the clerestory level (in the tradition of Gothic linearity); more than ample molding in the main arcade and upper levels; and an ambulatory with interconnecting chapels (as at Vézelay) furnished with numerous false-bedded shafts. All of these elements create an effect of sophistication comparable to that of such late twelfth-century French and Burgundian buildings as Soissons and Vézelay. However, when discussing Caen, the contacts with Early English Gothic must also be taken into account.

MAINE, ANJOU, POITOU. THE PLANTAGENET STYLE

During the twelfth century, a complex of territories in western France united politically to the Anglo-Norman kingdom—the Anjou, Maine, and Poitou regions—became organized into the so-called Plantagenet state. One need only consider the art of this area to realize that the creation of Norman-inspired French Gothic was not the only new path blazed by Romanesque architecture. It was only in the decades following the fall (1206) and subsequent political transformation of this feudal power that northern Gothic managed to penetrate the region. Originating in the middle of the twelfth century, Plantagenet architecture first appeared in the vaulting and nave of the Cathedral of Angers (1148-53) and in the

reconstructed nave of the Cathedral of Le Mans (1135-58). According to the most recent studies of this style (André Mussat), the reconstructed west towers of the Cathedral of Chartres also should be included in this initial phase.

The most obvious characteristic of the churches in this region is the design of the cross-ribbed vaults: their extremely curved, dome-shaped form necessitated the support of thick walls reinforced with piers. The twelfth-century tendencies toward opening the wall and toward rhythmic linearity are not to be found here. The building traditions already established in these lands during the Romanesque era might explain the use of such a system. In any event, three basic structural types stand out. First, immense churches whose single, wood-ceilinged naves had later to be vaulted and, in some cases, subdivided (Angers, Saint-Hilaire at Poitiers). Second, churches with three naves of approximately equal height, in which the side naves serve as counterthrusts to the central nave at the roof level (Saint-Savin-sur-Gartempe). Lastly, the Aquitainian type, with its rows of domes (Fontevrault, near Saumur, and the Cathedral of Angoulême). Vaulting procedures in these provinces had already reached a fairly advanced stage when the ribbed vault was taken over from England, Normandy, and the Île-de-France. It was adapted to traditional structures, and could be used in the construction of the immense square bays of the Cathedral of Angers or the low, massive bays of Le Mans. Strictly speaking, there was no attempt at a multitiered arrangement. At Le Mans, as at Avenières near Laval, a decorative band of flat arcatures, connected to the roof by narrow openings, extends between the arcade and the clerestory windows, which are pierced through an ample, solid wall. In the nave at Angers, extremely solid piers, comparable to those supporting Aquitainian domes, protrude into the nave, while a passage, conceived as an unarticulated balcony, runs along the wall. The same principle obtains in the nave of Saint-Pierre-de-la-Couture at Le Mans (1180-1200), where the sexpartite vault takes on a lierne (a subordinate rib parallel or perpendicular to the axis of the building). The Cathedral of Poitiers, an unquestionable masterpiece, defined the Plantagenet style even more decisively. Begun in 1162, the essential plan remained unaltered despite the fact that the building was not completed until the second half of the thirteenth century. It has three naves of approximately equal height and width, well illuminated by the large windows of the apse and lateral walls. Supported by slender, yet powerful interior piers, the dome-shaped vaults buttress each other by means of reciprocal counterthrusts. Even though the interior space is clearly articulated by the piers and vaults, the large, amply interconnected bays create a spatial interpenetration that brings to mind the German or Italian *Hallenkirchen* of the thirteenth and fourteenth centuries. This is undoubtedly a Gothic space, but one that differs from the northern French variety. During the construction of the bays of the transept

and nave, the vaults received supplementary ribs, resulting in slightly changed proportions.

Allowing for its exceptional dimensions and powerful effect, the Cathedral of Poitiers is nevertheless not unique from either the structural or the aesthetic point of view. In the chapel and main hall of the Hospital of Saint-Jean at Angers (1180-88), interior supports separating bays of equal height point to the same quest for spatial unity. The same holds true for the Maison de Coëffort at Le Mans (1180-82). These are small edifices, it is true, but astonishing in the virtuosity of their architects: witness the slenderized interior piers, above whose capitals radiate bundles of ribs leading to the roof, of these structures. In the last decades of the century, the Angers vault underwent two important refinements: the addition of liernes and the subdivision of the vault sections by diagonal rib branches perpendicular to the wall. The result was a complex linear network. The fact that all of the ribs share the same thin profile underscores their nonstructural function. Of all the examples of this style—the loveliest are from the thirteenth century—the most curious is to be found in Saint-Serge at Angers (c. 1200-20), with its rectilinear apse and triple choir, subdivided by extremely elegant and slender supports. Closer to the Poitiers model are the churches at Cunault, Le Puy-Notre-Dame, and Candes, where the bays are arranged according to the *Hallenkirche* principle. We might wonder whether there might possibly be a relationship between this proliferation of vault-and-support linearity and the development of contemporary English architecture. (From the point of view of general plan, there is no link whatever between the two). As in England (Lincoln), Anjou architects soon made use of fan-ribbing under barrel vaults—for example, at Airvault and in the demolished Church of La Toussaint at Angers.

By its extraordinary formal quality and its admirably accomplished nature, Plantagenet architecture in the first half of the thirteenth century may be likened to the stage at which northern Gothic had, by 1200, realized its most successful constructions at Soissons (transept) and Vézelay (ambulatory). But whereas development beyond the status quo was possible, logical, and even necessary in the Île-de-France and those provinces already conquered by Gothic, Plantagenet architecture was preoccupied with subtleties of detail and did not have the impetus to surpass this phase. Beginning in 1220, the northern models gained the upper hand, first in the Cathedral of Le Mans, followed quickly by Tours and Bordeaux.

THE EXPANSION OF EARLY GOTHIC OUTSIDE OF FRANCE

By the middle of the twelfth century, the use of the cross-ribbed vault had already spread significantly to areas of Europe lying outside of the original breeding ground of Gothic architecture. But only in the last third of the century did the new spatial and formal concepts manage to assert themselves, and even then with difficulty. The evolution toward Gothic in these lands occurred almost exclusively by dint of the influence of French architecture. The case of England is typical, as illustrated by the historical term generally accepted there to designate the first phase of the evolution—*Early Gothic*, successor to Anglo-Norman Romanesque art at the time of the reconstruction of Canterbury Cathedral after 1174. Necessitated by a fire, this project was admirably documented by the contemporary chronicler Gervase of Canterbury. The architect, Guillaume de Sens, was called from France, but four years after the start of work, he fell from the scaffolding and was replaced by another William, an Englishman. Most of the new structure was completed in 1185. We know that, although only the central part of the choir (between the two transepts and the crossing of the eastern transept) had been completed at the time of Guillaume's accident, he had probably planned the entire choir. The French contribution is considerable: sexpartite vaulting, the form of the gallery openings, and the piers, whose double columns echo the Cathedral of Sens (Canterbury presbytery). The upper gallery at the clerestory level is a hallmark of English tradition, while a system of wall buttresses under the roof and curious flying buttresses above the roofing assure the equilibrium of the whole. The interior space—its proportions, divisions, very high arcade, and luxuriously illuminated side aisles—is a perfect expression of the characteristics of Early Gothic. In addition, one peculiarity of major importance must be noted: the linearity of the vaulting, walls, and supports is accentuated by the innovative use of black Purbeck marble. Perhaps the use of Tournai marble in Notre-Dame at Valenciennes was its inspiration (Bony). Canterbury was not the only building whose architectonic quality profited from this polychromy; it was applied to an entire series of slightly later structures that were to develop fully the English variant of Gothic.

A quick mention should be given to the choirs at Chichester (1187-1200) and at Rochester (c. 1190-1200). More important was the work done on Lincoln Cathedral at the end of the twelfth century (beginning in 1192). Of this immense and highly complex structure, the two transepts and the choir joining them belong to this phase of evolution. The Canterbury system is used for the structure, with flying buttresses supported above the level of the traditional mural gallery. The vaulting, sexpartite in the transept, is disarticulated in the choir in a curious manner by means of a unique system of oblique movements accentuated by ribs. The principle of the crossribbed vault has now been abandoned. The spatial forms, too, are here drawn with an even greater decisiveness than at Canterbury. Moreover, an abundance of colonnettes (in Purbeck marble or limestone) not only dresses the piers, but also appears in dense groups at the gallery level. All of these features indicate a great inventive freedom that surpasses Early Gothic art and marks the movement away from the kind of French-influenced art that characterizes Canterbury. At

42. Poitiers, Cathedral, interior
view.

Lincoln, truly English Gothic established itself forcefully and enduringly. Its influence was quickly felt in Norway: witness the transept of the Cathedral of Trondheim (third quarter of the twelfth century).

With the exception of those provinces affiliated with the northern French development (dioceses of Cambrai and Tournai) and the southern fringe of Burgundy (Lyons, Geneva, and Lausanne), Early Gothic architecture entered the Holy Roman Empire with great difficulty. At the beginning of the twelfth century, the deep-seated traditions of Ottonian and Salian imperial art of the Meuse region provided highly elaborated Romanesque architectural types that were ripe for development. With its rounded transept arms and central complex of five towers, the Cathedral of Tournai shows that it benefited from this design, but its monumental four-story elevation is a Norman borrowing. Moreover, the pre-1150 use of colored marble colonnettes in the nave of Tournai in order to heighten the linear effect may have been the source of inspiration for such efforts at Canterbury and in English Early Gothic in general (via the now-destroyed Church of Notre-Dame at Valenciennes). Although the cross-ribbed transept at Tournai (c. 1150-60) is heavy and its walls imperfectly hollowed out, its overall proportions afford a vertical sweep that is highlighted by the molding.

During the second half of the century, a style termed Late Romanesque (*Spätromanisch*) reigned along the Meuse (Maas) and Rhine rivers. Its period of duration and even certain of its characteristics more or less correspond to Early French Gothic. As illustrated by Murbach (c. 1140) and the transept of the Cathedral of Speyer (1154-56), the cross-ribbed vault made its appearance in the Rhineland at a fairly early date. However, its use led neither to the lightening of walls nor to the concept of a subdivided and outlined interior space. The walls do include a number of rhythmic elements (such as half columns or pilasters, applied against piers, that extend the ribs of the vaulting). But these projections do not promote a framework effect. A complex superposition of levels is lacking in the elevation, and the wall space between the arcade and the clerestory is often bare or covered with a band of blind arcades or niches (Sankt Aposteln and Sankt Kunibert at Cologne, after 1210). Occasionally, the placing of a gallery at this intermediate level (Sankt Quirinus at Neuss, nave of the Collegiate Church of Bonn) produces a closer and more conspicuous tie to Gothic elevations. The general proportions remain heavy. Inside, strictly Romanesque walls demarcate the volumes evenly and uninterruptedly; outside, piers that would ordinarily punctuate the mass are omitted in favor of a continuous wall decoration of great richness and beauty. Such features as superimposed blind arcades (occasionally decorated) and a continuous, colonnaded gallery thoroughfare at the upper level of the façade are, to be sure, part of the Romanesque repertory, but here it has been surpassed in plasticity. The formal variety of the apertures—round or multifoil, oculus or "fanned" (as at Sankt Gereon in

Cologne)—bears witness to the subtlety of this magnificent decorative system. Although almost all of the elements of this style differ from those used in the Île-de-France, it is nonetheless possible to parallel, on the one hand, exterior Rhenish elevations to the overall effect of the façade at Laon, and on the other hand, Cologne elevations to the interior at Noyon.

Thus, we feel that Late Romanesque and Early Gothic are not totally antithetical. Despite the formal conservatism of the "great century of Cologne architecture" (1150-1250, according to W. Meyer-Barckhausen)—as opposed to the inventive dynamism of the Île-de-France and vicinity—the spirit of Gothic structure, its notions of linear divisions and separations, did slowly infiltrate Germany. True, French Gothic began to be accepted by the early thirteenth century, as in the cathedrals of Magdeburg (from 1209) and Limburg an der Lahn (after 1211-35); and after 1225, it would produce truly pure, coherent works (Liebfrauenkirche at Trier and Elisabethkirche at Marburg an der Lahn). Yet, Late Romanesque cannot be completely excluded from the general schema of the expansion of French Gothic. The old theory of Dehio, who observed all of these analogies while distinguishing several evolutionary phases, is certainly more accurate than the more categorical oppositions proposed by certain present-day writers (Hans E. Kubach).

Italy did not attempt a coherent Gothic style during the twelfth century, even though cross-ribbed vaults appeared quite early, at Sant'Ambrogio in Milan (1098 or 1117) and at Rivolta d'Adda (early twelfth century). The exception to this trend are the Cistercian structures, which we will discuss shortly. Whether derived from Early Christian traditions, influenced by Byzantine solutions, or faithful to Early Romanesque designs, the diverse forms of Italian architecture did not play a totally passive role in nascent Gothic. The creation of the façade rose window can probably be attributed to Italy (San Zeno at Verona, and the cathedrals of Trani and Troia). Moreover, the Cathedral of Modena and the northern Italian churches with alternating naves helped spread this rhythmic principle to Germany and elsewhere. However, San Francesco at Assisi (begun 1226) marks the real beginning of the history of Gothic art in Italy.

The situation was just the opposite in Spain. From the tenth-century beginnings of Romanesque art, there were innumerable ties between those countries that had escaped Muslim conquest (or that had been reconquered in the eleventh and twelfth centuries) and both southern French and Burgundian artistic centers. These links were strengthened by the Cluniac and Cistercian expansions. For the time being, we will pass over the Cistercian monasteries, where Gothic made its debut. At this stage of its evolution, noteworthy structures include the Cathedral of Zamora, the Collegiate Church of Toro, the Church of San Vicente at Ávila, and the choir of the Cathedral of Tarragona. Planned in 1171, construction at

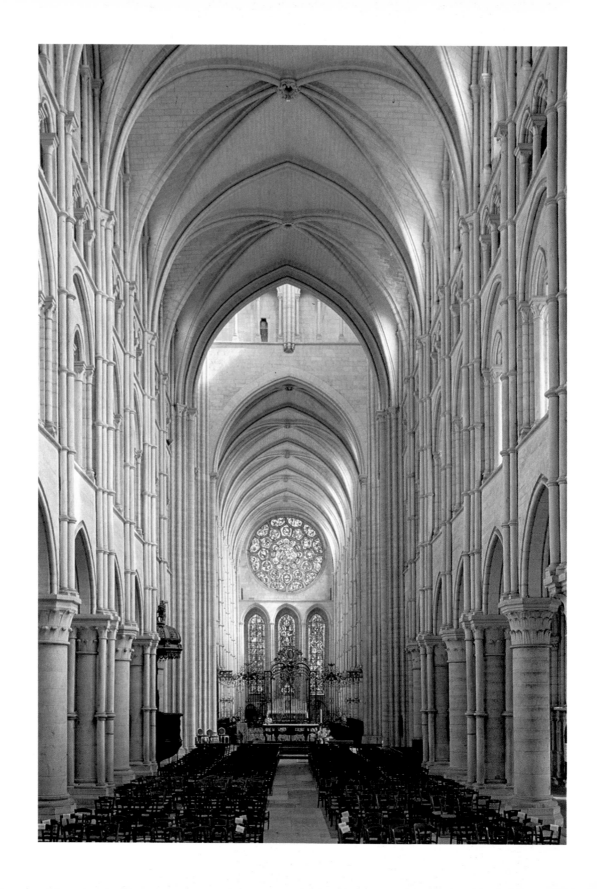

47. Cologne, Sankt Kunibert,
interior.

I. Laon, Cathedral, interior.

II. Paris, Notre-Dame, south side.

50. *Chiaravalle Milanese, Abbey Church, interior.*
51. *Poblet, Monastery of Santa Maria, refectory.*

50. *Chiaravalle Milanese, Abbey Church, interior.*
51. *Poblet, Monastery of Santa Maria, refectory.*

Tarragona began only toward 1200, based on a Romanesque plan: a two-story elevation in the Cistercian style, without ambulatory. Despite a scrupulous application of the Gothic system, this work remains hesitant and archaic. The Cathedral of Zamora (begun 1151, partially dedicated 1174) includes cross-ribbed vaulting in the central nave, not to mention a typically Spanish ribbed dome, but it displays nothing more than an early interest in French techniques. Founded in 1160, the Collegiate Church of Santa María la Mayor at Toro, related technically and formally to Zamora, received a beautiful Gothic portal as its construction continued into the thirteenth century. It is, however, the edifices at Ávila that best exemplify the contact made with French Gothic. In its plan and interior effect, the Cathedral of Ávila (choir built at the end of the twelfth century, according to Elie Lambert) echoes the Burgundian arrangement of the choir at Vézelay, despite the imposing, massive piers of the sexpartite-vaulted bays on the right side of the sanctuary. The three-story elevation and the gallery furnished with wall piers confirm its relationship to Vézelay. In San Vicente at Ávila, the nave is Gothic-inspired, with a Burgundian three-story elevation that is strongly punctuated by members protruding from the supporting piers. Thus, it is with a certain heaviness and awkwardness that Spanish architecture followed the lead of Early French Gothic. Perhaps no other country in Europe accepted it as rapidly as did Spain, a fact that presaged the magnificent development of Gothic art in the Iberian peninsula during the thirteenth, fourteenth, and fifteenth centuries.

CISTERCIAN ARCHITECTURE AND THE DISSEMINATION OF GOTHIC

Although the monastery at Cîteaux was founded in 1089, the Cistercian Order—the "reformed" Benedictine rule—was not officially inaugurated until 1119. By that time, the first "daughters" of Cîteaux had already been established: La Ferté in 1113, Pontigny in 1114, Morimond and Clairvaux in 1115. At the moment of their founding and of the pope's acceptance of the new order, there appeared on the scene the towering personality of Bernard des Fontaines, Saint Bernard of Clairvaux (1091-1153), adviser to the kings of France and the pope, and an anti-Cluniac for both moral and political reasons. The order of Cîteaux spread with lightning speed. From the first days of this expansion, Cistercian architectural efforts shared a common plan dominated by a spirit that was, in its severity and humility, resolutely opposed to that of Cluniac architecture. Pompous, grandiose interior configuration combined with an abundance of exterior volumes marks both Cluny III and the Saint-Denis of Abbott Suger as the very antithesis of the Cistercian aesthetic. Earlier Benedictine modes undoubtedly influenced the disposition of monastic buildings flanking the church (cloister, chapter house, dormitories, kitchens, annexes for manufacture [Fontenay] or agriculture [Noirlac]). But thanks to a more logical and economical arrangement, the

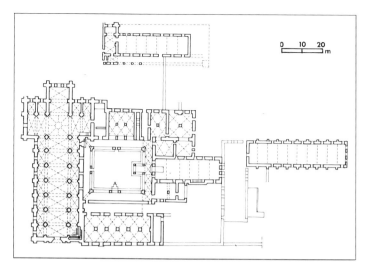

52. Fossanova, Abbey, plan
of the complex.
53. Fossanova, Abbey Church,
interior.

Cistercian church emanates naked, functional monumentality. Almost all of the first Cistercian structures (that is, prior to the mid-1100s) have disappeared. Only Fontenay in Burgundy (c. 1130-47) provides an excellent example of a "Romanesque" abbey, complete with pointed barrel vaulting, simple plan, and very restrained decoration. But it is the abbey at Clairvaux (Clairvaux III) that furnishes the most accomplished model for Cistercian architecture. Cross-ribbed vaulting was adopted quite early, if not in the nave and side aisles, at least in such auxiliary areas as the chapter houses (Fontenay, c. 1150). The entirely cross-ribbed nave at Pontigny (Pontigny II) marked the next chapter in the history of the partnership between Gothic and Cistercian architecture.

The Cistercian style obviously cannot be defined according to the same criteria as those of the twelfth-century cathedrals in northern France. With respect to the general plan, the Cistercians rejected rich Cluniac effects in favor of bare, rectilinear apses, with chapels protruding from the transept. There are no splendid towers at the crossing, no harmonious façades, no bell towers; these were forbidden by the order. Inside, there are only two levels of arcades, opening into the side aisles or side chapels, and clerestory windows of rather diminutive proportions. Even when the cross-ribbed vault was adopted, the clear, rigorous spatial division that would have resulted from vault lines extending to the ground via colonnettes did not take place. Twelfth-century Cistercian architecture has been called "simplified Gothic" (Dehio): that is, reduced to the principle and technical devices of a new luminous and divided spatial definition, one that incorporated the new molding and decoration of the carved foliate capital typical of nonmonastic edifices. In fact, the Cistercian architects eventually abandoned their original strict simplicity and turned more toward the style of the great Gothic structures.

Beginning in the middle of the twelfth century, the Cistercians spread their simplified Gothic into regions not yet answering the Gothic call: the south of France (chapter house at Le Thoronet, c. 1175); Spain (Santas Creus, after 1174); Catalonia (Poblet, last quarter of the century); Aragon (Veruela); Italy (abbeys at Fossanova, Casamari, and Chiaravalle Milanese); England (Rievaulx and Fountains Abbey); and the Holy Roman Empire (Himmerod, founded 1135, and Heiligenkreuz in Austria, after 1136). The chapter house at Zwettl in Austria (c. 1180) is a perfect copy of Burgundian models, and many other examples could be cited. We should also add that, after 1200, the influence of severe, rudimentary early Cistercian architecture extended far from France, into Poland (Sulejów) and Hungary (Eger). Within France, it rejected its original primitiveness (Ourscamps, Royaumont, Maubuisson) and evolved into an imitation of the more luxurious cathedral models.

In certain German Cistercian structures—in particular, at Maulbronn and Heisterbach—one can observe not only the Cistercians' role as propagators of French Gothic, but also the flexibility of their art, its capacity

to absorb highly diverse influences. The plan of Heisterbach (c. 1210), given the continuity from ambulatory to chapel niches, is an obvious imitation of Clairvaux III, but the execution of the plan utilized all of the refinements of Rhenish and especially Cologne Late Romanesque. The subtlety of design and the slender supports in the choir are related to the phase of formal sophistication expressed about 1200 in such a structure as the transept of Soissons (the latter stemming, however, from utterly different principles).

Consequently, an analogy between the formal treatment characterizing Late Romanesque and later Early Gothic is frequently proposed (Frankl, H.G. Franz). As an example, one might point to the western choir of the Cathedral of Worms, with its polygonal shape, cross-ribbed internal structure, and abundant use of foiled motifs and rose windows. It is also one of the most sophisticated and involved examples of the excessive proliferation of certain traditional elements of Romanesque decoration.

Today we use the term *classical Gothic* or *High Gothic* to describe that stage in the evolution of Gothic marked by the complete realization and intelligibility of its essential traits. It is a term used most recently by Jantzen, who, in turn, refers to previous writers on the subject. This notion of the Classical phase of a given style is related to an evolutionary schema that nineteenth-century art historians—notably Heinrich Wölfflin—elaborated in the their description of the stages of modern art since the Renaissance. It must therefore be understood that this classicism refers neither to Greco-Roman civilization nor to French art of the seventeenth century. According to Focillon, it denotes a full blossoming, the arrival at a perfect balance through a series of formal experiments. The disciples of Wölfflin hold that the definition of Classical must have "exemplariness" as its hallmark. For others, such as Dvořak and, more recently, Panofsky, the key issue is achieving a balance between the containing form and the spiritual content.

Archaeologists, for their part, have asserted that several new types of religious edifices that appeared during the late twelfth century were the most accomplished and fully elaborated models and commanded architectural creation for more than a century. In particular, the Chartres type is believed not only to have served as a model for the great cathedrals both in and outside France, but also its formal and structural success is believed to have made it a kind of masterpiece sui generis whose historical value surely matches that of the most celebrated creations of world architecture. However, upon closer examination of thirteenth-century architecture, we realize that the influence of this model was, in fact, not universal and that other masterpieces based on a different design—Bourges, for instance—appeared at the same time. Certain writers since Dehio have even maintained that the most logical and accomplished product of the Gothic style is not to be found in the Chartres type, but instead in mid-thirteenth-century art: namely, the so-called Court Style (Branner) or, to use the more widely accepted term, Rayonnant Style. According to this viewpoint, the transept and nave of Saint-Denis, the choirs of the cathedrals of Troyes and Tours, and Sainte-Chapelle in Paris all share certain features—the lightening of the structural system, the hollowing out of the spatial limits, and the absolutely logical linearity of the interior configuration—that mark the real culmination of the Gothic principles of space and construction. Moreover, this stage would accord with an explicitly expressed spiritual meaning. Assuming we follow the evolutionary outline of Focillon and of Wölfflin's students, to what extent did a fundamental stylistic change occur about 1270, giving rise to a new phase of development that might be labeled Mannerist? And to what extent did diverse regional reactions contemporaneous with the family of Gothic cathedrals and French Rayonnant structures manage to assert themselves—reactions that would have at least partially broken up the presumed stylistic unity of thirteenth-century art? These are the kinds of problems that we will consider in this chapter.

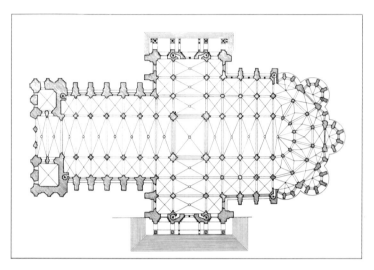

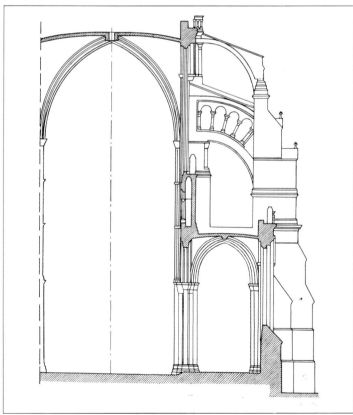

CHARTRES AND ITS DESCENDANTS

Notre-Dame at Chartres, an eleventh-century Romanesque cathedral
whose western portion had already been altered in the middle of the
twelfth century, was destroyed by fire on June 10, 1194. A very moving
account of this catastrophe has survived. The immensity and magnifi-
cence of this edifice were due not only to the fact that Chartres was the
seat of a very wealthy bishopric, but also because it was the site of a well-
known Marian pilgrimage. Reconstruction began immediately; the foundations of the original structure were retained as much for reasons of
economy as for pious respect. Inspiring extraordinary generosity on the
part of the faithful, work on the project proceeded rapidly. It has been
fairly well established that the nave was built first, sometime prior to
1210 (L. Grodecki, F. Van der Meulen), during which time the foundations of the choir were laid out, to be completed about 1220. The arms of
the transept were probably finished shortly after 1230. Owing to the successive intervention of several architects, the plan underwent some
modification in the course of construction. But it was the general conception established in 1194-95 that determined the basic design, one that
is nothing short of revolutionary in the development of Gothic art
(Focillon, Jantzen).

Grandiose in its dimensions, the plan of Chartres includes a double
ambulatory with chapels, thus combining the plans of Notre-Dame at
Paris and of Saint-Denis. The layout of the transept, with its large side
aisles, is derived from the transept of the Cathedral of Laon. The extraordinary originality and genius of the architect of Chartres are borne out in
the interior elevation and the general structure of the building. The elevation comprises three stories and thus resembles Sens, with this one difference: the arcade and clerestory, separated by the kind of triforium
found at Laon, are of equal height. This feature contradicts the twelfth-
century structural principle that dictated the superposition of arcade,
gallery, triforium, and clerestory in such a manner that the size of the
clerestory windows was unavoidably reduced. It has sometimes been said,
and rightly so, that the architect of Chartres sacrificed the gallery and ad-
justed the elevation to much more monumental proportions in order to
enlarge these windows and thereby to allow more light into the building.
The result is a complete realignment of the scale of the edifice: immense
bays covered with large oblong vaults whose springings extend to the
abaci (uppermost elements) of the supporting cylindrical or octagonal
piers, each of which, in turn, is flanked by four huge columns. The
clerestory consists of two lancet windows beneath a huge multifoil rose
window; it fills the entire space beneath the wall ribs. As for the exterior, the master of Chartres categorically altered the twelfth-century
flying buttress: the two struts linked by arcatures make up a rich, forceful
pattern that blends in well with the overall plastic effect of the exterior
structure. Seven towers—framing the choir, at the arms of the transept,

57

and atop the crossing—had originally been planned. Together with the two towers of the façade, they were to have given the Cathedral of Chartres an imposing appearance comparable to that of the cathedrals of Tournai and Laon. The design of the interior volumes, the delineation of bays by piers and colonnettes, the rigor of proportions between the central volumes and those of the side aisles and ambulatory—these features comprise one of the most logical spatial arrangements known to Gothic architecture. In addition, by virtue of its incredible abundance of 166 stained—glass windows on biblical narratives and its six thirteenth-century sculpted portals, the Cathedral of Chartres must be considered one of the monuments that states most explicitly the Scholastic or mystical purpose of medieval art.

A great deal of thought has been given to the possible origins of such a masterpiece. Chartres, however, cannot be easily explained either as a derivative of Laon or as a reaction against such small-scale, poorly illuminated structures exemplified by Notre-Dame at Paris. The hypothesis of a precedent in the Laon tradition—the Church of Saint-Vincent, now demolished (Lambert)—cannot be totally disallowed, but it does not account for the authoritative creativity of the first master of Chartres. In both plastic and structural terms, there are noticeable differences between the nave on the one hand, and the transept and choir on the other. Not only have the flying buttresses of the choir been lightened, but a third row has been added in order to support more effectively the upper portion of the wall. The molding of the transept façades is much more sophisticated than had originally been conceived by the first architect. The arrangement at either extremity of this transept is especially noteworthy: the placing of large, partitioned rose windows above a single row of windows creates a group of light sources whose unified and awe-inspiring illumination is made even more glorious by the use of multicolored stained glass. We are a long way from the lovely, but nevertheless hesitant composition of the transept at Laon. Although later masters imposed these modifications in an attempt to modernize Chartres according to early-thirteenth-century artistic standards, they were unable to undermine the profound unity of this cathedral.

The influence of this extraordinary structure was immediate and widespread. Its first effects were felt in the plans for the choir of the Cathedral of Soissons (1197-98) and in the construction of Saint-Laumer at Blois (prior to 1200), as well as in the plans for such great northern French cathedrals as Reims (1211) and Amiens (1221). The hallmark of Chartres is the nearly universal adoption of the three-storied elevation—without gallery, but with enlarged clerestory windows; this, in turn, necessitated the systematic use of a new double-row type of flying buttress. Other distinguishing features include a cylindrical pier flanked by four columns (in the semicircular apse, by a single columns) and a window group consisting of two lancets beneath a rose window of varying

62, 63. Chartres, Cathedral, south side aisle and vault of the ambulatory.

III. Chartres, Cathedral, detail of the apse.

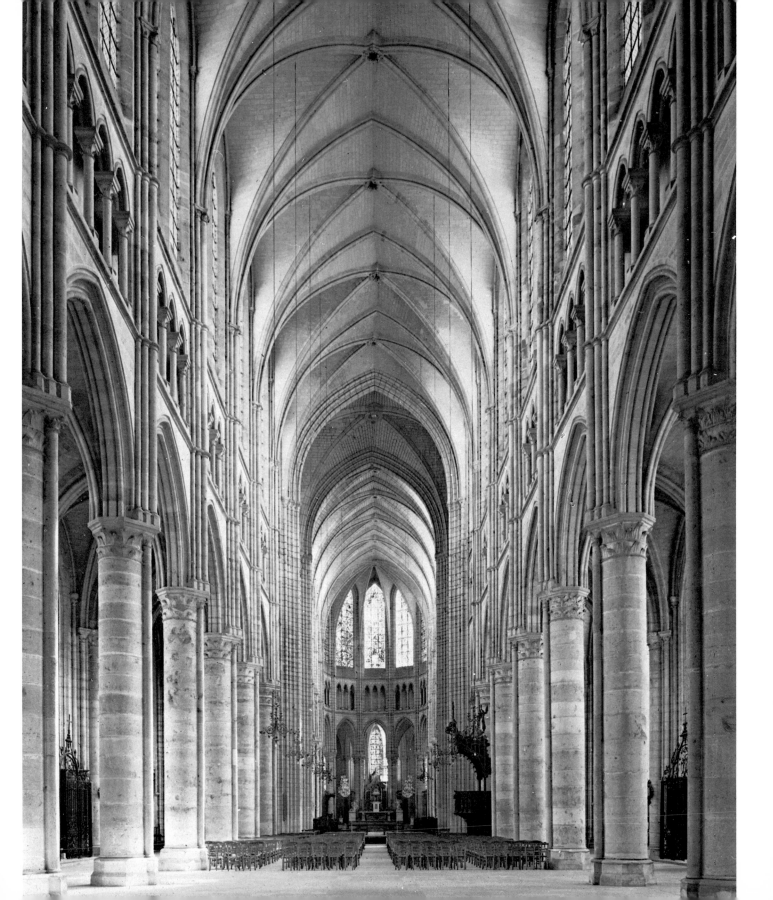

65. Orbais, Abbey Church
of Notre-Dame, choir.
66. Reims, Cathedral, plan.
67. Reims, Cathedral, section.

65. Orbais, Abbey Church of Notre-Dame, choir.

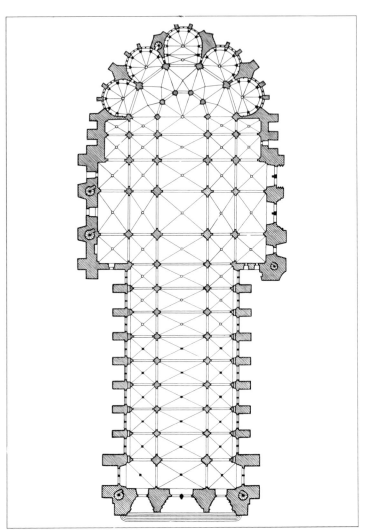

66. Reims, Cathedral, plan.

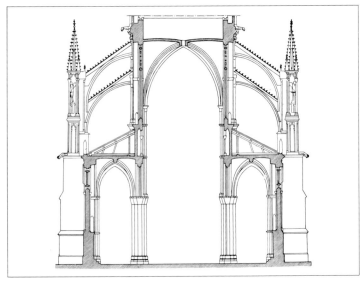

67. Reims, Cathedral, section.

68. Reims, Cathedral, aerial view.   70. Reims, Cathedral, nave wall.
69. Reims, Cathedral, façade.

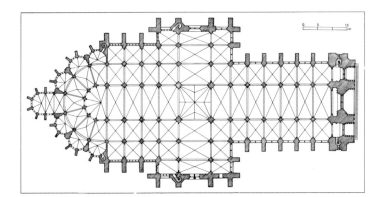

elaborateness. At Chartres, this arrangement was not only applied in the clerestory level, but also was extended to the windows of the side aisles and chapels during the thirteenth century. The treatment of the interior space is marked by a strong, even cadence of bays and powerful plastic highlights, but also by a kind of mural dullness in the principal alignments (Bony). In several large-scale projects begun about 1200—such as the cathedrals of Meaux and of Rouen—the Chartres plan prompted the abandonment of the gallery during construction and the rejection of certain characteristic Champagne features (for instance, the triple window, as in the choir at Orbais). The complicated twelfth-century design of Notre-Dame at Paris had now been definitively surpassed. Nowhere was this more evident than at Notre-Dame itself, where the model of Chartres was responsible not only for the easternmost bays of the nave (c. 1215), but also for the complete remaking of the upper levels (c. 1225).

Owing to its more limited dimensions, the choir at Soissons (completed c. 1212)—first descendant in the Chartres line—constitutes a somewhat simplified version of the model. There are three stories, including a triforium, and tall but narrow clerestory windows underneath small rose windows. Its system of abutment is lightened and marks a progressive step beyond the heaviness of Chartres. As Carl F. Barnes has observed, the result is a building that emanates great elegance. It is especially revealing to compare the choir of Soissons to the adjoining south arm of the transept, one of the outstanding products of twelfth-century architecture. The disparity in dimension and scale forcefully underscores the profound changes that Chartres had wrought over a period of only a few years.

More significant is the Cathedral of Reims. Like Chartres, Reims is extraordinary for historical as well as architectonic reasons. Seat of a large diocese and part of the crown lands, Reims is the cathedral in which the monarchs of France were traditionally consecrated. These exceptional circumstances doubtless influenced the splendor of the edifice, the opulence of its decoration, and its heightened political and religious status during the thirteenth century (Hans Reinhardt). Clearly an imitation of Chartres, its plan includes a transept flanked by side aisles that are doubled along the choir. As in the Chartres plan, there were to have been seven exterior towers altogether, including two on each arm of the transept and one at the crossing, but the only two completed were those on the western façade. The interior space of Reims is a perfect example of the Chartres type: the same heaviness, plastic force, and abundance of light filtering through double windows in the clerestory as well as in the side aisles and chapels (Jantzen). Although the transept arrangement of large rose windows over lancets resembles that of Chartres, Branner has observed that there is a certain archaic quality indicating that it may have been designed a few years prior to Chartres. However, not everything at Reims derives from Chartres—for example, a passage cut into the wall that runs along the base of the windows of the chapels and side aisles.

Moreover, the sculpted vegetation that decorated the portals, the friezes beneath the cornice, and especially the columns capitals—almost naturalistic in its variety and profuseness—runs counter to the dearth of ornamentation at Chartres. This feature is the mark of a style that truly belongs to Champagne. It may also be found in the Abbey Church of Notre-Dame at Orbais, south of Reims. The construction of this church began in the twelfth century but continued into the first third of the thirteenth under the influence of Chartres and Reims. But let us return to Reims.

Outside, the flying buttresses and abutments—double-strutted from pier to wall in the nave, with an additional double-strutted row in the choir—are integrated into the overall style and form of the structure. Furthermore, the pinnacles echo the form of the towers and house statues of angels, again pointing to the unusual imaginativeness with which the architect of Reims transformed the original model. Architectonic and decorative elements alike contribute to the creation of this cathedral as a cosmic image: the Heavenly Church guarded by angels, its lofty western towers rising in hollow transparency. The history of the construction of Reims is quite complex. Work was interrupted in 1223, the choir was not vaulted until 1241, and the upper sections of the towers were still under construction at the beginning of the fourteenth century. We also know that the project was directed by four architects in succession. Although we cannot be certain of their order, it is generally agreed that Jean d'Orbais, active from 1211 to 1228?, was responsible for the initial plans, which were somewhat modified later (Reinhardt, Salet). These shifts in architects can be seen in the structure of the choir (H. Deneux) and most revealingly in the obvious disorder of the sculpted decoration of the portals (R. Hamann McLean).

The weight of this evolution now passed to Notre-Dame at Amiens, whose plans were probably created in 1221 by Robert de Luzarches. At this moment, the choir of Chartres was being completed and construction of the transept and choir of Reims was well under way. Compared to the large structures that preceded it, Amiens marks a step forward by virtue of its gigantic dimensions. Its principal vault soars to almost 138 feet, whereas Reims rises to about 131 feet, Chartres to almost 125 feet. The width of the bays and the dimensions of each level of the elevation are equally colossal: the triforium is 10 feet high and the total length of the edifice is more than 492 feet. Its plan resembles that of Reims, except that the choir is more fully developed and the axial chapel (dedicated to the Virgin) is longer. In the nave elevation, the starting point of construction, the architect doubled the Chartres window, thereby creating groups of quadruple windows under three rose windows. In addition, the Laon variety of triforium was rejected in favor of two triple-arched openings to each bay. As a result, a subtle, yet rather distracting rhythm takes shape from floor to roof: to each bay of the main arcade correspond two triple

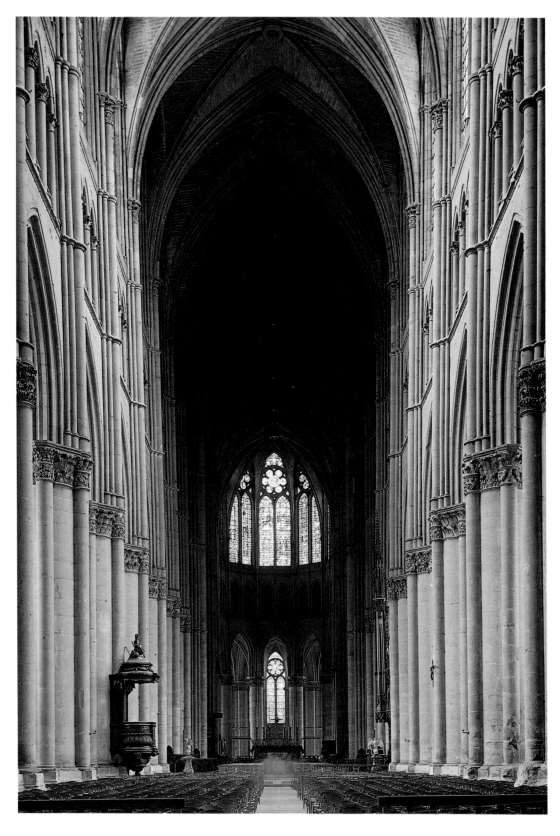

V. Reims, Cathedral, nave.

VI. *Amiens, Cathedral, façade.*

76. *Beauvais, Cathedral, exterior of the south arm of the transept.*

openings in the triforium and two double openings in the clerestory. In the choir, which was built later, these rhythms are even more complex. However, it is only in these highly subtle details that Amiens distinguishes itself from Reims and Chartres, for it retains the same plasticity of piers and ribs highlighted against the plane surfaces of the walls. Viewed from the outside—in this case, the exterior profile is not dominated by the towers—the volumes of the cathedral are admirably harmonious and readable, despite the forest of double flying buttresses linked by arcatures in the Chartres manner. More slender and inclined at a greater angle, these flying buttresses have acquired a new functionality: they carry channels for water drainage. All of these refinements notwithstanding, the Cathedral of Amiens may be considered the most Classical of French cathedrals, for it achieves a perfect balance between impressive monumentality and subtlety of detail (Viollet-le-Duc, Jantzen). At least, this is the case in the nave and in the lower part of the transept; the work on the choir (begun 1236-37, completed 1269) already belongs to the Rayonnant phase of Gothic. It is likely that Thomas de Cormont, who, in 1230 or 1233, succeeded Robert de Luzarches, exerted a sizable influence in the Île-de-France and even in Paris (Branner). We cannot take leave of Amiens without mentioning the sculpted decoration of the western and southern façades. No other French cathedral approaches the logic, coherence, and formal abundance of its comprehensive, almost encyclopedic iconographical repertory (John Ruskin, Mâle).

The last great edifice in the Chartres line of descent is the Cathedral of Beauvais. Only its choir and the western part of its transept were constructed in the thirteenth century, probably from 1225 to 1272. Moreover, this choir does not retain its original form. In 1284, a considerable part of the vaulting collapsed, necessitating a forty-year campaign to repair the damage through reinforcement of the entire structure. However, work stopped at that point and was not resumed until the sixteenth century. Even more ambitious than Robert de Luzarches, the architect of Beauvais wanted to raise the principal vaults to a height of more than 144 feet and, in general, to build a structure of greater proportions. The original plans, reconstructed by Viollet-le-Duc and Branner, attest to his audacity. The three right bays of the choir, more than 49 feet wide and almost 33 feet deep, rest on extraordinarily high and slender piers of the Chartres variety. The more than sixty-five-foot height of the choir side aisles and ambulatory alone matches the entire height of the naves of twelfth-century Gothic churches. Consequently, tall and powerful abutments were required at the level of the lateral wall and immense clerestory windows, not to mention double flying buttresses resting on dangerously cantilevered intermediate piers. After the collapse of the vaulting, the bays had to be divided in two, so that there are presently six along the length of the choir instead of three. Moreover, new sexpartite vaults had to be constructed, along with twice as many external supports

as before. In its original state, Beauvais unquestionably evolved from the plan of the Cathedral of Amiens: there was an immense triforium made up of four double arcades whose main divisions corresponded to those of the clerestory windows. In the side aisles and ambulatory, the architect placed a row of windows above a small triforium. This is an idea that calls to mind the Cathedral of Bourges, but one that is especially noticeable in the choir of the Collegiate Church of Saint-Quentin, probably built at the same time as Saint-Pierre at Beauvais (P. Héliot).

By virtue of its truly fantastic spatial proportions and its maximum reduction of wall area—already a part of Rayonnant art—Beauvais constituted a real effort to surpass the standard established by Chartres. In a sense, the cathedral was a failure. Structurally speaking, the church collapsed; economically speaking, it could not be completed. Aside from the Cathedral of Cologne, which was begun in 1248 following this model, no structures took up the lead of this incredible project at Beauvais. Signaling the end of the gigantic Gothic undertakings of the thirteenth century, Beauvais also stands at the threshold of a new phase of development. Buildings belonging to the generation of 1230 would now tend toward reduced monumentality and toward a higher degree of sophistication.

BOURGES AND RELATED STRUCTURES

The present-day Cathedral of Bourges was, together with Chartres, most probably begun about 1195. In certain respects, it is a more archaic edifice; but Bourges is, in any case, the product of a wholly different architectonic vision. Its construction progressed at a very rapid pace: the choir was being completed at the time of Saint William's death in 1210—he had been archbishop since 1199—and was in service by 1214. The nave required a longer period of construction and was probably completed between 1255 and 1260 (Branner). It is interesting to note that the original plans were adhered to (with minor modifications) right up to the end of the project, but what is truly remarkable is that these plans took into account neither the singular creation at Chartres nor its repercussions.

It has always been pointed out that Notre-Dame at Paris was the source of inspiration for the plan of Bourges—no transept, double side aisles, and double ambulatory. Although, as at Paris, radiating chapels had not been planned for Bourges, they were added in the course of construction, perhaps about 1200. In any event, the plan can hardly give an adequate idea of the monumental quality of this cathedral. Rising to a height of almost 125 feet, the interior elevation of the nave consists of a very high arcade level, a noteworthy compound triforium beneath a relieving arch, and fairly diminutive, but numerous clerestory windows arranged two to each curved bay, three to each straight one. The arcade opens up spaciously to the first side aisle, whose fifty-nine-foot elevation is composed of a three-storied arrangement of arcade, triforium topped

79. Saint-Quentin, Collegiate Church of Saint-Quentin, nave and transept.

80. Bourges, Cathedral, aerial view.

VII. Amiens, Cathedral, interior.

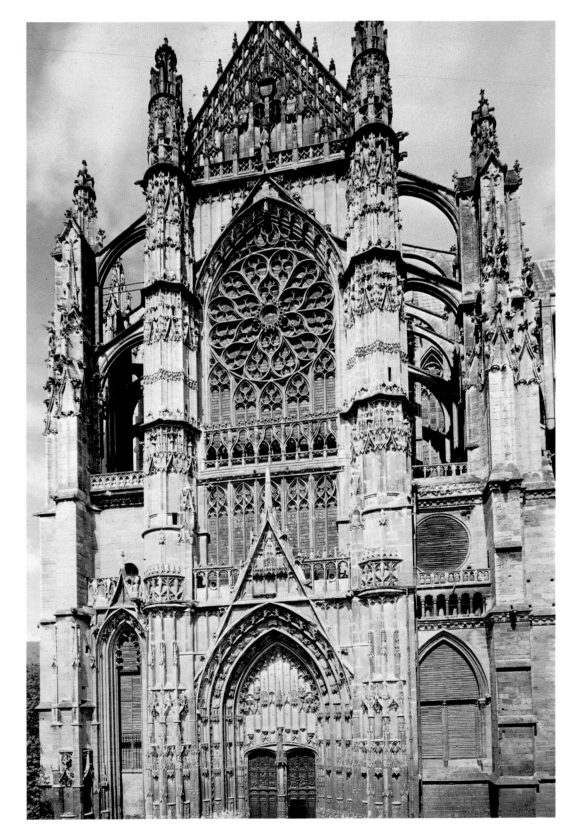

VIII. Beauvais, Cathedral, façade
of the south transept.

81. *Bourges, Cathedral, plan (reconstruction of the thirteenth-century plan).*

82. *Bourges, Cathedral, transverse section.*

83. *Bourges, Cathedral, interior.*

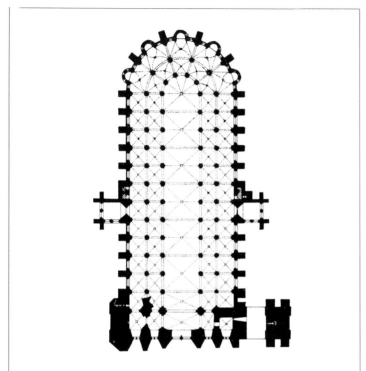

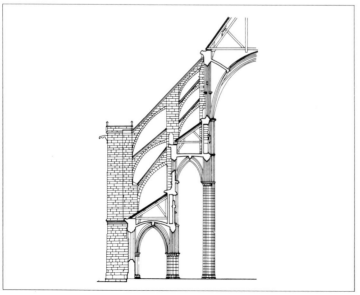

84. Le Mans, Cathedral, plan
of the choir.
85. Le Mans, Cathedral, aerial
view.

86. Le Mans, Cathedral, choir.

87. Le Mans, Cathedral, vaults
of the choir.

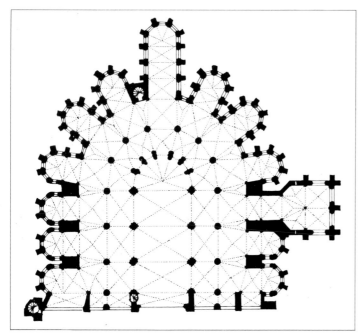

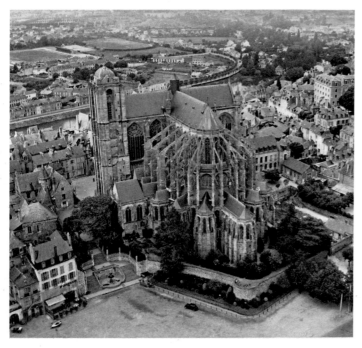

88. Coutances, Cathedral, apsidal view.
89. Coutances, Cathedral, choir.

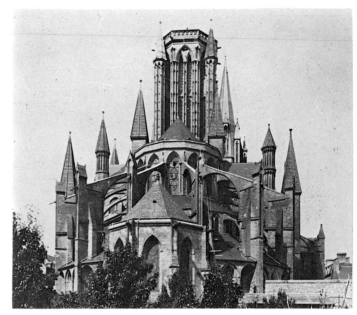

with relieving arch, and clerestory. Lastly, a second, rather low side aisle encompasses the whole; this outer ring features simple windows and tiny radiating chapels in the ambulatory, each of which is lighted by three windows. Thus, the lateral perspective reveals a superposition of five stories illuminated by either six or nine windows; the contrast with the colossal scale of Chartres can be readily perceived. The interior space has been opened up, "liberated." Whether viewed from a lateral or oblique perspective, the impression is one of unified, open, immense space (Focillon). Despite the fact that light, slender colonnettes flanking each cylindrical central pier effect a certain linearity, the divisions between the bays, rigorously aligned and combined in and of themselves, are not clearly delineated by the principal supports. In the nave, the vaulting is archaically sexpartite, but much more complex in the ambulatory: there, triangular vault fields juxtapose regularly crossed ribs. In all of the structural subdivisions, the use of slender diagonal ribs seems almost out of scale with their span. As for the external support system, three are double-ranked, double-strutted flying buttresses of the type possibly used for the nave of Notre-Dame at Paris. However, their arches and piers, unlike the imposing structure at Chartres, are of very slender proportions. It has recently been observed that, compared to buildings in the Chartres family, the Bourges structure is remarkably light. This quality was undoubtedly achieved thanks to the very layout of the building, with its vertically graded volumes and lofty side aisles serving as buttresses to the nave.

This then is a wholly original edifice for which there exists no real prototype. The occasionally proposed idea that Bourges is simply the Notre-Dame of Paris type minus a gallery does not stand up under analysis. Only one, nearly contemporaneous building may be compared to it—the choir of Saint-Martin at Tours, begun about 1202 but no longer extant. Certain details of molding and decoration indicate that the master of Bourges came from the Soissons region. Moreover, the use of triple windows under a rose window points to a possible influence from Champagne. According to Branner and Héliot, the complexity of the ambulatory vaulting probably derives from either Paris or Saint-Martin at Étampes. Yet, none of these speculations sufficiently explain the truly visionary art of the master of Bourges. In fact, its Augustinian and mystical spirit has been contrasted to the Scholastic nature of the Cathedral of Paris (Bony).

One may wonder why the influence of a majestic creation as formally and technically successful as Bourges did not match that of Chartres. The archaic quality of certain parts—combined with a design lacking a transept that otherwise affords a beautifully unified outline—has the disadvantage of confining the requirements of the liturgy. Furthermore, Bourges lacks magnificent arrangements of transept rose windows of the kind found at Chartres. It is also quite probable that the Bourges type

90. Toledo, Cathedral, plan.
91. Braine, Saint-Yved, apsidal view.

92. Braine, Saint-Yved, transept and choir.

was less amenable to evolution and adaptation in accordance with new technical demands.

Nevertheless, several structures did copy the fundamental Bourges concept of an elevation with a towering arcade and a very tall inner side aisle. These include the choir of the Cathedral of Le Mans (begun shortly after 1217), the choir of Coutances (begun shortly after 1220), the choir of the Cathedral of Toledo (begun in 1227), and, according to some, the choir of the Cathedral of Burgos (begun 1221-22).

At Le Mans, the decision to imitate Bourges was complicated by the intervention of a second architect of Norman origin, resulting in a significant modification in the principles laid down by the first architect, a native of Bourges. Stretching out over three vast bays, the extensive choir adjoins an ambulatory radiating thirteen chapels, all of which—especially the elongated central chapel—are fairly deep. As a result, when viewed outside atop its rocky escarpment, the choir of Le Mans creates an impression of numerous, highly articulated gradations rising toward the summit of the apse. This effect is totally at variance with the great unity of mass found at Bourges. In addition, the piers and struts of the flying buttresses—whose outer components are doubled in an innovative manner—envelop the apse in a diaphanous cage that reduces the readability of the central mass. Inside, the master from Bourges managed to complete only the lower story and the lofty piers of the principal arcade. The second architect simplified the plan and decoration of the intermediate piers and imparted to the vaulting a dry, linear quality typical of Norman art of that time. He also did away with the triforium of the nave in order to enlarge the clerestory windows. Probably built between 1245 and 1254, the upper level of the church displays the kind of hollowing out of the walls and the multiple and very narrow subdivision of windows that already announce the Rayonnant Style. Thus, the very lovely effect of the interior—its great height, verticality, linearity, and luminosity (even with dark stained—glass windows)—is the cumulative product of several transformations, each of which corresponds to a different architectonic concept. One could say that this choir embodies all the dynamism of Gothic architecture during the thirteenth century.

The choir of the Cathedral of Coutances, completed about 1250, is a Norman copy of the Bourges design. Its plan reveals radiating chapels that merge into the outer ambulatory, as at Saint-Denis. Only the central chapel juts out from the apsidal contour. As for the elevation, the proportions of the nave and side aisles seem squeezed together in both height and length. The quantity and severity of the linear accents against the walls, supports, arcade contours, and vaulting combine to produce a tense, almost stark effect. This element opposed the Coutances interior to the impression of emptiness that characterizes Bourges, and this contrast extends to the structural aspect as well. For example, the cornice at

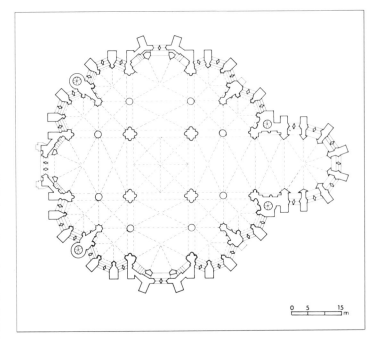

74

93. Trier, Liebfrauenkirche, plan.
94. Trier, Liebfrauenkirche, vaults.

95. Auxerre, Cathedral, nave.
96. Auxerre, Cathedral, choir
vaults.

the clerestory level is a mark of Norman technique, and the flying buttresses have been simplified. Observed from the outside, the apse is articulated with admirable clarity, a quality accentuated by the linear network of colonnettes that appears at every story. The overall effect is further enhanced by an extraordinary tower over the crossing that dominates the already sophisticated composition.

At Toledo, too, the basic idea of the Bourges space has been lost, due to the width of the bays, the heaviness of the supports, and the greatly lowered proportions of the entire structure. Granted, certain structural traits typical of Bourges can be observed in the triforium and buttressing system; granted, the smallness of the radiating chapels and the alternating triangle/rectangle vaulting in the outer ambulatory recall the configuration of the French model. Even so, the spatial effect is a far cry from Bourges; and the profuse, typically Spanish decoration removes Toledo even farther from its architectural source. As for the Cathedral of Burgos, only its plan can be compared to Bourges, except that the outer side aisles and the ambulatory have now been replaced by chapels. However, the design, technique, and decoration of the piers recall French forms. We shall discuss these buildings at a later point within the framework of the development of Spanish Gothic.

RESISTANCE TO CHARTRES IN NORTHERN FRANCE AND BURGUNDY

The creation of Bourges and the Bourges type proves that, about 1200, it was possible to conceive of a Gothic architectural style different from the one established at Chartres. In fact, a group of structures, extending from England and Normandy to the Rhine and the Alps, shows that additional forms participated in the resistance against the artistic influence of the great cathedrals. One such trend had its origins in the Abbey Church of Saint-Yved at Braine, not far from Soissons. Its construction began about 1195 and continued until the early thirteenth century, but the building is today incomplete. Saint-Yved is well known to historians of architecture: its singular plan features four chapels, between the choir and transept, that radiate on a 45-degree axis running diagonally to the principal axis of the church. Adapted in various ways to churches with or without ambulatory, this kind of chapel met with some success during the thirteenth century in Champagne, Brie, Flanders, at Toul (in the Holy Roman Empire), and especially in the Liebfrauenkirche at Trier. However, this plan does not constitute in and of itself a fullfledged stylistic variant; it merely illustrates a related tendency. Braine is a relatively small building; there is no ambulatory, and the extension of the transept is quite limited. Even though the elevation is three-storied, the windows have not been enlarged and, consequently, do not follow the Chartres tendency toward the hollowing out of the walls. The oldest sections of Saint-Martin at Ypres (begun 1221), Sainte-Chapelle at Dijon (begun 1220?, demolished), and a certain number of small churches in the

Brie region may all be compared to Braine and classified in the same category of traditional structure. In addition, the plan of Braine, with its simplicity of spatial design (modified by later contributions), was also responsible for two great works of Gothic architecture—Notre-Dame at Dijon and the Liebfrauenkirche at Trier (begun only after 1235). We will return to Dijon shortly; it is, along with Auxerre, the masterpiece of thirteenth-century Burgundian art. Based in many respects (for instance, the design of the windows) on Reims models, the Liebfrauenkirche deserves special mention for the exceptional beauty of its effect and the originality of its plan. It is a centrally arranged structure whose four arms—one of which extends to become a choir—radiate from the crossing. Eight chapels placed diagonally are fitted in pairs into the spaces between the four arms of the cross. The tall, slender interior supports allow an open interpenetration of all parts of the church. Abundant light enters through the windows of the chapels and choir; the latter features two stories of superimposed windows, a beautiful arrangement unknown to Chartres-derived art. The interior space is both unified (by virtue of the plan) and dispersed (by virtue of the four axes radiating from the center). Even if, based on the choir plan, an analogy can be drawn between this church and either Lorraine architecture in general or the Elisabethkirche at Marburg an der Lahn (begun c. 1225), the Liebfrauenkirche recalls just as strongly the Champagne style that was independent of Chartres (H. Bunjes, Bony).

In northern France and Burgundy, as well as in Normandy, the system derived from the Anglo-Norman thick or double-shell wall joined forces with the movement of independence from Chartres. This category includes galleries carved out of the walls as well as interior and exterior galleries running across the vault supports at the upper-window level. Especially in Burgundy, these solutions gave rise to highly successful instances of mural diaphanousness produced by windows either sunken beneath deep-set casement arches or doubled on the exterior by an additional wall. Structurally speaking, this type of interior abutment perforated with a passage not only contributes to the stability of the walls, but also doubles, in a sense, the depth of the triforium. Moreover, the use of an exterior gallery running above the triforium roofing, across the piers supporting the tops of the flying buttresses, both facilitates movement and reinforces the plastic highlights of the exterior. The opulent results obtained from this procedure were to be enthusiastically utilized in Burgundian architecture and later in the Île-de-France (Bony, Jantzen). Without devoting too much space to the prototypes of these Burgundian schemes (choir of the Cathedral of Loussane, similar to English arrangements), we will mention that accomplished examples of these galleries appeared simultaneously at Saint-Martin at Clamecy and at the Cathedral of Auxerre (from 1215 to 1217).

It is obviously at Auxerre that this Burgundian variant of High Gothic

97. Dijon, Notre-Dame, detail of the façade.
98. Dijon, Notre-Dame, interior.

IX. Bourges, Cathedral, nave.

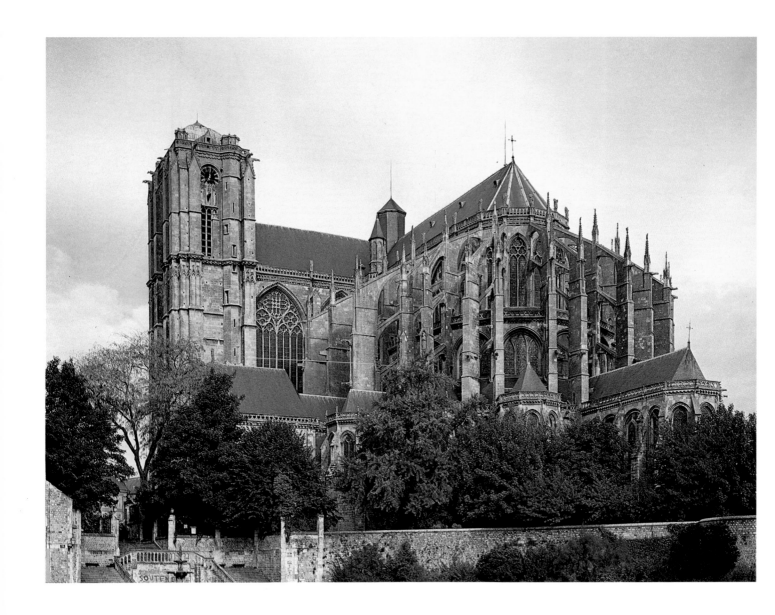

X. Le Mans, Cathedral, apsidal view.

can be fully appreciated. The architect clearly did not aspire to the gigantic monumentality of the buildings of the Chartres family: here one finds no double ambulatories, no proliferation of chapels, no soaring height in the nave. The elevation is the three-storied type, but the height of both arcade and clerestory is reduced by a very tall interposed triforium. The scaled-down dimensions facilitate lighting, as the clerestory windows (two lancest beneath a large rose window) are no longer at a great distance from the ground. The lower level opens generously to the outside by means of windows set quite close together. The interior articulation of the bays is ensured by ultraslender, false-bedded colonnettes that dress the piers, elegantly separate the tall triforium bays, and extend along the base of the side aisle. We have already noted this predilection for stone placed against the grain of surrounding material during our discussion of the Abbey Church of Saint-Madeleine at Vézelay. Corresponding to the delicacy of these linear accents is the structure of both the high, pointed arcade and of the wall at the level of the windows, which are pushed outward toward the church exterior by the passage across the vault springings. The treatment of the single ambulatory chapel, dedicated to the Virgin, is significant. Here the master architect achieved an extremely lightened arrangement by borrowing the Champagne principle of isolated columns at the chapel entrance cut in very hard stone (as in Saint-Remi at Reims). The exterior flying buttresses linked with arcatures blend harmoniously with the overall style of the building.

Though utilizing the same procedures and structural principles, Saint-Martin at Clamecy comes no closer to the perfection of Auxerre than do other churches in the same group, such as Auxonne and Semur-en-Auxois. The second Burgundian masterpiece is the parish church of the palace at Dijon—called Notre-Dame—possibly begun in 1220, in any case before 1225. It is this church that enabled Viollet-le-Duc and Jantzen to elaborate several theories about Gothic architecture. The plan of the church is modest: no ambulatory, diagonally positioned chapels like those at Saint-Yved at Braine, a standard-length transept, a nave comprising three double bays, and an impressive galleried porch. The edifice is practically homogeneous, despite the fact that construction was not completed before 1251. According to Viollet-le-Duc, the structural system of Notre-Dame at Dijon is the perfect example of the use of false-bedding as part of support technique, the thirteenth-century use of the *tas-de-charge* (springing stones on a pier), and the reduction of the entire structure to a logical framework. As in the Cathedral of Auxerre, the elevation is three-storied: the very tall triforium reduces the size of the arcade and clerestory alike. A system of superposed galleries characterizes the choir. Two of the galleries open toward the interior, one at the lower window level, the other at the triforium level (where, incidentally, the outer wall is pierced with oculi). Lastly, a third gallery at the clerestory level runs along the exterior wall, crossing the pier abutments

103. *Saint-Germain-en-Laye,
Palace Chapel, interior.*

of the apse. In the nave, all three galleries face the interior at every level, augmenting the effects of diaphanousness and of the doubling of the wall. Certain archaic traits draw Notre-Dame at Dijon into the camp of resistance against Chartres: single windows (triple in the nave) without oculus, sexpartite vaults, and, in the transept and crossing tower, large circular windows that lack partitioning mullions. The interior space is divided with great clarity, thanks to both the false-bedded colonnettes that outline the springings and the perfect readability of the structural skeleton. We should also point out the immense porch, divided into three naves and topped with a gallery; it forms a kind of rectangular, two-storied façade-screen, luxuriously adorned with tall, false-bedded colonnettes. Found in a less spectacular form in the Church of Saint-Pierre-sous-Vézelay and in the Cathedral of Lausanne, this phenomenon can doubtless be compared to façades in Romanesque Italy (the Pieve at Arezzo and the Cathedral of Pisa). We ought to bear in mind the southern origin of this enchanting arrangement.

The Burgundy variant, which reached its zenith between 1215 and 1225 at Auxerre and Dijon, proved to be a hardy strain. Imitations—indeed, near-duplicates—are to be found at the Cathedral of Châlon-sur-Saône, the naves of the cathedrals of Nevers and Lyons, Semur-en-Auxois, and Notre-Dame at Cluny. In some instances (Saint-Pierre-sous-Vézelay and Villeneuve-sur-Yonne), the triforium has been absorbed into the clerestory level. However, the more characteristic feature of the interior passage in the wall persists into the thirteenth (Saint-Bénigne at Dijon) and fourteenth centuries (Saint-Germain at Auxerre). Architects of the Rayonnant period succeeded in eliciting admirable effects from this principle: an example is Saint-Thibault-en-Auxois (near Dijon), one of the most delicate structures in the Burgundian Gothic style.

In our previous discussion of the cathedrals of Le Mans and Coutances, members of the Bourges family, we touched upon Norman architecture in the thirteenth century. Despite its annexation to France in 1206, Normandy proved to be another case of "disobedience" in the face of the dominating currents of French architecture. This may be explained, at least in part, by Normandy's strong traditions and the maintenance of a special contact with England. Curiously, certain commonly shared traits link Burgundy and Normandy. Until the fifteenth century, the latter retained the crossing tower, abandoned elsewhere in France about 1200. The Norman structural system was based on a clerestory-level passageway derived from the traditional double-shell wall. Furthermore, the quest for an abundance of linear decoration, effected by quantities of colonnettes and a wealth of arcade molding, points to a relationship with Burgundian trends, despite certain differences in formal detail. This sort of subtle interplay is the very antithesis of the grandiose monumentality of Chartres or Amiens. Thus, the interior division into bays or spatial

XI. Le Mans, Cathedral, choir vault.

XII. Saint-Denis, Abbey Church, nave.

104, 105. Saint-Denis, Abbey Church, apsidal view, choir and transept.

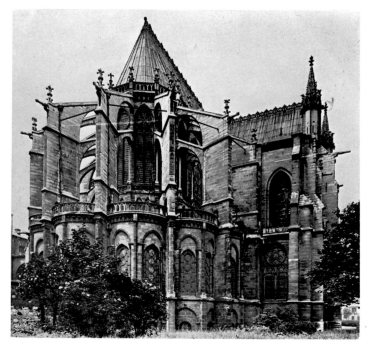

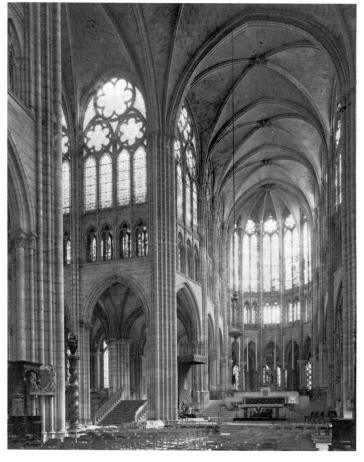

cells could indeed be obtained by means other than those applied in France, albeit sometimes at the expense of clarity.

Apart from Coutances, the chief Norman edifices are the choir of Saint-Étienne at Caen (already discussed in the previous chapter), the Cathedral of Rouen, and, toward mid-century, the Cathedral of Bayeux. After 1250, the great building projects often were original applications of French Rayonnant art. The Romanesque Cathedral of Rouen was destroyed by fire in 1200, but it is possible that work on the Gothic structure had already begun a few years prior to this date in the nave. The plan included a four-storied elevation with galleries above the side aisles. After 1201, the entire nave was erected over a period of approximately 30 years under the direction of the architect Jean d'Andely. Although the gallery was eliminated, its traces subsist in the braces midway up the main piers of the nave and side-aisle elevations. In addition, these piers are trapezoidal and flanked by numerous colonnettes: they may be compared to those in the choir at Salisbury. False-bedded shafts in the side aisles are arranged in a highly original manner. Likewise, the triforium is unconventional in form. However, the choir—with its large, simple cylindrical piers supporting narrow, pointed arcades and its slender triforium—offers a totally different picture. A relationship may exist between this choir and the work of both the master of Coutances and the Norman master of Le Mans. If the influence of Laon or of Soissons is seen to be operating at Rouen, the essential elements actually belong to twelfth-century, not thirteenth-century art. The transept already expresses the Rayonnant phase of Gothic.

We should also mention the Cathedral of Bayeux (dates uncertain). About 1230, its Romanesque nave was transformed by the construction of immense Gothic windows. Though the choir was not built until the middle of the century, it followed the traditional model established by Saint-Étienne at Caen: three stories with a tall triforium and a passageway at the clerestory level. Articulated and molded by arcatures framing deep-set casements, the exterior of the apse at Bayeux matches the apse of Coutances in linear beauty. We could enumerate other Norman projects of this period, many of which are charming and exquisitely decorated. But these did not prove to be the source of the great thirteenth-century renewal of Gothic style that Normandy itself would soon accept and follow.

THE MID-THIRTEENTH CENTURY AND THE FIRST PHASE OF RAYONNANT ARCHITECTURE

Nothing proves the characteristic dynamism of Gothic art more convincingly than the appearance of a new structural formula 25 or 30 years after the introduction of the Chartres concept. In the opinions of such historians as Dehio and Panofsky, this phase marks the real fruition of the formal principles elaborated between 1150 and 1230. The structural

*109. Paris, Notre-Dame, exterior
of the south arm of the transept.*

*110. Paris, Notre-Dame, rose
window of the north arm
of the transept.*
*111. Saint-Sulpice-de-Favières,
Church, apsidal view.*

heaviness of Chartres and Reims was not so much a derivation from Romanesque predecessors as the inability to harmonize the lightness of the upper levels with the solidity of the supports. Moreover, if Gothic space is to be defined as a skeleton outlined by a linear interplay of colonnettes, then the Chartres- or Bourges-type churches were not fully successful in realizing this principle. From its inception, Gothic architecture moved in the direction of formal sophistication and spatial subtlety, which attained complete expression only in buildings designed about 1230 or later. To demonstrate this process, one may observe and analyze different types of windows and piers, or compare the overall effect of various interiors. The real difficulty lies in distinguishing between this stylistic phase and its successor (c. 1280 or 1300), called Rayonnant. By dubbing this particular Gothic mode the Court Style, Branner recently resolved the dilemma, at least in part. The so-called royal style of the Île-de-France proved to be a decisive inspiration for the evolution of European architecture.

The building still traditionally considered the first example of this phase is the Abbey Church of Saint-Denis, whose reconstruction began in 1231 and was completed in 1281. During these years, the upper sections of Abbot Suger's choir were rebuilt, and the newly constructed transept and nave were joined to the twelfth-century narthex. It has long been agreed that this work was directed by Pierre de Montreuil: a text of 1247 alludes to his presence at Saint-Denis (Aubert). However, Branner has shown that at least two architects participated in this project and that the plan was modified during the construction of the nave. What innovations are to be found at Saint-Denis? The most obvious is the form and function of the bays. Using the three-storied church as a model, the architect filled the entire space beneath the wall ribs with several lancet windows (either two or four) separated by slender mullions and topped with rose windows (themselves partitioned by mullions). This arrangement may be seen as a development of the Chartres type, one that had already been utilized by 1230 in the clerestory of the Cathedral of Amiens. However, what does not occur at Amiens is the further enlargement of the windows of Saint-Denis, brought about by perforating the exterior triforium wall. Instead of functioning merely as a wall space between the arcade and clerestory, the triforium now participates in the overall lightening of the wall. The second trait peculiar to Saint-Denis is the systematic replacement of the round pier by a rhomboid support entirely covered with colonnettes that respond to the numerous vault ribs. This design was not entirely unknown to previous generations: it had been used for the piers of the twelfth-century transept crossing and could also be found in the cathedrals of Rouen and Salisbury, beginning in the first third of the thirteenth century. From the time of the Saint-Denis nave until the fifteenth century, the full linear potential of this architectonic form would be realized in a truly systematic fashion. The major characteristic of Saint-Denis and its progeny is the emphasis placed on the lightening of the wall,

on a kind of "loss of heaviness" (Jantzen calls this trait "antiheaviness"). Needless to say, certain exterior elements still ensure the stability of the structural mass: protruding abutments, tall flying buttresses supported by pinnacled piers, and the like. From this point of view, the choir of the Cathedral of Amiens or the upper level of Beauvais may be numbered among buildings in this group. We also note that, in buildings conceived after 1230 as well as in Saint-Denis, the "gigantism" typical of Chartres has given way to more modest dimensions and less towering proportions.

It is one thing to try to explain Saint-Denis as the logical outgrowth of previous principles. But can we pinpoint any specific sources of inspiration? It is possible that the Cistercian Abbey Church of Royaumont (begun c. 1225), founded by Louis VIII and Blanche of Castile, had already featured some of the elements discussed above (Branner). Moreover, the addition of side chapels to the nave of Notre-Dame at Paris (also begun c. 1225) points to certain similarities with the Saint-Denis forms. In Champagne, work on the Cathedral of Troyes, begun at the turn of the century, was resumed after 1228 under the direction of a new architect. He abandoned the Chartres forms previously utilized and built the side aisles and clerestory windows of the choir (before 1241). In 1231, work began on the Abbey Church of Saint-Nicaise at Reims (demolished), which evidently was the great masterpiece of this architectural style. (The tomb of its architect, Hugues Libergier, survives.) The only clue we have as to the style of Saint-Nicaise is an old engraving of the façade, whose style seems to belong more to the years 1245-50 than to the time of its founding. At Troyes, the lovely windows and perforated triforium in the upper level of the choir resemble the same areas of Saint-Denis so closely that we may assume that they were both designed by a single architect of widespread influence. The stylistic evolution in the side chapels of Notre-Dame at Paris (until 1245); the general design of the nave of the Cathedral of Strasbourg (1236-37); and the formal evolution of the choir at Amiens (after 1237)—all of these seem to be derived from the same movement, one that evolved simultaneously in Paris and Champagne.

One of the most charming examples of this style may be found in chapels built as part of castles or great abbeys in the region surrounding Paris. Constructed between 1235 and 1238, the chapel of the palace at Saint-Germain-en-Laye, near Paris, already displays elements of Rayonnant design in its windows, western rose window, and molding. However, the presence of a double-shell wall bears witness to a kinship with the art of Burgundy and that of Champagne. Even more decisive were the efforts of Pierre de Montreuil at Saint-Germain-des-Prés in Paris: namely, a large refectory and, later, a chapel dedicated to the Virgin (neither extant). The slightly more recent Sainte-Chapelle, part of the Palais de Justice complex in Paris (c. 1241/42?-48), is surely one of the most exquisite accomplishments in this group. Even similar projects

112. Meaux, Cathedral, choir.

erected in the second half of the century—for example, the great apsidal chapel at Saint-Germer-de-Fly—were unable to surpass it. In fact, it may be considered a building species that might enable us to pinpoint the essential criteria not only of the Rayonnant phase, but also of Gothic art in general. Built as a repository for the precious relics—in particular, Christ's Crown of Thorns—that Louis IX (Saint Louis) had purchased from the Byzantine emperor, Sainte-Chapelle is a monumental reliquary and shrine surrounded by translucent walls. Its stained glass and sculpted decoration underscore both the sacred and royal functions of this personal tabernacle of Louis IX. Its base consists of a lower chapel for the use of the parish, while the upper chapel is flush with the palace and opens onto it through a porch and gallery. The incredibly light interior effect was obtained by solid exterior abutments as well as by such technical procedures as the use of iron braces. A work of supreme virtuosity, this edifice seems to have been at least partially inspired by the central chapel in the choir of the Cathedral of Amiens (1240-41); but the details of workmanship are typically Parisian, with connections to Saint-Denis, Notre-Dame, and what we know about the Chapel of the Virgin in Saint-Germain-des-Prés. Should we trust the eighteenth-century text that attributes this splendid work to Pierre de Montreuil? Or was it Thomas de Cormont, the master of Amiens, who supplied the plans (Branner)?

Another Parisian creation of this period is the transept of Notre-Dame at Paris, enlarged (beginning in 1245-50) by Jean de Chelles and Pierre de Montreuil. The end walls of both the north and south arms of the transept are adorned with immense stained-glass rose windows that crown a long perforated gallery similar to the triforium. The corner spaces between this horizontal band and the rose window have been hollowed out, thereby integrating all components of the arrangement. Obviously, the transept of Saint-Denis (built 1240-50) provided the model for these rose windows; they are the culmination of efforts that began in the transept of Laon and continued at Reims and Chartres. Designed by Jean de Chelles, the older north façade of the transept is, in terms of decoration, a magnificent creation, for it surpasses all such compositions occurring in the cathedrals of the first half of the century. A complex tracery of blind arcades topped with pointed gables covers the wall with a network of miniature false architecture. In executing the southern façade after 1258, Pierre de Montreuil copied the work of his predecessor quite faithfully; this design served as a model both in and outside France. The first plan of the façade of Strasbourg (c. 1260?) is a direct descendant of this structure.

Unfortunately, several important Parisian structures of this period have disappeared, especially those churches erected in the midthirteenth century by the mendicant and Carthusian orders. However, certain structures located in the *domaine royal* (crown lands) do reveal an unadulterated Parisian inspiration. One of the most interesting is Saint-

Sulpice-de-Favières (begun c. 1245), whose choir, though reduced in size, exhibits Parisian virtuosity in both its structure and decoration. Especially significant is the design of the triforium: the hollowing out of all the corner spaces produces a panel of square-shaped tracery lighted from the outside. The same pattern may be found in the choir of the Cathedral of Meaux. In reconstruction from the end of the twelfth century, this building underwent modifications in the thirteenth century that severely altered its upper levels and the interior of the transept. The abundance of blind tracery found there undoubtedly derives from Notre-Dame at Paris. The triforium at Meaux is not glazed in the choir, whereas it is at Saint-Sulpice-de-Favières (in the latter, both exterior and interior sides are cut in the same manner). Contemporaneous with these structures, but quite different in spirit, is the Church of Saint-Martin-aux-Bois in northern Valois, where the influence of Amiens made itself more strongly felt. Its high choir, entirely perforated with tall lancet windows braced at midheight, gives the impression of a stone grating supported only by exterior abutments. A small royal building, the Church of Nogent-les-Vierges features a different arrangement consisting of a nave and two side aisles of equal height lighted by large Rayonnant windows. As we can see, Parisian art was not expressed uniformly and was clearly subject to several formal discoveries in rapid succession. Beginning in the 1240s, this style may be considered a source for eclectic imitations in several regions of France.

Begun in 1234-36 according to the Chartres plan and with borrowings from that cathedral's repertory of forms, the Cathedral of Tours later underwent modernizations that were not completed until about 1260. The upper level now included clerestory windows and a triforium based on the Saint-Denis and Paris models. However, it is perhaps the choir of the Cathedral of Troyes that provides us with the purest expression of the Court Style, to use Branner's terminology. One other astoundingly precocious, eclectic work is the Cathedral of Strasbourg, begun 1236-37 and completed in 1276. In the triforium and windows, as well as in the piers of the main arcade, the architect meticulously adhered to Parisian formal principles. In the side aisles, a passage running across the responds was placed beneath vast Rayonnant windows, a procedure typical of Champagne art. The flying buttresses, of considerable length and sophistication, are a copy of the Parisian flying buttress of the 1230s. The one aspect of Strasbourg that does not follow French solutions is that of proportion: namely, the extraordinary width of both nave and side aisles, which yields uninterrupted transverse and oblique perspectives. These unusual dimensions may be explained by the fact that the foundations of the original Ottonian cathedral were retained. The nave of Strasbourg is of great historical importance. It is from here that Rayonnant models quickly spread, from the banks of the Rhine into Alsace, Swabia, and, at a later point, toward the Lower Rhine. As the nave of Strasbourg is be-

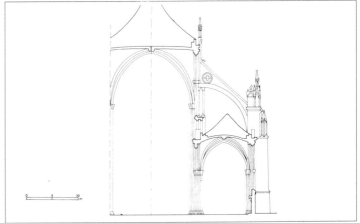

ing completed, the construction of the western façade of the cathedral was already being prepared: it took two centuries to complete and incorporated new, characteristically Germanic Gothic elements.

Beginning about 1250-55, Rayonnant architecture asserted its influence throughout the greater part of France as well as in several foreign projects. We should first mention the important series of cathedrals in the central and southern areas of France, several of which were designed by Jean Deschamps, the royal architect. Perhaps the oldest of these is the Cathedral of Clermont-Ferrand, whose construction began shortly before 1250 and actively continued until after 1262. Its greatly elongated choir, Parisian-type transept, and nave with double side aisles (the western sections of which are modern) are elements that added nothing new to the definition of Rayonnant art. In the structure of its high walls and its more thick-set proportions, the Cathedral of Narbonne is a partial modification of the Paris type. Despite the coarse building material and a lack of forcefulness in the application of the larger windows, the Cathedral of Limoges (begun 1273) can still be considered an imitation of Clermont-Ferrand. Farther south is a masterpiece that, though officially part of Spanish art, is nonetheless very much a French work—the Cathedral of León, begun between 1255 and 1258. Nor was Italy totally isolated from this current: it was felt particularly in those southern regions that, for a while, had been under Anjou rule (see, for example, San Lorenzo at Naples).

In Normandy and vicinity, all forms of Rayonnant art were included in the upper level of the Cathedral of Le Mans (prior to 1254) and in the two great cathedrals undergoing renovation at this time, Sées and Évreux. Although its dates are uncertain, the construction of the upper level of the choir of the Cathedral of Sées was probably under way toward 1260. It reveals a mixture of Rayonnant and typically Norman elements, the latter deriving from the choir at Bayeux. At Évreux, work on the clerestory windows (c. 1250) transformed the Romanesque nave; construction of the choir must have begun sometime after 1260, and it was completed at the beginning of the fourteenth century. Here, French forms and the French structural system were unabashedly adopted without concessions to Norman tradition. It should be pointed out that the original thirteenth-century church was somewhat altered by fifteenth- and early-sixteenth-century work on the triforium, transept, and crossing. Two sumptuous façades, direct descendants of the transept of Notre-Dame at Paris, were added to the transept of the Cathedral of Rouen after 1265-70. The small, but highly sophisticated Church of Norey-en-Auge dates from the same period. In England, the two principal structures that expressed this style were Westminster Abbey at London (begun before 1245) and Old Saint Paul's, at London, begun in 1258 (demolished). Although the French influence left its mark in Westminster's structural and spatial design, it could not displace the typically English tendency to

decorate with Purbeck marble or other colored stone. Nevertheless, the French current did take on the proportions of an artistic hegemony. In the north, the choir of the Cathedral of Tournai, begun in 1242 but built very gradually, patterned itself after the nave of Saint-Denis. In addition, the Cathedral of Utrecht (begun 1254)—despite restrained windows in the nave walls at the levels of the clerestory and ambulatory roofing—shows that it, too, came under the sway of Rayonnant Gothic.

THE END OF HIGH GOTHIC. RESISTANCE TO RAYONNANT ART. MONASTIC ARCHITECTURE

During the years 1260-80, several regions of western Europe witnessed the appearance of buildings that, to varying degrees, conflicted with the dominant formal principles of what is called the Classical age of Gothic art. In England, this was marked by the emergence of the Decorated Style; along the Rhine, by the initial work on the façade of Strasbourg; and in Catalonia, by the design of the choir of the Cathedral of Barcelona. Within France itself, two edifices, though products of Île-de-France Rayonnant art, may be considered the clearest examples of this development: Saint-Urbain at Troyes and Saint-Nazaire at Carcassonne. We should pause here to point out that the evolutionary rhythm of Gothic art was an unsteady one. Just as the previously mentioned structures were orienting Gothic toward a kind of Mannerism, the Rayonnant Style that originally produced them had not yet completely overtaken all areas of western Europe. While southern France, Bavaria, and Saxony were still in the process of adapting Rayonnant to more archaic designs, Bohemia and Austria were barely emerging from their Romanesque past (with the exception of monastic structures of French origin). Even within France, Burgundy held on to traditional construction techniques (as in Saint-Bénigne at Dijon) and applied Rayonnant forms only to certain details. One may legitimately speak of resistance to Rayonnant art lasting until the end of the thirteenth century. The years 1260-80, however, constitute the most revolutionary period.

What was the nature of this revolution? There seem to be three essential principles that must be taken into account. First, a radical change in the system of illumination brought about a significant redefinition of interior space. Second, the system of spatial division into stories was altered by reduced dimensions and by a quest for a unified interior space (the finest examples are Spanish and German *Hallenkirchen*). Finally, the preoccupation with decoration—exterior or interior painting, sculpture, or molding—that we have already observed in Sainte-Chapelle and in the transept of Notre-Dame at Paris, now took precedence over those principles of architectonic logic that had overshadowed all churches of the mid-thirteenth century. In this respect, the change in the relationship of glass to wall is especially typical. Those churches that had retained their stained glass—Sainte-Chapelle, the choirs of Le Mans and Troyes—were enclosed in veritable walls of vivid, sometimes dark color. Beginning about 1260, the luminous, variegated effect of the interior volumes was transformed by the blending of a nearly white *grisaille* with the colored sections of the glass, resulting in enhanced opalescence. Consequently, subtleties of molding and decoration became highlighted, and spatial divisions were partially effaced by a new profusion of light (Grodecki). Even if this tendency was more widespread in Germany and Spain, the augmented luminousness of stained-glass windows still played essentially the same kind of role in the late fourteenth and fifteenth centuries there as did the use of *grisaille* in France and England.

The perfect example of this formal development is the Collegiate Church of Saint-Urbain at Troyes. Founded in 1262 by Pope Urban IV on the site of his birthplace, the church was rapidly erected until 1266, at which time the choir and transept must have already been completed. That year, however, a fire slowed construction, and work continued at a reduced pace until the end of the fifteenth century. The nave was not finished until the twentieth century. Both its plan and elevation limited in size, Saint-Urbain features an unequivocal two-storied elevation, with clerestory windows occupying fully one-half of its total height. In the apse, the completely hollowed-out, stained-glass clerestory is reminiscent of the lower galleries in Rayonnant art. In addition, an exterior passage runs along the abutments at the clerestory level. The steady rhythm of Rayonnant art is no longer respected: each right bay of the choir presents a different number of lancet windows as well as a different system of arcades. The glass panels in *grisaille* that frame bands of colored glass make an effective contribution to the extreme sophistication of this building. In an almost exaggerated development of the decorative system of Sainte-Chapelle's exterior, the architect of Saint-Urbain increased the number of gables and miniature architectural forms. Each part took on the appearance of a reliquary, recalling the work of contemporary goldsmiths. This phenomenon may also be found on the exterior of the chapels added to the choir of Notre-Dame at Paris after 1260. As for the side portals of the Saint-Urbain transept—long believed to postdate the choir by a century—the rigidity of design and assembly, together with the removal of capitals on the imposts of the arcades, brings to mind a piece of carpentry. It would not be too presumptuous to qualify such a creation as Mannerist.

The same label may be applied to Saint-Nazaire at Carcassonne, built in the upper town between 1269 and 1329. It may have been Louis IX himself who provided the initiative for replacing the choir and transept of the old Romanesque church, and the architect may have been called from northern France. The dimensions of the church are restrained: the transept is a little more than 30 feet wide and the vault is about 53 feet high. What is truly remarkable about this structure is its plan. It has a shallow choir whose proportions are nearly those of a chapel, and the transept is flanked by a side aisle of equal height adjoining, in turn, six in-

123. *Albi, Cathedral of Sainte-Cécile, exterior.*
124. *Albi, Cathedral of Sainte-Cécile, axonometric section through the nave.*

terpenetrating chapels. These mesh with the side-aisle space. The overall interior effect is very nearly that of a hall church; even the tall columns that stand in the middle of the interior space do not succeed in imposing a subdivision into bays or cells. The linear interplay of blind tracery lining the wall and of colonnettes no longer assumes the demonstrative role it does at Saint-Denis or at Tours. Not only do the transept rose windows recall the great northern edifices, but also the eastern windows—whose single upward thrusts of glass fill most of the elevation—indicate that the architect took Sainte-Chapelle into account. As at Saint-Urbain at Troyes, the moldings of the supports and base are remarkably refined, and statues adorn the piers at the choir entrance. The illumination is abundant, though modified by recent additions to the stained-glass windows. Thanks to the height of the transept side aisle, which provides a counterthrust to the nave, the external support system could be simplified and reduced to wall abutments. The use of completely exposed metal braces to unite the tall interior piers to the springings of the vaults had already appeared in the form of iron armatures in the Cathedral of Amiens and especially in Sainte-Chapelle. Since the interior supports were positioned from the point of view of the walls, the effects of Gothic diaphanousness ended up destroying the internal logic of Gothic space. Even though the Saint-Nazaire design did not, strictly speaking, lead to any exact copies, it nevertheless played an undeniably significant part, not only in fourteenth-century Catalonian Gothic, but also in Languedoc and Gascony (the Cathedral of Bazas). In any event, this church certainly no longer fits into the framework of Classical Rayonnant Gothic.

Several secondary examples of the same trend may be added to the two key monuments just described: in Champagne, the Church of Mussy-sur-Seine; in Burgundy, the choir of Saint-Thibault-en-Auxois; as well as other English and Spanish structures. It is above all the fourteenth century that was to witness the development of this second Rayonnant style, especially beyond the borders of France.

At the same time, however, Rayonnant art met with some rather powerful local resistance, due to a stubborn adherence either to Classical spatial principles or to deep-seated regional traditions. Thus, even though the Rayonnant window was accepted at Saint-Bénigne at Dijon (reconstructed beginning in 1281), the church's basic structure and effect imitated Notre-Dame at Dijon, built a half century earlier. At Poitiers, neither the completion of the nave of the cathedral nor the reconstruction of the nave of Sainte-Radegonde—both from the second half or perhaps the last third of the thirteenth century—fully obeyed the dictates of French Rayonnant Gothic. In particular, whole areas of southern France, such as Languedoc, developed a highly innovative architectural style that did not derive from northern sources and that accepted Rayonnant elements only with great reluctance.

Beginning with the Romanesque era, southern France had witnessed

125. Toulouse, Church of the Jacobins, interior.

some experimentation with cross-ribbed vaulting (the bell tower of the Abbey Church of Saint-Pierre at Moissac and the crypt of the Abbey Church of Saint-Gilles-du-Gard). The Cistercians added the rudimentary elements of Gothic art to the monastic buildings at Silvanès and at Flaran. When, at the beginning of the thirteenth century, the reconstruction of the Cathedral of Toulouse was begun, this single-nave church received both cross-ribbed vaults and decoration of northern origin. Then, the scourges of the Albigensian Crusade and the Anglo-French struggles put a halt to this evolution, and building activity resumed only toward the middle of the thirteenth century. As a result, southern France was not exposed to the Chartres expansion of the first High Gothic phase, although a faint echo of the major architectural trends occurred, for instance, in Saint-Michel at Gaillac (after 1271). Just at this time, northern Rayonnant art was flourishing everywhere, thanks to the work of Jean Deschamps at various great cathedrals. After Clermont-Ferrand and Limoges came the cathedrals of Narbonne, Bayonne, and, after 1300, the choirs of Saint-André at Bordeaux and of the Cathedral of Toulouse. However, southern French art confronted this northern proliferation with its own kind of church, based on the single-nave principle. In addition, several important examples of monastic structures built by mendicant orders are better preserved here than in northern France.

The single-nave church was already common in southern France, first during the Romanesque era, then in Cistercian art. Square-shaped side chapels often opened directly onto the main nave, as in the Abbey Church of Silvanès; and the southwestern phenomenon of single-nave churches crowned with rows of domes probably helped acclimate architects to this design. We will shortly see that the mendicant orders—the Franciscans in particular—adopted this plan from the beginning of their expansion (for example, San Francesco at Assisi). Thus, owing to either Romanesque tradition or Franciscan influence, several great and celebrated southern French buildings were designed in accordance with this structural principle. Although one of the earliest instances may still be seen in the remaining bays of the nave of the Cathedral of Toulouse, the most accomplished example is the Cathedral of Sainte-Cécile at Albi. This church was planned in 1247, and work on it probably began about 1276 and progressed slowly during part of the fourteenth century. The impressive size of the building, the fullness of the nave, and the monumentality of its profile were all made possible by a structural peculiarity—the fact that the main vault is supported by the vaults of the side chapels, themselves topped with galleries. Moreover, brick—a substance that is light, strong, and malleable—was chosen as the building material. Twelve bays long, the interior space of the church is strongly outlined by both the ribs of the oblong vaults and the colonnettes that extend their springings. The walls of this central volume are opened up by the chapels and their galleries, thereby creating a configuration that runs counter to the subtleties of Rayonnant Gothic. Only the contours and tracery of the windows—even these are narrow and do not fill all the space beneath the wall ribs—suggest the forms of northern Gothic art. The importance of the Cathedral of Albi stems from its position as first in a series of southern French churches: the Cathedral of Notre-Dame at Saint-Bertrand-de-Comminges and the cathedrals of Béziers, Perpignan, and Mirepoix. These, in turn, are closely related to such significant Catalonian edifices as Santa Catalina at Barcelona and the extraordinary nave of the Cathedral of Gerona. In a sense, the trend of the large single space also influenced the design of Catalonian churches with tall side aisles, such as Santa María del Mar at Barcelona and the Cathedral of Palma de Mallorca.

Closely linked to this local architectural variant is the building activity of the mendicant orders in southern France. In fact, it is quite likely that the major Dominican structures erected during the middle of the century had a role in determining the evolution of the Albi design. Except for some old documents, our knowledge of the development of mendicant-order architecture in Paris and northern France is very limited. In 1250, there were four great Dominican churches in Paris; the most notable was the Church of the Jacobins, the place of worship of an immense convent on the Rue Saint-Jacques, at the gates of the city. According to old plans, we know that the church had two parallel naves supported along the center by a row of very tall piers. This may have been the model for that masterpiece of French Dominican art, the Church of the Jacobins at Toulouse, the burial site of Saint Thomas Aquinas. To a certain extent, the theory of Raymond Rey concerning the derivation of this type of church must be accepted, however illogical it may seem: namely, that the double-nave design was an outgrowth of the primitive single-nave church flanked by side aisles. Such was actually the case of the original Church of the Jacobins at Toulouse: it was founded in 1227, erected beginning in 1240, and rebuilt into its present form after 1260. Its status as a masterpiece of Dominican architecture is due not only to its vastness and unified spatial effect (the central row of piers notwithstanding), but also to the magnificent linearity created by its vaulting. The latter effect is especially evident in the choir, where a palmetto design results from the "sprouting" of multiple ribs. The structure is analogous to that of the Cathedral of Albi, with this one difference: instead of chapel galleries, powerful exterior abutments linked at their summits by arcades ensure the stability of the edifice. In this respect, the Church of the Jacobins may be categorized with such buildings as the Church of the Augustinians at Toulouse and the Church of the Jacobins at Agen (1254-81). There is also a singular lighting effect in the Jacobins at Toulouse: almost all illumination filters through the clerestory and is concentrated in the upper reaches of the church. None of the previously mentioned phenomena have anything to do with the formal tendencies of northern French Rayonnant architecture of the middle and second half of the thirteeenth century.

A certain number of late-thirteenth-century Franciscan and Dominican churches still survive in the south of France (for example, at Perpignan and Béziers). However, to get a better idea of the architectural style of the mendicant orders at the time of their initial thirteenth-century expansion, special attention should be given to German, Rhenish, and Italian structures. If one compares the great single naves of the churches in Perpignan or Agen to Dominican structures in Germany, the difference in design becomes quickly evident. The typical German church—as at Regensburg, Esslingen, Erfurt, or Strasbourg (demolished)—is based on a basilican plan with side aisles. Destined to accommodate crowds of worshipers, these vast structures can be more easily compared to the models of Rayonnant art. However, this comparison cannot—in the thirteenth century, at least—pertain to the complex design and formal richness of the second Rayonnant phase, which we have termed Mannerist Gothic. Italy, for its part, witnessed the construction of marvelous Franciscan and Dominican monasteries at the end of the thirteenth century and the beginning of the fourteenth. Here, too, we have the case of a region that followed its own rhythm of development, one that we will examine in a later chapter.

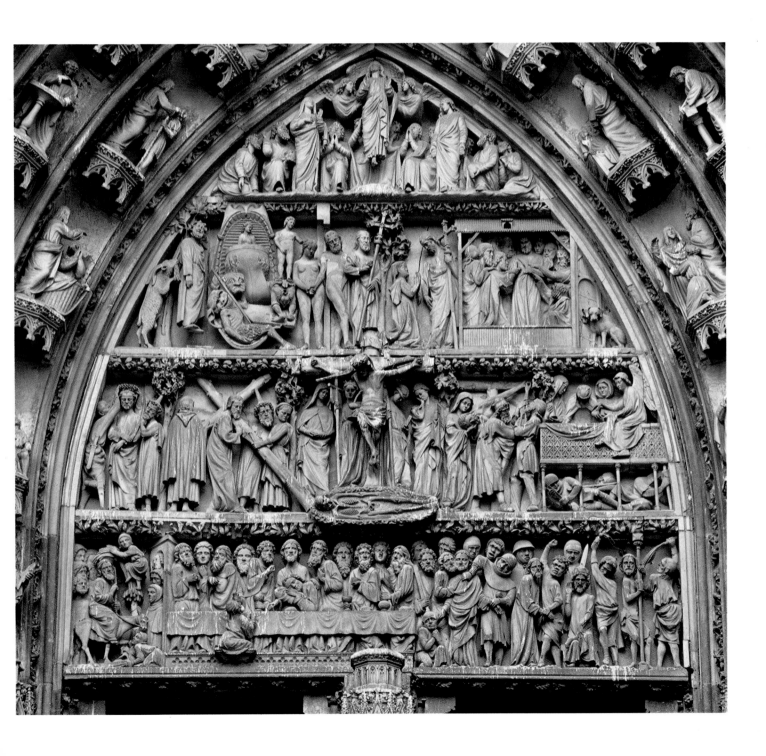

If we have been able to describe the origins and initial expansion of Gothic architecture as a unified movement — one that, of course, admitted diverse modes, local resistance, and variants floating against the general current — it is because the evolution of this style was based essentially on the spread of a certain building technique and, in particular, a way of conceptualizing and organizing space. It was northern France and England that gave birth to these seminal architectonic principles. However, beginning in the thirteenth century — and even earlier in England — various national reactions transformed the acquired models into a series of regional Gothic styles (*Sondergotik*), each of which merits special analysis. At times, we will have occasion to seek the origins of regional variants. However, these technical changes should not be attributed solely to reasons of convenience. About 1300 complex political, economic, and social conditions were bringing about the demise of French hegemony. On the one hand, French building activity was slowing its pace: the country was being subjected to a serious, ever-recurring conflict during the fourteenth century and part of the fifteenth. On the other hand, the star of Italian and German cities was fast rising; these urban areas were developing into thriving artistic centers. Modern nations were taking shape, and the formation of the world order that we call the Renaissance was proceeding rapidly, both culturally and economically.

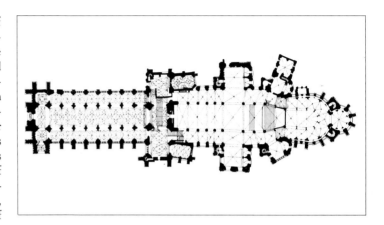

We have divided our study of Late Medieval trends into three sections. The first deals with English architecture, which appeared as a distinct form (Early English Gothic) about the beginning of the thirteenth century; the second section treats the architecture of Germanic countries and their dependencies, whose reaction did not crystallize until the end of the thirteenth century; and the Latin Gothic of Italy and Spain, produced by particular climatic conditions as well as traditional techniques, is discussed in the third.

EARLY ENGLISH GOTHIC

It would be pointless to reexamine the Anglo-Norman sources of Gothic architecture, but we should keep in mind that it did not originate in England. One might say that this style was first introduced in the Paris region and northern France, then imported to England in 1174 by Guillaume de Sens in the choir of Canterbury Cathedral. Prior to this date, no religious structure deserving of the label Gothic could be found beyond the Channel. Once it appeared, however, the new English current — adapting at once the double-shell or thick wall (Bony), as well as traditional Romanesque spatial concepts, to French building techniques — showed promising signs of undisputed originality. Moreover, English art sought inspiration especially from those buildings — for example, the well-illuminated transept of Noyon — that had themselves interpreted the Anglo-Norman double-shell wall according to new architectural formulas.

At Canterbury Cathedral, Trinity Chapel, that is, the apse and the ambulatory erected between 1179 and 1184 by William the Englishman, features the kind of ground-floor mural passage that had already appeared in the oriented chapels in the transept of the Cathedral of Laon (Bony). Although Romanesque England had never abandoned the use of false-bedding, the freestanding, false-bedded columns surrounding the central core of the piers derive, too, from Laon. Northern French Gothic — more so at Laon than at Paris — had favored protruding supports to accentuate structural linearity and to add rhythmic highlights to the walls. This taste for plastic and lighting effects fit in well with the English Romanesque tradition of thick, forceful moldings. Thus, England's selected borrowings from the Gothic architecture of the Continent were limited to those elements that corresponded to its own stylistic predilections.

The apse of Canterbury Cathedral exerted substantial influence beyond the Channel, not only by virtue of its double-shell walls, false-bedding, and multicolored marbles, but also by virtue of its two transepts and its single axial chapel. Canterbury is the cathedral of the primate of England, and its axial chapel, called Becket's Crown, was dedicated to an earlier primate, the martyr Saint Thomas à Becket. In later cathedrals, this chapel was invariably dedicated to the Virgin Mary (Lady Chapel). However, Canterbury was not the unique point of entry of Gothic art into England. In northern shires, such as Yorkshire, numerous Cistercian establishments served as architectural intermediaries. For example, Roche Abbey (now in ruins) was, like the apse at Canterbury, begun about 1175. At its extremity there is a rectilinear choir with rectangular ambulatory. Although this design probably dates back to the early twelfth century in England (Romsey Abbey, Old Sarum), a Gothic version may be found at Morimond, one of the four "daughters" of Cîteaux (c. 1155-60). The elevation of Roche Abbey consists of three stories with blind triforium; its ambulatory piers, topped with round abaci, are compounded with engaged columns arranged around a central core; and the strongly molded transverse arches are markedly pointed. The church at Ripon, built by Roger de Pont-l'Evêque, archbishop of York, dates from approximately the same period. Only two western bays remain of its original unvaulted nave; its three-storied elevation had sharply pointed arches and, in the Romanesque tradition, an interior passage at the clerestory level.

Gothic at first appeared in southwestern England about 1175 — thanks again, in all probability, to Cistercian contacts — in the three-storied west bays of Worcester Cathedral and, shortly thereafter, in the rectangular axial chapel of the former Benedictine Abbey Church of Glastonbury. Dating from 1184 to 1186, this chapel blends decidedly Romanesque elements — round-arched windows and chevron (that is, zigzag) patterns carved into the ribs — with cross-ribbed vaults on

pointed wall ribs. A contemporary of Glastonbury, Saint David's Cathedral at Saint David's, Wales, has an unvaulted nave with single side aisles. The round-arched arcade rests on alternately round and octagonal piers, each of which has four engaged, margin-drafted columns. Except for their much heavier proportions, these piers almost duplicate those in the Cathedral of Chartres. Deep round arches mark the upper level: each bay contains four triforium openings topped with two clerestory windows, the whole recessed from the plane of the arcade. This seems to be the same kind of attempt to simplify the articulation of stories that occurred in twelfth-century northern France. However, the English architect of Saint David's exploited the idea of the double-shell wall in order to position the framework and storied elevation on two separate walls. The use of an offset, deeply recessed triforium and clerestory was repeated at Dublin and, in a later and different style, at Lichfield, York, and Winchester. The circular foliage carving between the bays of the triforium in Saint David's is a decorative pattern typical of Early Gothic art in western England and was imitated in Normandy during the thirteenth century (the cloister of Mont-Saint-Michel).

Structures in the northern and western regions show that England was ripe for Gothic architecture toward 1180; but it was the eastern and southeastern areas that, under the influence of Canterbury, took the really decisive steps in that direction. In 1187, Chichester Cathedral was damaged by fire; and its east end was rebuilt in accordance with the proportions of the tall, three-storied Romanesque nave. The main arcade remains round-arched but rests on piers encircled by freestanding black marble shafts that are exact copies of those in Canterbury. The mullioned apertures of the gallery, as well as the arches positioned in front of the clerestory-level passage, are pointed.

Begun in 1192, the choir of Lincoln Cathedral also derives from Canterbury before its reconstruction. It has two transepts and a three-sided apse with ambulatory opening onto a polygonal axial chapel whose form recalls Becket's Crown. The five-ribbed vaults of the side aisles echo the southern arm of the east transept at Canterbury; the sexpartite vaults of the two transepts, as well as the piers surrounded by freestanding columns, can also be traced to this model. However, beginning with the end of the twelfth century, Lincoln proclaimed certain innovative traits that were in no way linked to the Continent. Saint Hugh's Choir, with its three stories and single side aisles, extends between the two transepts. Unlike Canterbury, the intermediate level is not a triforium: it opens instead to the roofing, in accordance with a technique often utilized during and after the Romanesque period. The walls of the tall nave are quite thick and colored with numerous marble shafts that also highlight the pillars of the triforium openings. Recalling the Romanesque *mur épais*, the wall here doubles in the clerestory: the outer shell is pierced with groups of simple, pointed windows, while the inner shell consists of ar-

130. *Worcester, Cathedral, nave.*
131. *Glastonbury, Abbey Church,*
ruins.

132. *Mont-Saint-Michel, Abbey,*
cloister.
133. *Chichester, Cathedral, façade.*

ches supported on false-bedded marble colonnettes. Although the entire choir is Gothic and its architect did not feel constrained to respect Romanesque proportions — as was the case at Chichester — the clerestory windows are relatively low, while the main arcade is fairly elongated. The resulting spatial effect is comparable to that of certain Romanesque naves, such as that of Durham or to the nave of the Cathedral of Sens. That is, the side aisles merging with the nave space produce an overall impression of elongated massiveness. This spatial concept, inherited from previous generation, prevailed in England during the thirteenth century.

The vaults in Saint Hugh's Choir spring from beneath the clerestory-window supports and are thus securely sustained by the thick upper walls that bear their thrust. Consequently, the flying buttresses normally needed to stabilize the roofing are practically superfluous. Though they do exist at Lincoln (as a derivative of Canterbury), they protrude only slightly above the lateral roofing. The simultaneous occurrence of the double-shell wall and an upper story of reduced height virtually eliminated the development of the flying-buttress system of support in thirteenth-century English architecture. The volumetric masses were to remain quite simple, marked only by gradations of roofing. Another result — essential to an understanding of this architecture — was that, owing to the thickness of the walls, the thrusts did not have to be directed toward points spaced at great distances from one another. The vaulting of Saint Hugh's Choir provides one of the earliest examples of this procedure, one that contradicts the principles of Gothic rationalism and structural clarity.

All of the ribs originate from fixed, regularly spaced points positioned between the clerestory windows, above the piers of the arcade. However, the rib branches do not meet at a single crown or boss, as had been dictated by the vaulting technique of Early Gothic architecture on the Continent. Instead, the ribs extending from either side of a window group come together to form a triangular vault field, only one branch of which, shorter than the other, reaches the top of the vault. As a result, this triangle is "out of joint" with the one formed by the ribs extending from the opposite wall. Additional ribs delineate groups of narrow, oblique triangles that alternate with the vault fields framing the windows. A bold ridge rib highlights the crown of the vault, which is also punctuated by carved bosses at each rib intersection. The resulting effect is, to use W.R. Lethaby's term, "linear". The customary structure of bays has been annihilated, giving way to a continuous roofing whose identically molded ribs create a linear pattern apparently more decorative than structural in function (Frankl).

The second innovation in Saint Hugh's Choir is the decoration of the lower part of the side-aisle walls. The interior wall beneath the windows is decorated with two intersecting arcatures, one in front of the other. A

134. *Lincoln, Cathedral, plan of the church and of adjoining buildings.*

135. *Lincoln, Cathedral, façade.*

136. *Lincoln, Cathedral, Angel Choir and eastern window.*

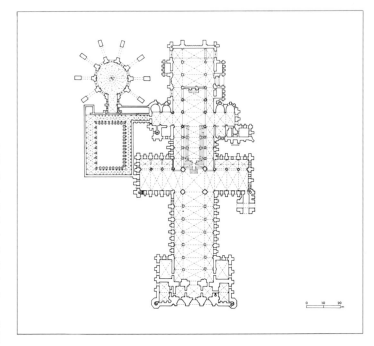

possible origin may be the intersecting round-arched arcatures so common in English Romanesque architecture and even used in the axial chapel of Glastonbury. What is truly novel about Saint Hugh's Choir is the arrangement of the arcatures in two separate planes: the rear row consists of pointed arches on falsebedded columns set against the wall, in front of which a staggered row of trefoiled pointed arches rests on freestanding shafts of black marble. The corners between the trefoiled arches are adorned with angels carved in high relief. This invention reflected the English taste for double-shell walls and rich, polychromatic plastic effects; it was further exploited in the triforium of Beverley Minster, begun in 1225 and the axial chapel of Ely Cathedral. In addition, it was a possible source of the cloister at Mont-Saint-Michel.

Although the influence of Canterbury and Lincoln can be seen in the eastern part of Rochester Cathedral (begun c. 1200), the most original project in eastern England (after Saint Hugh's Choir) was unquestionably the western part of Peterborough Cathedral. The beginning date of Peterborough is uncertain: according to C. Peer, it was begun about 1190; according to J. Bilson, about 1205. Two partially constructed towers were demolished to make way for a vaulted west transept based on those at Ely and at Bury St. Edmunds. During a second building campaign, a colossal porch was added to the façade; its three pointed arches, stretching to the full height of the transept, probably hark back to the niches of the Romanesque façade of Lincoln Cathedral. The three gables, decorated with statues and rose windows, are flanked by turrets. This façade was not meant to serve as a monumental entry to the cathedral, for the main entrance is on the north. The wall of the west transept, at the back of the porch recesses, is decorated with arcatures that imitate perforated windows and recall a scheme developed by Rayonnant Gothic in the Île-de-France. It was not until between 1220 and 1230 that the façade was completed. Its effect is bizarre: the colossal arches are juxtaposed between two side towers, with a horizontal lime of molding running from one to the other beneath the gables. Thus, instead of accentuating the verticality of the façade, the arches create an impression of expansion in breadth. Here again, the double-shell wall was a source of plastic effects, and as with the vaults in Lincoln, a readable structure was sacrificed for the sake of decorative interests that have little to do with logical clarity. As was the case on the Continent, one goal of Early English Gothic architecture was increased illumination. Thanks to its familiarity with the thick wall, the English variant achieved diaphanousness by expertly blending the spatial volumes of the doubled walls as well as the numerous highlighted moldings.

As the choir of Lincoln Cathedral was being erected, work was beginning on the choir of Wells Cathedral in western England. Only the westernmost bays have survived. The nave, which dates from the early thirteenth century, is somewhat more recent.

Sustaining the vaults are short supports that stop above the triforium; and the two lower stories, a continuous succession of vertically unconnected arcades, recall the "aqueduct" profiles of Romanesque architecture (Southwell). As at Peterborough and at Lincoln, this arrangement contradicts the logical structure so dear to French Gothic. The north porch — which, like the one at Peterborough, is the main entrance to the cathedral — is a variation on the double-shell theme, its gable doubled by a gallery of arches of descending height. The turrets above the angular pier abutments may also be found in Gothic transepts in Normandy (Coutances, Bayeux).

Built about 1230-40, the west front of Wells is developed along its breadth: its two massive towers stand outside the central volume (as on the façade of the Cathedral of Poitiers, a possible source), and the decoration is spread over two stories. Pierced by three modest doors, the lower level is decorated with arcatures or cusped double windows beneath relieving arches crowned with gables. Above, niches housing statues appear as part of much taller arcading carved into strongly protruding abutments. All of the false-bedded shafts of the arcades and arcatures are fashioned from a stone that is darker than that of the walls. Although the architect William Wynford modified the upper level in the fourteenth century, the statuary is, even today, remarkably well preserved. The west front of Wells was to remain the prototype of broad, richly decorated English façades from Salisbury to Exeter. This preference for walls and abutments runs counter to the French insistence on framed windows; only the presence of certain motifs (canopied statues, cusps, quatrefoils, and gables) bears witness to contact with France.

The same decorative motifs occur in the eastern section of Worcester Cathedral (much restored), which also features an interior passage at the level of the ground-floor windows, possibly derived from the Cathedral of Reims. They may also be found in the nave of Lincoln and in Beverley Minster, both begun about 1225. This period can also lay claim to Salisbury Cathedral, begun in 1220 and completed in 1266, which Gainsborough's paintings have made world-famous. Actually, the lofty crossing tower and spire that dominate the profile — according to J. Evans, this is the single most important source of the church's beauty — date from only the fourteenth century. Relationships to Lincoln and Wells are to be found everywhere: the three-storied elevation of low proportions; the double-shell wall with low, simple windows; polychromatic effects in marble; forceful moldings and trefoiled or quatrefoiled decoration. Salisbury holds special interest for art historians: its rectangular axial chapel (erected 1220-25) includes side aisles as tall as the nave that merge into the rectangular ambulatory. The quest for diaphanousness thus led to fusion of space and unification of components, both abetted by the extreme slenderness of the marble pillars. In addition, this chapel offers the first example of a small-scale English hall church, perhaps in-

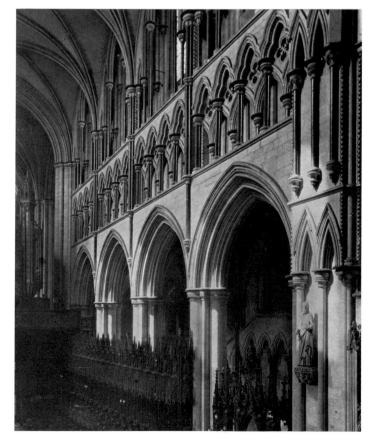

*137. Beverley, Minster, northwest
arm of the transept.*
*138. Beverley, Minster, southeast
choir.*

*139. Wells, Cathedral, plan of the
church and of adjoining buildings.*
140. Wells, Cathedral, façade.

spired by Saint-Serge at Angers (J. Harvey). It directly influenced the axial chapel of Winchester Cathedral.

WESTMINSTER ABBEY

During the second quarter of the thirteenth century, the majority of
religious structures in England shared similar characteristics. But the
reconstruction of Westminster Abbey west of the City of London under
the auspices of Henry III breathed new life into English architecture. In
1220, an axial chapel had been added to the Romanesque abbey and it
was retained in the new plan. The walls of the ambulatory and radiating
chapels were probably being erected even before the demolition of the
Romanesque apse in 1245 (G. Webb). The plan of Westminster breaks
with the English tradition of a single axial chapel: its multisided apse surrounded by an ambulatory and five radiating chapels derives from French
models. Prior to Westminster, this type of apse could be found in only
one other thirteenth-century English structure — the Cistercian Abbey
Church of Beaulieu. In the choir, the three bays that decrease in depth
recall the choir of the Cathedral of Reims. As in Notre-Dame at Paris, the
piers of the apse are spaced as far apart as those in the rectilinear bays;
but this scheme had already occurred in eleventh-century England
(Gloucester and Tewkesbury). The side aisles of the transept bring to
mind Chartres and Reims, and the rhythm and proportions of the elevation are also comparable to those of the great French edifices. The choir
has the sweeping narrowness of the lofty nave at Royaumont (Branner).
The windows are of the Reims variety — two lancets beneath a traceried
rose window with hollowed corner spaces (spandrels) — and they extend
to well below the springings of the vaults. The upper walls are thin and
constructed in the French manner, rising from a single *tas-de-charge*
(springing stone). The columns engaged in the piers rise uninterruptedly
along the wall and up to the vaults, thereby giving a sweeping, punctuated effect to the bays.

The first master of Westminster was Henry of Reynes, and it has been
proposed that he may have come from Reims. However, the research of
Lethaby indicates that, although he had traveled in France, he was in fact
an Englishman. Indeed, certain features of Westminster are decidedly
English. The piers and their engaged shafts are in Purbeck marble,
establishing a polychromatic effect that is taken up by the two-toned
motifs covering the spandrels of the principal arcade. The arcade itself
consists of sharply pointed, heavily molded arches that are a great deal
taller than the clerestory windows. The middle story comprises, not a
triforium, but a full-fledged gallery lighted from the outside; each of its
interior bays includes two cusped arcades beneath a relieving arch, the
whole crowned with a rosette perforation. This arrangement recalls the
triforium openings in the nave of Amiens, except that the latter is carved
in much higher relief. As for the clerestory windows, they are recessed

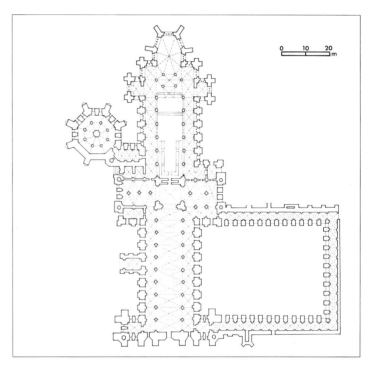

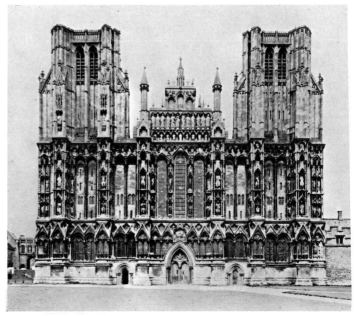

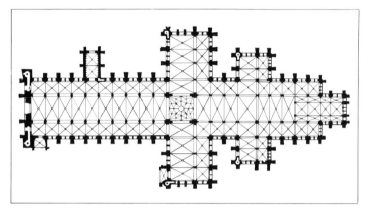

from the wall ribs, resulting in a plasticity quite different from that of French schemes. With its superposed galleries between the windows, the end of the north arm of the transept is even more typically English, despite the presence of an upper rose window derived from the north rose of Notre-Dame at Paris (Branner).

Westminster is a happy confluence of French borrowings and local traditions. Characteristic elements of Rayonnant Gothic can be detected in the treatment of the windows and gallery bays, and this phenomenon is even more obvious in the chapter house, completed in 1253. In accordance with English custom, this is a separate building, whose octagonal form had a direct effect on the chapter house of Salisbury. Proceeding upward, the elevation consists first of cusped arcatures (not set in pointed arches), then very large windows composed of four lancets within two pointed arches perforated with quatrefoils and topped with a sexfoil rose window. This composition comes from the side-chapel windows in Notre-Dame at Paris (Branner) and demonstrates that the master of Westminster was well informed about the latest projects in the *domaine royal* of Louis IX. We can even observe curvilinear profiles in the gallery windows, evoking the rounded triangles carved in the interior of the north arm of the transept of Notre-Dame.

Even though Westminster Abbey was not completed in the thirteenth century — only the apse, transept, and four east bays date from this period — its influence was deeply felt throughout England. The chapter house launched the craze for the great compound tracery windows that afforded such abundant illumination. The north rose window, as well as Rayonnant decorative motifs (cusps, multifoils, curvilinear forms, and hollowed spandrels), was succeeded by countless imitations. The Reims-style mural passage in the apse was copied in the east part of the nave of Durham Cathedral (begun 1242). However, the undeniably French plan of the apse in Westminster — its vertical sweep and its *tas-de-charge* vaulting system supported by flying buttresses thrusting themselves audaciously into space — had no durable offspring. Be that as it may, the nave of Lichfield Cathedral and the Angel Choir of Lincoln Cathedral (that is, the rectilinear eastern end reconstructed from 1256 to 1280) did follow in the footsteps of the royal abbey. The proportions of the Angel Choir match those of Saint Hugh's Choir; but in the former, trefoils decorate the arcade spandrels, while the triforium spandrels are adorned with angels carved in high relief. Both clerestory windows and interior arcades are compound. An immense glass surface, derived from those in the Westminster chapter house, lights the rear of the choir. Owing to the double-shell walls, there is a return to English vaulting traditions, complete with ridge ribs and tiercerons and liernes (supplementary ribs).

Another London structure probably played a major role in the development of English Gothic: Old Saint Paul's, no longer extant but known to us through the engravings of Hollar (Lethaby, Branner). Its rectilinear

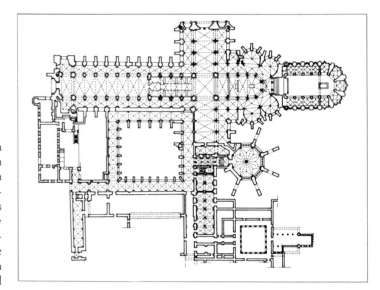

apse was built about 1280-85. In the east wall were juxtaposed seven pointed windows; they were topped with a large rose window that was, in turn, set in a square frame with hollowed-out spandrels. This composition must have given the impression of a single immense aperture that completely opened up the rear of the choir. The profiles of both the windows (cusped lancets beneath an outer gable) and the traceried rose window (concave and fourcentered arches) broke with Rayonnant tracery and inaugurated a decorative scheme that had no French counterpart until the Flamboyant period. Here too are the beginnings of foliate tracery, which though conceivably derived from Rayonnant art, underwent novel decorative applications in England. Thus, of all French influences operating at Westminster, English architects retained only two essential features: broadening and lengthening of the windows (facilitated, as at Lincoln, by the double-shell wall supporting the vaults) and a new ornamental imaginativeness evolving from intricate window tracery.

DECORATED STYLE

The traditional starting point of the new phase of English Gothic called Decorated or Curvilinear is placed about 1290. This was the moment when Edward I (1272-1307) had so-called Eleanor Crosses erected to commemorate the resting points of the cortege of his queen, Eleanor of Castile, who died in 1290. Three of them remain; the one at Waltham was built by Nicolas Dymenge de Reyns (from England or Reims?). Their bases are covered with floral decoration carved in vertical bands; arcatures outlined beneath gables are, in turn, accompanied by finials (ornamental top pieces) and rampant arches bristling with foliage. In addition, gabled and pinnacled arches hollowed into the base frame statues placed within. These crosses tend to confirm both the royal (that is, London) origin of the new style and its contacts with French Rayonnant Gothic. To be sure, the Eleanor Crosses did not constitute the sole source of the next Gothic phase, but they did signal a stage of development already prepared by projects after Westminster — in particular, Old Saint Paul's.

It would be incorrect to think that the Decorated Style was nothing more than a new approach to decoration. The characteristic features of the various phases of Gothic were determined in the mid-nineteenth century on the basis of window form and design. One should realize, however, that to these decorative elements correspond specific structures. For instance, because English architects were captivated by immense glazed surfaces, they preferred rectilinear to curved apses. It is perhaps this taste that led them to retain thick walls, thereby allowing them to hollow out the upper levels with greater ease (Evans). But this may also point to a refusal to accept Continental buttressing systems. English builders took great liberties with the French cross-ribbed vault, not only because of the thicker walls but also because their island was not

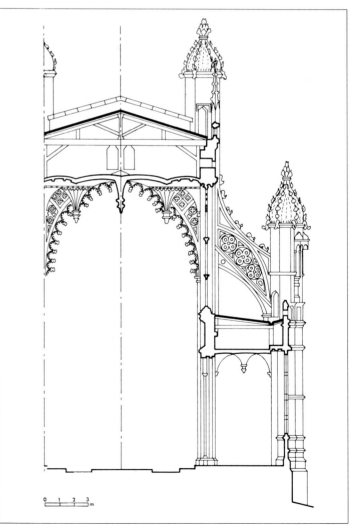

144. London, Westminster Abbey,
plan of the church and of adjoining
buildings.
145. London, Westminster Abbey,
Chapel of Henry VII, section.

XV. Salisbury, Cathedral, façade.

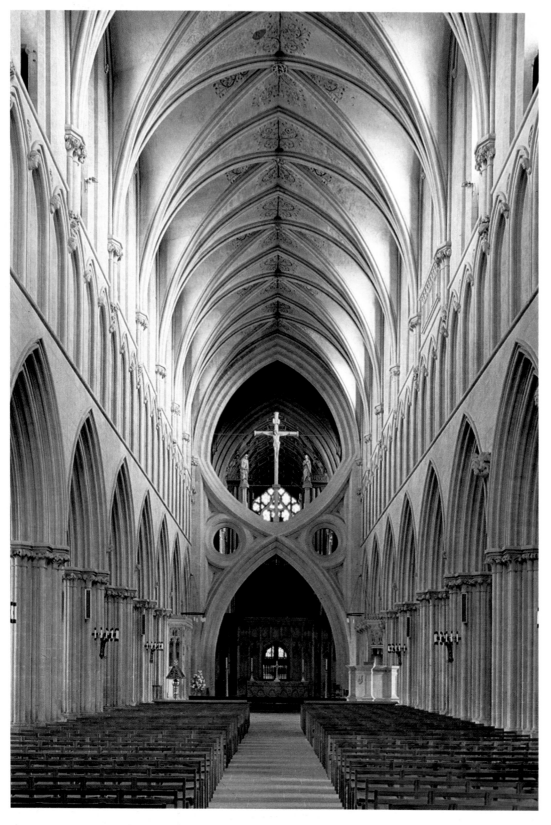

XVI. Wells, Cathedral, nave.

146. London, Westminster Abbey, nave.

rich in stone quarries. England's natural wealth lay in wood; and, like all maritime countries, England produced excellent carpenters trained in shipbuilding. In thirteenth- and fourteenth-century England, it was not at all uncommon to encounter large churches covered with false wood vaulting (Lichfield, Ely, York, Winchester). As the components of timber roofing were lighter and of greater length than those of stone vaulting, the use of wood favored imaginative ornamental treatment of ribs and bosses.

The English also frowned upon the slender, narrow proportions of Westminster. When art historians come upon exceptions to this rule (Beverly Minster, for example), they immediately deduce a French influence. During the entire Gothic period, English religious structures remained elongated, broad, and relatively low. In a word, their proportions were a good deal more squat than those of their French counterparts. Even when English architects did adopt foreign decorative elements, they adapted them to their taste for richness of general effect. One of the best examples of this attitude is the manner in which they accepted naturalistic foliage carving from the Île-de-France (the façade of Notre-Dame at Paris) beginning about 1210-20). The French design was transformed into repeating patterns (such as garlands of small, formalized rosebuds called ball flowers) or into thicker, more uneven foliage that emphasized seaweed and other motifs from marine life (Lady Chapel at Ely). Juxtaposed to these lively organic forms are geometric designs in which curves predominate-triangles, lozenges, rosettes, and multifoils. Moreover, countless moldings expressed the predilection for surfaces carved in high relief. At the end of the thirteenth century, the sharpening of edges and the addition of longitudinal ribs to convex surfaces further enhanced the play of light and shadow.

Some scholars have wondered if the appearance of the Decorated Style coincided with increased contacts with the East: witness vault ribs arranged in star patterns that recall certain Islamic domes. The oldest example of this phenomenon is unquestionably the choir of Old Pershore Abbey, reconstructed after a fire in 1288. Perhaps the most curious building in this group is the North Porch of Saint Mary Redcliffe in Bristol (first quarter of the fourteenth century), a two-storied hexagonal structure that was attached to an early-thirteenth-century rectangular porch. Its decoration is quite intricate and, indeed, Flamboyant in its use of curves, countercurves, and Eastern-style multifoils in the apertures. With respect to this stylistic aspect, Harvey has pointed out that the journey to Persia by an emissary of Edward I confirms the very real existence of contact between England and the Mongol Empire. We should not omit borrowed themes and motifs that were "imported" to England by navigators; this was later the case of the Manueline Style in Portugal.

The key monuments of the Decorated Style include Exeter and York cathedrals, the choirs of Lichfield and Wells, the towers of Ely and

Salisbury, and the cloister of Norwich. The construction of Exeter Cathedral must have begun shortly before that of York, between 1280 and 1290. Though the nave was completed about 1300, the choir took 25 more years to finish, and work on the façade continued until the third quarter of the fourteenth century. Its plan utilized a typical Early Gothic arrangement: two transepts, rectangular apse and ambulatory, and rectilinear axial chapel. The three-storied elevation, though traditional, was treated in an innovative manner. The vault supports rest on corbels above the arcade piers and vertically punctuate the interior space, forming rigorously articulated bays. The walls seem flatter that in preceding buildings for several reasons: the spandrels are unadorned; the triforium arcatures lie on but a single plane, as does the Norman-style clerestory balustrade; and there is no inner gallery at the upper level. However, the closely fitted columns engaged in the piers, the arcade moldings, and the clerestory windows recessed from the balustrade all bear witness to an exceptional concern for surfaces in relief. The vaults — complete with ridge ribs and tiercerons — boldly spread their ribs from the walls above the balustrades like palm leaves sprouting from their trunk. The cusped triforium arcatures, balustrade quatrefoils, and noninscribed, superposed cusps in the clerestory window tracery all point to Rayonnant decorative sources. In joining an odd number of lancets to the rose window by a group of ogees, the more recent window of the façade marks the culmination of Old Saint Paul's rose-window-over-lancet arrangement.

The dates for York Cathedral can be stated with greater certainty: the large transept dates from the thirteenth century; the chapter house was begun in 1290, the nave in the following year; the façade was completed about 1340; and the nave was ceiled with wood in 1346. Work on the choir did not begin until 1361. As at Westminster and Salisbury, the chapter house is octagonal; it is lighted by a large number of windows comprising an odd number of lancets and a multifoiled rose window. A passage runs beneath the windows, its arcades standing free of the interior wall. These stalls are crowned with cusped, three-sided canopies beneath gables whose finials create the effect of an unbroken ripple. The walls of the passage between the windows lie obliquely — not perpendicularly — to them, and this underscores the undulation of the walls. Although consisting of three stories, the nave seems to have only two: the triforium and clerestory are offset and the window mullions extend downward between the bays to the base of the triforium. There are indeed traces of Rayonant here (Saint-Denis), but the great west façade window reveals a tracery whose curves, countercurves, and fillets branch out like tree limbs above the central mullion.

This wavy wall rhythm can also be found in the choir clerestory windows of Lichfield Cathedral, where a balustrade tops the arcade and the two upper stories rise at the rear of a deep, carved recess (allowing room, incidentally, for a passage). The axial chapel added at the beginning of

150. *York, Cathedral, plan.*
151. *York, Cathedral, aerial view.*

152. *York, Cathedral, interior.*

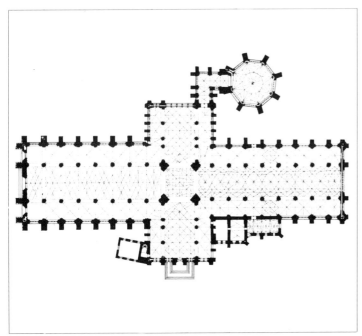

XVIII. Gloucester, Cathedral, choir vault.

the fourteenth century has a single story made up of immense traceried windows in trefoil motif. Above, the gables are ogeed, while two levels of niched statues decorate the abutments (as in the Wells façade). The Lady Chapel of Wells Cathedral is somewhat older: it dates from the time of the building of the apse and was completed in 1306. Polygonal in shape, its west piers interpenetrate the shorter ambulatory, resulting in a spatial effect as curious as that at Salisbury. The vault ribs branching out like palm leaves recall the nave at Exeter, and the window tracery is reminiscent of Lichfield. The slightly more recent vaults of the chapter house likewise accentuate the bundles of ribs. The most noteworthy axial chapel of this period is without doubt the Lady Chapel at Ely Cathedral, begun in 1321. The low-set arcade has been transformed into veritable niches whose decoration brings to mind the zigzag patterns in Saint Hugh's Choir at Lincoln. The niches are crowned with gables that are in turn flanked with pinnacles and carvings in relief. The arch of the niche opening is not only multifoiled, but also tilted forward, and each of its lobes is made up of asymmetrical ogees. Another ogee interposed between the opening and the gable above twists asymmetrically, curving outward like the tip of a leaf. All of the interstices of the foils, gables, and rampants are carved in a seaweed or leaf motif. An openwork balustrade tops the entire composition, one whose dynamism, high relief, and ornamental intricacy mark the triumph of this decorated, curvilinear English style.

In 1322 — the year after the beginning of work on the Lady Chapel at Ely — the square lantern (tower) atop the Romanesque crossing collapsed. It was rebuilt from 1328 to 1340, but according to a new spatial scheme: the corners of the crossing were eliminated and replaced by walls pierced with large windows. Above this was positioned an octagonal lantern built entirely of wood, together with an abundance of balustrades and pinnacles (the work of the master carpenter William Hurley). The wood tower at Ely corresponds to the stone tower and spire at Salisbury, constructed about 1320 by Richard of Farleigh. At this same moment, the addition of a tall central tower to the crossing at Wells was proving to be too great a burden for the crossing piers. To remedy this problem, the crossing was braced in 1340 with massive pointed arches between the piers. Equally massive but inverted arches were then positioned above them, and all of the components were united by two large oculi. The resulting curve and countercurve produce a particularly vigorous effect as well as an extraordinary division of space. To the list of towers that modified the long, horizontal lines of the English cathedral, we will add the towers and steeples at Lichfield and the graceful towers of the York, Beverley, and Westminster façades. Their source of inspiration may have been the once-renowned steeple (demolished) of Old Saint Paul's in London.

Another example of this style is the cloister at Norwich Cathedral

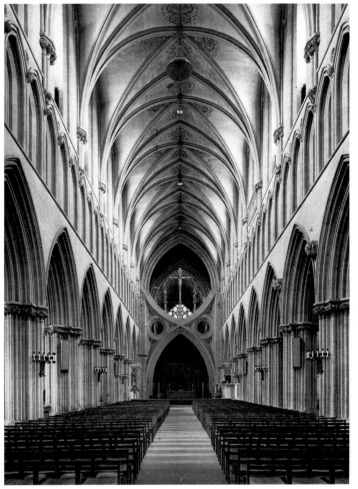

(begun 1297). Here there are vaults with ridge ribs, tiercerons, and many ornate bosses, as well as bays consisting of trefoiled lancets beneath curvilinear triangles, within which appear noninscribed trefoils and rippled quatrefoils. However, this decorative exuberance, this proliferation of naturalistic ornamentation, this dynamism of curved, pointed, and twisted arches elicited a reaction that was not long in coming.

PERPENDICULAR STYLE

Through renewed structural rigor and uninhibited use of right angles, this new form of English Gothic proved itself to be a genuinely national style — a true "opus anglicanum," as Evans puts it. However, because it appeared more or less simultaneously in London and western England, its origins are subject to debate. For Evans, its birth-place was Bristol Cathedral (Saint Augustine's), completed in 1341. Harvey and Webb see London as its place of origin and William Ramsey as its inventor. A native of Norwich and architect to the king from 1336 to 1349, Ramsey was one of the countless victims of the Black Death that ravaged England in the mid-fourteenth century. He designed the chapter house of Old Saint Paul's in 1332 and worked at Windsor, where the Dean's Cloister was constructed soon thereafter. M. Hastings also perceives London origins, but this time at Saint Stephen's Chapel (the royal chapel at Westminster). Finally, the nineteenth-century historian R. Willis proposed a compromise hypothesis: although the new style may have taken shape in western provinces — at Gloucester, where the Romanesque choir and the south arm of the transept were reconstructed about 1330 — the idea for it originally came from London.

The dates are so close together that one can hardly justify leaning toward one region or the other, especially in light of the fact that the London structures have all but completely disappeared. In any case, the current tendency is to favor London, as the royal architects and court atmosphere in general are seen as important factors in the development of both Decorated and Perpendicular styles. It is believed that the rectangular paneling that gave Perpendicular Gothic its name was derived from French models either introduced or already known to London (viz. the windows of the royal chapel of Saint-Germain-en-Laye, the triforium of Saint-Sulpice-de-Favières, and the apse of Saint-Urbain at Troyes). We should add that this term was also arrived at from observations of window tracery designs, often composed of rectangular glass panels. Moreover, narrow juxtaposed lancet windows, like those in Old Saint Paul's, were often separated by vertical mullions with horizontal subdivisions, and the rose window above would itself be set within a square. The tiers of arcatures and niches on church façades (Wells, for instance) also created a paneled effect. Therefore, in its long-standing insistence on horizontally continuous divisions with occasional vertical accents, English art already contained the seeds of Perpendicular Style.

Be that as it may, the precociousness of new architectural forms in western England cannot be denied; it was here that a singular vaulting technique, the fan vault, first appeared. Although not truly perpendicular — or even Gothic in the sense that it no longer adhered to the idea of a roof resting on arches — this was the characteristic vault of the Perpendicular phase. It was used to cover the chapter house at Hereford (c. 1360-70, now demolished) and was quickly reapplied in the cloisters at Gloucester. The fan vault uses the walls for support, lining them with a succession of flared, umbrella-shaped conoids whose upper lips are joined together by a nearly flat section of vaulting. The resulting undulation of the interior surface follows in the footsteps of the early-fourteenth-century "undulating wall." Every trace of diagonal ribbing has vanished, giving way to a veritable embroidery of raised multiple decorative elements — fillets, rosettes (at Gloucester), ogees, trefoils, and quatrefoils. Here again we see the imaginativeness of Decorated wall ornamentation and tracery. As for the windows, the cusped lancet tips are no longer set within a pointed arch, but within a rectangular frame.

Through not entirely abandoned, cross-ribbed vaulting did take on additional liernes (ridge ribs), tiercerons, and, as in the nave at Canterbury, numerous bosses. These ribbed subdivisions result in a reticulated effect not much different from that produced by net vaults. Diversity reigns supreme: there are even vaults resting on arches detached beneath the vault fields, joined only at their crowns by bosses or transverse arches (skeleton vault). These arches make one think of indoor flying buttresses, like those in the ground-level side aisles of Sainte-Chapelle in Paris and especially the arches reinforcing the crossing at Wells. In the early fourteenth century, this kind of arch could be found at Bristol Cathedral, a hall church, and in Saint Mary's at Warwick toward the end of the century. As illustrated by the south porch of the Cathedral of Prague, this vaulting system did have German counterparts, but the fan vault in particular remained an English idiosyncrasy.

Perpendicular Style, which dominated Gothic architecture in England from about 1330 until the end of the Middle Ages, is divided into two distinct periods. The first includes the last two-thirds of the fourteenth century. At the turn of the fifteenth century, international conflict (the Hundred Years War) as well as civil strife (the Wars of the Roses between the houses of York and Lancaster) interrupted several building projects, including the nave of Westminster. Only after the return of Edward IV from exile could work be resumed (c. 1480): there was then a second wave of important Perpendicular structures. The style finally died out about 1525-30, not of its own accord, but a victim of the Reformation and the suppression of monasteries by Henry VIII.

Numerous documents provide us with information about Late Medieval building activity in England as well as the role of royal architects throughout the island nation. Among the fourteenth-century

158, 159. *Gloucester, Cathedral, aerial view and presbytery.*

XIX. *Winchester, Cathedral, façade.*

masters, we have already mentioned William Ramsey, and we must add William Wynford, together with the pair responsible for Westminster Hall, Henry Yevele and the carpenter Hugh Herland. Although the architects active in the western provinces and at York remain anonymous, they probably came into contact with court architects. In particular, Harvey has noted that the great window in the south arm of the transept at Gloucester (erected before 1337) is a direct descendant of the windows designed by William Ramsey in 1332 for the chapter house (now demolished) of Old Saint Paul's. The murder of Edward II in 1327, his subsequent interment at Gloucester, and the influx of pilgrims to his tomb were surely factors related to the resumption of work on the Romanesque cathedral. In fact, this may serve as a basis for establishing a direct link between Gloucester Cathedral and royal architects from London. Even though the eleventh-century choir was not destroyed, the interior walls of the three-storied, galleried nave were decorated with a network of rectangular panels framing pointed or ogeed lancet tips. These panels either form arcatures raised directly from the wall surface or stand independently in front of the arcade apertures, like a window tracery without glass. The entire rear of the apse above the ambulatory was hollowed out to allow for an enormous tripartite window regularly divided by panels similar in shape to those just described. Since the panels lie in a single plane and all of the tracery moldings share the same profile, one has the sensation of being surrounded by flat surfaces. This violent break with the traditional double-shell wall and moldings in high relief had actually been presaged by the treatment given the upper stories of the nave at York Cathedral. Moreover, it was a belated outgrowth of Rayonnant Gothic. The engaged supports that rise in a single thrust from the ground to the springings of the vaults; the two great posts separating the main sections of the apse window; and the "mullions" rising from the middle of each bay's "tracery," uninterrupted by the horizontal lines of the paneling — all of these features create the impression of sweeping vertically, much as at York. It is this flatness and verticality that are the hallmarks of this style's originality of formal structure and spatial design. The continuous paneled subdivision of wall and window, combined with the dense tissue of vault ribs, effects an extraordinarily unified interior volume, one that resembles a rigid net through which air and light are allowed to filter. The choir at Gloucester is the masterwork of the Perpendicular Style at its most diaphanous. The cloister, built a few years later, complements the unique choir perfectly, with its fan vaults, niched walls, and traceried windows featuring close-set ogees that animate the rigidity of the mullions.

Aside from Bristol Cathedral (a contemporary of the choir at Gloucester), we should also mention Tewkesbury Abbey, whose Romanesque upper stories were torn down about 1340 in order to erect a two-storied apse. Especially picturesque are the vaults, which combine

the triangular motifs of Gloucester with starribbing. In London, certain sections of Saint Stephen's Chapel at Westminster have survived: it was refashioned into a House of Commons in the sixteenth century, restored by Wren, then destroyed by fire in 1834. Because of its two-storied elevation and its lofty, gabled clerestory windows — undoubtedly patterned after those in the chapter house of Old Saint Paul's — it has been compared to Sainte-Chapelle in Paris. The windows were framed in perpendicular moldings, the spandrels adorned with narrow, vertically arched tracery. The interior was filled with the vivid colors of stained glass and paintings, taking up where the two-toned marble of the preceding century had left off. The entire building was probably completed between 1360 and 1370.

In 1376, Henry Yevele (in the king's service since 1360) and two other architects resumed work on the nave at Westminster, leaving the choir untouched. However, he proved to be more original in reconstructing the nave of Canterbury Cathedral, which dates from the eleventh century. Its dimensions are the same as those of the Norman church at Lanfranc, but, like Gloucester, its verticality is emphasized by supports extending from the ground, along the piers, and up to the ribbed vaults. The walls are not hidden behind tracery; in fact, they take up more that half of the elevation and open generously onto the side aisles. The triforium is flush with the arcade, and its subdivision into elongated panels seems to continue the decoration of the spandrels below. Only the clerestory windows are recessed from the wall ribs, whose supports descend to the floor unbroken by intervening capitals.

The work of Yevele is often compared to that of his rival on the nave of Winchester Cathedral, William Wynford. Wynford did not completely eradicate the Romanesque nave, but he did alter it radically by molding the piers, refashioning the arcade, and reconstructing the upper stories. Verticality of supports and filleting of ribs were the rules. The principle of "flatness" was abandoned: witness the forceful molding on the piers and arches. Moreover, the two upper stories — triforium and low clerestory — are set in behind a balustrade that frames the arcade in large rectangles. The towerless façade is pierced with an immense central window whose tracery of perpendicular panels seems to continue into the narrower arcatures of the gable above.

Under construction since the thirteenth century, York Cathedral was completed in its eastern part from 1361 to 1373. The rectilinear apse, with its great window, is comparable to the façade at Winchester, except that the decoration at York is more reminiscent of Decorated Style.

Ushering in a phase of formal renewal, the second period of Perpendicular Style was dominated by a few outstanding individuals: William Orchard, John Wastell, the brothers Robert and William Vertue, and Henry Redman, architect to Thomas Cardinal Wolsey. It was probably

Orchard who, in 1379, first used pendant vaulting (at the Oxford Divinity School), the consummate example of which is Henry VII's Chapel in Westminster. He was also the architect of Magdalen College at Oxford, one of the key monuments of English civil architecture.

Continuing the tradition of fourteenth-century towers, John Wastell erected the tall Bell Harry Tower over the transept at Canterbury from 1493 to 1505. He was perhaps also responsible for adjoining the transverse hall (c. 1500) to the Romanesque apse of Peterborough Cathedral. The fan vaults here recall those in the cloisters of Gloucester, except that the corollas at Peterborough are joined at the center, and the ridge ribs are punctuated by apparently functionless raised bosses. Wastell's most famous work remains his 1508-15 completion of King's College Chapel at Cambridge, begun in the fourteenth century by Reginald Ely. The design of the enormous nave is Ely's: there are immense windows positioned above an even base that opens here and there to very low side chapels. But it was Wastell who erected the gigantic fan vaulting, regularly marked by bold pointed transverse arches whose supports rest upon corbels placed halfway up the windows. There are also protruding bosses (like those at Peterborough) that clearly indicate the center of each bay. Powerful mullions dividing the façade window — recalling the choir window at Gloucester — draw attention to the magnificent unity of the interior space. The unbroken walls along the base bring out all the more the glazed latticework of color and light that takes the place of walls directly above. Perhaps nowhere else did the English taste for tall, broad windows express itself more unequivocally. Although a far cry from thirteenth-century designs, this kind of reduction to skeletal supports framing translucent walls is nevertheless quite Gothic in spirit.

Robert and William Vertue were architects to Henry VII and Henry VIII. Together they erected the new Abbey Church of Bath and Henry VII's Chapel at Westminster (the latter replaced the axial chapel of 1220). Constructed between 1503 and 1519, this chapel is the size of a small church with single side aisles ending in a five-sided apse. A wide, flattened arcade separates the central area from the side aisles, and the openings of the five radiating chapels seem to continue the arcade openings. The chapel windows consist of rectangular panels that bend obliquely like the shutters of a screen. Instead of a triforium, there is a series of statues resting on corbels; their canopies form an undulating line along the base of the clerestory windows. The pendant vaults are a further refinement of the fan vault: between half cones that line the wall are placed full cones whose tips take on the appearance of hanging bosses. Seemingly suspended in midair, these elements are covered with profuse ribbing that leaves no surface untouched; even the crowns of the transverse arches are hidden, their lower section detached from the walls. This is the ultimate expression of fan vaults as joined to skeleton vaults. Its extraordinary, petrified foliage gives the impression of some fantastic, luminous grotto encrusted with stalactites.

William Vertue worked alone on Saint George's Chapel at Windsor, later completed by Henry Redman, as well as at Corpus Christi College at Oxford. His pendant vaults were the last generation in a long line of imaginative English vaulting techniques. With this final display of independence and originality, English Gothic architecture came to an end. To be sure, its sources were many, and there were contacts and exchanges between England and the Continent. But thanks to deep-rooted traditions (such as the double-shell wall) and a desire to unify interpenetrating volumes, English Gothic managed to produce many singular works of art. Its development of window arrangements led to highly original and intricate systems of roofing. Finally, we should emphasize the taste for opulent decoration, highlighting, and polychromy, which, in the final analysis, means illusionism and the play of the reflections of light.

TRADITIONS AND LOCAL RESISTANCE

During the twelfth century, while architects in northern France and the *domaine royal* were gradually developing the elements of Gothic art, a fundamentally different architectural aesthetic was taking shape in the more dynamic areas of the Holy Roman Empire. These regions lie, for the main, in the western part of the Empire, along the Rhine Basin from Basel to Cologne. From the time of Charlemagne, architects had exercised to the fullest the resources of their imagination in these regions. Under the Ottonians, Cologne witnessed the establishment of many religious edifices; then the Salians made Speyer Cathedral the greatest basilica in western Europe. During the century of Hohenstaufen rule, the region of contact and exchange known as the Pfaffengasse gave rise to particularly splendid efforts.

The western reaches of the Empire have long been singled out as a pocket of especially strong resistance to Gothic. A crossroads of international contact, it is here that the incursions of the new architectural style from the west were first felt. That this opposition was firmly rooted until 1230 can perhaps be explained by the fact that architectural thought here was not satisfied with patterning itself after "imported" Gothic from Chartres or Reims. The churches in Cologne provide us with a revealing example of the situation peculiar to Rhenish lands. At Sankt Gereon, the old fourth-century shrine had been constructed on an oval plan. Although work beginning in 1219 transformed it into a decagon and its exterior niches were covered with masonry, the supports, vaults, and window tracery assumed Gothic forms.

Sankt Aposteln was reconstructed with a large Ottonian arcade. However, instead of a triforium, the early-thirteenth-century architect enlivened the wall with blind arcatures, a procedure already utilized in Ottonian architecture.

Begun in 1215, Sankt Kunibert obeyed the principles of alternating supports and sexpartite vaulting. Thus, these buildings reveal that they were not totally impervious to French Gothic, but the basic principles of structure and elevation were never put into question.

The new style also met with strong opposition in the northern region as well as in the colonized areas. In this case, however, the development of a counteraesthetic was due, not to preestablished architectural traditions, but to the preference for brick as a building material. The compactness of brick structures was antithetical to the Gothic tendency toward extreme lightness. Only in the second half of the century did these regions produce Gothic structures: at this time, architects managed to combine the new architectonic language with the use of brick, resulting in a regional style that German scholars termed *Backsteingotik*.

These two examples illustrate how stubborn this opposition could be when confronted with a conception that, at least at first, seemed inimical to German architectural thought.

CISTERCIAN ARCHITECTURE DURING THE TWELFTH CENTURY

The oldest Cistercian structures in Germany are Altenkamp (1122); Walkenried, in the Harz (1127); Ebrach, in Franconia (1127); Eberbach, in the Rheingau (1131); Amelungborn, near Brunswick (1135); Heiligenkreuz (1136); and Maulbronn (1138). The expansion of the order fostered the spread of such architectural concepts as the cross-ribbed vault. Consequently, whereas the naves of the oldest buildings are still covered with flat roofing, the nave of Eberbach (reconstructed in 1186) is vaulted. Just the same, the nave of Heisterbach, near Bonn, received groin-vaulting between 1202 and 1237.

Actually, the cross-ribbed vault was introduced into the Empire about 1120-30 (that is, a generation after Normandy): namely, at Petersberg (near Erfurt), Hersfeld, Madgeburg, and in Alsace. However, in the case of Alsacian or Rhenish buildings that we know of, the use of this vault never led to the same structural consequences that occurred in France and Picardy. At the Abbey Church of Murbach, the ribs — rectangular in contour, without a central boss — rest on columns engaged in the reentrant angles of cruciform piers. Although the date of Murbach is subject to controversy, its builders, like those of Heiligenkreuz (1187), had certainly become acquainted with Lombardian vaults. The churches of Rosheim and Saint-Jean-Saverne adopted cross-ribbed vaulting shortly after 1150; the rib contour developed into a torus (convex curve) applied to a flat strip. In the Collegiate Church of Bonn, the ribs were likewise extended onto columns engaged in pier-angles. A different scheme was adopted in Lorraine and those areas under her sway (Saint-Dié and Sélestat): the crossed ribs are supported on a simple corbel. In some cases, this technique was applied to limited spaces before all of its logical consequences could be weighed. Thus, these ribs were built in the apses of the east choir of Trier Cathedral (1196), of Sinzig (Rhineland), and of Münster Cathedral, in Westphalia.

At the turn of the thirteenth century, Burgundian influences made their way into Germany with the help of Cistercian architecture. Burgundian Gothic designs were incorporated, to varying degrees and purposes, first at the churches of Bronnbach, Heisterbach, Bebenhausen, and Arnsburg, and later at Maulbronn and Walkenried (in Austria, at Lilienfeld, Zwettl, and Heiligenkreuz).

Since the nave of Heisterbach was destroyed in the nineteenth century, all that remains of this abbey church is a choir in ruins. The ambulatory encircling the sanctuary opens to a crown of apsidal chapels. With the exception of Hildesheim, this principle, patterned in all likelihood after the Clairvaux model, was totally foreign to German architecture. On the other hand, the subdivision of interior space and the multitude of slender columns both juxtaposed and superposed create an unmistakable fragility that belies the more compact view from the exterior. The example of Heisterbach illustrates how Cistercian Gothic

173. Worms, Cathedral, apsidal view.

174. Magdeburg, Cathedral, interior view toward the west.
175. Limburg an der Lahn, Cathedral, exterior.

could be modified by strong indigenous traditions.

Between 1201 and 1255, additions were made to the monastery at Maulbronn: a narthex, the north wing of the cloister, the refectory, and the chapter house. Most of the false-bedded columns are encircled with bands, and crockets decorate the capitals. In the cloister, the ribs of the sexpartite vaults rest on bundles of colonnettes or on corbels. Were it not for a certain heaviness that spoils the overall effect, one would almost think the structure Burgundian. Austria, too, felt the effects of Burgundian art: for instance, the choir of Lilienfeld, dedicated in 1230, restates the scheme of Cîteaux II (1193).

None of the aforementioned buildings admit of a comprehensive, coherent Gothic system. Only selected borrowings were made, and even these scarcely altered overall proportions. The new architectonic "syntax" was not yet responding to a new way of thinking.

THE PERIOD OF TRANSITION

We would like to substitute a less precise term for the expression *transition style* coined by Dehio and Albin Polaczek. When referring to those experimental years between 1190 and 1220 that saw the construction of Basel, Worms, and Strasbourg, one cannot really speak of stylistic coherence. It is more a question of a well-defined stylistic "void" than a neat aesthetic progression from Romanesque to Gothic.

Let us first consider the case of Basel Cathedral (after 1185-1229), which features galleries above the side aisles and a polygonal choir. The idea for the galleries probably derived from northern France. The nave piers are still cruciform, whereas the crossing piers are made up of bundles of colonnettes. The most noteworthy innovation at Basel is the polygonal choir with ambulatory: its origins may possibly be traced to the choirs at Trier and Verdun and especially those of Saint-Germer and Laon in northern France. This plan would eventually replace the rectilinear or semicircular apses being used along the Upper Rhine. In addition, a simplified, somewhat weaker version of the Basel arrangement would be taken up by a group of Rhenish buildings — Freiburg, Saint-Ursanne, and Pfaffenheim. Another original feature of Basel was the adoption of a tall gallery that runs along the transept arms, thus effecting a link between the nave gallery and the choir. The imposing west front of Worms Cathedral, which has yet to be satisfactorily dated, consists of a single bay topped with a dome, leading to a five-sided apse. It is a case of sophisticated proportions within a relatively heavy architectonic framework. Ottonian holdovers (the outer apsidal gallery) find themselves in the company of typically Late Romanesque traits (the abundance of rose windows). Built from east to west between 1170 and 1210, the three-storied nave alternates cruciform and simple piers. Although a century separates them, the nave of Worms recalls that of Speyer Cathedral: nothing in its spatial design evokes the Gothic style.

176. Limburg an der Lahn, Cathedral, south arm of the transept toward the nave.
177. Bonn, Cathedral, nave.

It is the transept of Strasbourg that most clearly reveals the contradictions inherent in the period we are currently examining. Architects began to bring about a series of changes beginning in the last quarter of the twelfth century. The plan of the choir and transept was based on an Ottonian scheme. But the old continuous transept is divided into three equal sections, the middle one raised above the others by a tall crypt. In the north transept arm, a huge central pier receives the springings of the oblong cross-ribbed vaults. The entire vaulting system is incongruous with respect to the type of wall masonry used here; over the span of only a few years, several different solutions were proposed in succession.

It is possible that Albrecht, the archbishop of Magdeburg, returned from a Paris journey with the idea of a choir with ambulatory and radiating chapels. In any event, the architect who, in 1209, undertook the construction of the choir at Magdeburg according to this plan was not a Frenchman. In the angles formed by the walls of the apse were placed colonnettes whose bases are too slender and whose summits are too heavy. The ponderous bases and cornices of the supports spoil the overall interior effect. Compared with buildings in the Laon family, these elements seem heavy and archaic. Despite its pointed arches and daring plan, Magdeburg remains tied to Romanesque and Byzantine traditions; it did not play a decisive role in the diffusion of Gothic.

Beginning in 1211, the Abbey Church (now the Cathedral) of Limburg an der Lahn was constructed atop a rocky height overlooking the river Lahn. The choir and the nave were already in use by 1235. This structure is exemplary in both its acceptance of new ideas (the western rose window borrowed from Laon) and its loyalty to old principles (the west front copied from Andernach). The nave and choir consist of four stories: arcade, gallery, triforium, and clerestory. There is an alternating rhythm of "strong" and "weak" piers; the first ones are not round (like those at Laon) but cruciform. In order to support the intermediate transverse arch of the sexpartite vaults, a technique was used that betrayed the weight of local tradition. Colonnette bases were extended from midway up the triforium and adjoined to other shafts on the upper wall. The eye is led to focus on these details, on this accumulation of elements that damages the coherence of the whole. When an observer views this majestic site from a distance, the numerous towers crowning the basilica remind him of Laon.

Although its plan was determined by the eleventh-century structure, the Cathedral of Bonn blends Rhenish elements with new influences. The arcade consists of round arches and the pier-cores are cruciform; the side-aisle windows recall Sankt Gereon at Cologne. However, the triforium and the clerestory windows spreading generously over the upper walls already echo Gothic tendencies. Outside, the transept extremities are polygonal and the crossing tower is exceptionally tall. Like Sankt Gereon and Zülpich, Bonn (under construction in 1221) made precocious use of the flying buttress.

127

The full impact of the Gothic system was dulled by strong local opposition during the transition period, but this resistance subsided after 1230. Such buildings as Trier and Marburg adopted new ideas with a certain degree of enthusiasm and made more coherent use of French Gothic spatial concepts.

The growing preference for Gothic among architects within the Empire can be especially discerned by examining the structure of the pier support. In the crossing at Basel, we have seen that the cruciform core was giving way to the bundled pier. However, this issue — one that would be crucial to the future of architecture — was far from resolved. In 1225, the direction of the Strasbourg project was placed in the hands, not of a Rhinelander, but of a young architect versed in the art of Chartres. As a result, the central support of the south arm of the transept was patterned after the Chartres octagonal core, compounded with eight instead of four colonnettes. The perfect balance between support, vault, and aperture struck a chord hitherto unheard in Germanic art. Granted, there had been attempts to group colonnettes in the cloisters at Zwettl and Maulbronn, but the arrangement did not realize its full potential at these sites. Likewise, the supports applied against the narthex wall in the Cathedral of Lausanne are unable — unlike the central transept pillar at Strasbourg, the Pillar of the Last Judgment — to command the attention of the onlooker.

In addition, Strasbourg was the birthplace of foliage decoration carved into capitals. These leafy crockets had, it is true, previously appeared at Bamberg, but at Strasbourg they acquired a freshness quite new to Germany. It was only natural that German architects did not forsake the central plan, which had existed in the western regions of the Empire since the days of Charlemagne. Its career as a modulation of Gothic expression, however, was short-lived. Aside from Ettal (fourteenth century), the only entirely Gothic edifice on German soil designed according to this plan was the Liebfrauenkirche at Trier. But one other building, Sankt Gereon at Cologne, does provide us with information about the attitude of German architects when dealing with the problem of modernizing an old structure.

This ancient, oval-shaped shrine was surrounded by nine apsidal chapels and flanked on the west by a narthex. Although the work undertaken in 1219 respected the original plan, the elevation of the building was completely altered. Both narthex and choir were enlarged. Outside, the triangular sections between the chapels were filled in with masonry, and the building took on the appearance of a decagon. This masonry work, in turn, was used to support flying-buttress piers. Those elements foreign to Gothic art — the Lombardian arcature friezes and the gallery (*Zwerggalerie*) atop the octagon — are still of only secondary importance.

The interior elevation consists of four stories: niches; a gallery opening

to the central space by double or triple apertures; and two levels of clerestory windows (the upper level, preceded by a passage, is offset). The treatment of the supports, which divide the elevation into tiers, accounts for the unity of the whole. A column positioned in front of the masonry joining the ground-level niches rises to the clerestory passage to receive the diagonal vault ribs. Then, two colonnettes, one on each side, support that section of the arch under the passage. This articulates a second level whose scale is reduced with respect to the first.

The design at Trier is quite different in that the choice of a central plan was intentional. Begun in 1235, the Liebfrauenkirche was built next to the Cathedral and was intended for secondary liturgical ceremonies. Its plan is more subtle than that of Sankt Gereon: two chapels on each of the four diagonal sides alternate with three larger chapels and a protruding choir. The polygonal exterior wall could be inscribed in a circle, while the interior apses form a Greek cross. The columns supporting the crossing tower are surrounded by colonnettes and encircled midway up with rings. The capitals are fashioned into wreaths of foliage — their abaci are barely visible — and the stories are delineated by a thin molding running continuously along the walls beneath the windows. Compared to Heisterbach, the divisions of the supports and masses are proportioned in an exemplary manner. Even though some of the windows are three-quarters covered by the sloping roofs over the "side aisles", the two tiers of windows still allow a great deal of light into the building. All of the windows consist of two lancets topped by a rose window. Those in the choir are recessed, with a passage at the sill line. The result is a veritable "dematerialization" of stone. The Liebfrauenkirche rivals those very northern French structures — Soissons and Saint-Yved at Braine — that were its sources of inspiration.

At the pole opposite the converging masses of the Liebfrauenkirche stands the expanding space of the Elisabethkirche at Marburg an der Lahn, the second great exponent of French Gothic within the Empire. As at Trier, the architect did not opt for a typically French plan; in fact, he rejected the basilican scheme in favor of the hall church (*Hallenkirche*) configuration. In any case, its proportions, supports, and windows are indeed of French origin.

The construction of the Elisabethkirche was begun in 1235, shortly after the canonization of Saint Elizabeth of Hungary. As both a mausoleum and pilgrimage church, it was intended to accommodate large crowds of worshippers. The body of the saint was interred in the area of the choir and transept: this east end — its trefoiled plan was previously used in Romanesque Rhenish churches (Sankt Marien im Kapitol at Cologne) — does not include an ambulatory. The division between the two stories of windows is strongly accented by a ridge running around both the interior and exterior of the church. Thus, in visual terms, the vertical lines of the piers and engaged supports are set off by the seemingly recess-

ed horizontals. The windows are composed of an oculus above two lancets; in accordance with a principle established at Reims, the window tracery is mounted in frames. The proportions of the windows have been refined, resulting in increased illumination.

The transept, crossing, and choir all rise to the same height, and the architect extended three naves — again, quite naturally, of equal height — west from the crossing and transepts. Already utilized in Westphalia, this scheme was here realized in an innovative manner. The arrangement of the piers shows that the architect of the Elisabethkirche worked from a plan "in the French style": that is, a wider central nave with oblong bays down the middle and square bays along the sides. Moreover, he was obliged to increase the height of the side-aisle vaults to compensate for his refusal to raise the point from which they spring (namely, the impost). The central-nave piers consist of huge columns flanked by four round colonnettes that respond to the transverse and arcade arches. These Reims-style columns are set rather close together, a procedure that runs counter to Westphalian traditions. By stressing the axiality of the nave, the architect exploited a principle that contradicts the kind of spatial expansiveness demanded by the *Hallenkirche* system. This conflict between plan and elevation was to be definitively resolved by the end of the century in four different hall churches: Minden, where the side vaults were lowered slightly and the supports spaced farther apart; Saint-Thomas at Strasbourg; and especially Soest and Schwäbisch Gmünd (beginning of the fourteenth century).

The exterior elevation of the west section and nave is continuous; a series of abutments stretches over the entire height of the wall. The two levels of windows that light the nave remind one of how much this elevation still owes to the basilican system. The transepts of Noyon and the apsidal chapels of Laon doubtless inspired the dense rhythm of the abutments, while Saint-Léger at Soissons was the model for the double-tiered window arrangement. Both the Elisabethkirche and the Liebfrauenkirche were way stations on the road followed by Gothic art from northern France. Indeed, the influence of this region was felt throughout Germany: the towers of Naumburg (1237), Bamberg (1250), Magdeburg, and Halberstadt were all derived from Laon. Like the master of the Elisabethkirche, the architect of Sankt Viktor at Xanten was familiar with Soissons. The vacillation between the newer and more traditional architectonic ideas was already disappearing from those areas of the Empire subject to French "imports". This was the beginning of the second generation of Gothic art in Germany.

THE SECOND GENERATION

Spanning the middle and second half of the thirteenth century, this period witnessed an initial wave of buildings that, although not comparable to the great contemporary projects in Champagne and the Île-de-

Schwerhörige
nehmen im Mittelschiff rechts
Platz und stellen ihr Gerät auf
„induktiv".

France, were nevertheless no longer tied to local traditions. These structures owed everything to the great French classics: Strasbourg looked to Saint-Denis and Troyes, Altenberg and Cologne to Amiens. The French architectural language became fashionable, even if spoken with a German accent; it was considered a mark of good taste that abbots and bishops should know how to speak it. It was, after all, not without pride that the chronicle of Burchard von Halle praises the architect of Bad Wimpfen for his familiarity with the *opus francigenum* and saying of him that *noviter de villa Parisiensi e partibus venerat Francie.*

However, the architect of Bad Wimpfen was probably inspired, not by Paris, but by that intermediary of Parisian art, Strasbourg. The nave of Strasbourg Cathedral was built between 1235 and 1275. Whereas the nave of Rouffach (begun 1210) was still dominated by alternating supports, the nave of Strasbourg follows the Saint-Denis and Troyes schemes (Branner). Its three stories — arcade, perforated triforium, and clerestory — are remarkably well balanced. The piers are compounded with colonnettes whose thicknesses vary according to their particular support functions. The stories are further balanced by the use of framing and a series of recesses along the wall that "carve out" space. All components are thus arranged according to a rational order. The similarity between the first nave bays and the south arm of the transept proves that, thanks to a team of architects that remained for the most part on the site, the passage from the Chartres model to Rayonnant was smooth and unhindered. The Strasbourg scheme gave birth to only modest imitations: for example, Freiburg im Breisgau, whose west bays were erected beginning in 1240. The absence of a triforium in this building can be explained by the first architect's cautious approach to the nave plan. But this is also a characteristic shared by other secondary structures (Gross, Schürenberg) that simplified the elevations of their prestigious model. The influence of French architecture on regions lying to the east was unremitting: witness the rood screen at Strasbourg, a derivative of Saint-Urbain at Troyes: the "A" plan of Strasbourg; and the façades and transepts of Bad Wimpfen and Colmar, both echoing the transept of Notre-Dame at Paris.

Begun in the 1260s, the so-called Reims west bays of the Cathedral of Halberstadt have only two stories: the height of the nave is twice that of the side aisles. The triforium has been eliminated; and the flying buttresses extend their struts (perforated with oculi as at Strasbourg) to the top of the lateral wall. As a result, their angle of inclination continues that of the nave roof.

Cologne and its sphere of influence reacted quite differently to the French models. Construction of Cologne Cathedral became financially feasible in 1248 under the brilliant episcopacy of Konrad von Hochstaden. Work has begun on the choir, according to the French cathedral design with ambulatory and radiating chapels. By 1304, it had reached a dizzying height of more than 141 feet. In many respects, one

might say that Cologne Cathedral surpasses Amiens, its model. In any case, what is certain is that Cologne displays both a perfect comprehension and an imaginative, innovative realization of Gothic principles. The piers are bundled: the colonnettes facing the sanctuary rise directly to the vaults, unbroken by arcade capitals. Compared with Amiens, the clerestory windows have been slenderized; next to Beauvais, the main arcade arches and triforium have been given sharper points. The tension created by the delicate triforium arcatures does indeed surpass the French "originals". The large statues of the Apostles positioned in front of the piers (recalling Sainte-Chapelle in Paris) serve as decorative counterpoints to this almost superhuman architecture.

Begun in 1275, the choir at Regensburg in no way follows up the French arrangement adopted at Cologne. The sanctuary consists of three parallel apses: the protruding middle one terminates at the east in a polygonal apse. The two-leveled arrangement of the windows is reminiscent of the Elisabethkirche at Marburg an der Lahn, but the windows at Regensburg are fuller. Outside, the gables topping the upper windows stand out against the roof balustrade. The superposed windows give the impression of a single opening filling an entire space between two abutments.

Amiens also inspired the architectural style of the Cistercian abbey at Altenberg. But whereas the archbishop of Cologne, sensitive to the brilliant development of French art, tried to surpass his model, the Cistercians of Altenberg expressed their fidelity to their ideal of moderation by pushing the Amiens elevation back into a more archaic direction. The tracery has been simplified; the flying buttress, rejecting the complexity of French versions, was returned to the style of the previous generation. The dignified clarity of the interior is heightened by the absence of stained-glass windows and the whiteness of the wall covering. Except for the crossing supports, all of the piers have been reduced to simple columns supporting unadorned corbels. The stories are clearly outlined by a band running along the wall between the triforium and clerestory windows.

Begun in 1255, the church at Altenberg is mixture of nostalgia for great wall surfaces and a concern for diaphanous structure (Jantzen). The result is a complete absence of superfluity that is a perfect expression of the Cistercian spirit. Thus, Altenberg managed to orient Gothic architecture in a path opposed to that followed by the French cathedrals. However, in the final analysis, it was not this already venerable monastic order that allowed German Gothic to express its particular concept of space. This would be the achievement of buildings erected by the newer Dominican and Franciscan orders.

THE MENDICANT ORDERS

The Dominicans and Franciscans in Germany created an architecture

whose development and consequences went far beyond what occurred in France. The reason is simple. Seeking support from the new bourgeoisie, these dynamic, ambitious orders established themselves in the cities, whose power expanded unchecked from the thirteenth century on.

The vast monastic movement of the mendicant orders provided the framework within which Germanic architecture could elaborate its own concept of space. Like the Cistercians, these orders aspired to a sober, bare architectural style. Although the choir reserved for the brothers could be vaulted, the nave — where they preached to the faithful — could be covered with no more than a simple, flat, wood ceiling. The church was to have neither transept nor towers.

However, unlike the Cistercians, the mendicant orders were to eliminate everything that stood in the way of spatial unification — transept, ambulatory, and radiating chapels. This was a phenomenon that did not obtain in the basilica and would be fully realized only in the hall church.

Begun at the choir in 1248, the Dominikanerkirche at Regensburg provides the perfect specimen with which to analyze the metamorphosis that was taking place in Germanic architecture. We should note in passing that 1248 also marked the beginning of the construction of Cologne Cathedral. But these two structures followed fundamentally different routes: Cologne signaled the end of the cathedral era, while Regensburg laid the foundation for a new aesthetic. The former had only developed an "imported" style; the latter proclaimed — albeit with a certain degree of hesitation — an autonomous direction.

The choir at Regensburg is an extension of the nave. The piers in the sanctuary rise from only midway up the wall, but those in the nave extend completely to the ground. The double-lancet apse windows stretch over the entire height of the wall. In the nave, a large bare surface fills the space between the arcade and clerestory, and the upper windows are limited to the triangular field described by the wall rib and the vault imposts on either side. This design reflected a desire to revive the twelfth-century open, unencumbered wall (school of Hirsau) as well as to simplify the elevation to two stories. According to R. Krautheimer, this structure is a harbinger of Late Gothic, whereas Gross believes that its "reduced" elevation system opposes it to French Gothic. Anything at Regensburg that did not contribute to spatial and volumetric stability was eliminated. The naves are terminated at the west by an uncomplicated gabled wall. Both the impulsiveness of Cologne and the structural sophistication of the nave at Strasbourg run counter to this variety of Gothic.

In other cases, the mendicant orders vaulted their churches: for example, the Minorites at Cologne and the Dominicans at Strasbourg. The Minoritenkirche at Cologne was dedicated in 1260. Compared to Regensburg, the windows here have been enlarged to the point that the wall rib now serves as a frame for the glass. Plans for a hall church were abandoned during construction. This basilica reminds one of Regensburg, except that the four colonnettes flanking the circular piers betray an influence from Reims.

Vaulted naves are vastly outnumbered, however, by those covered with a simple wood ceiling. The Dominikanerkirche at Constance (after 1236) reveals a certain kinship with Romanesque architecture: its two rows of piers (ten columns in each file) bear octagonal capitals — as in the eleventh-century church at Stein-am-Rhein — and a ceiling covers the nave. A cornice runs unbroken above the arcade, recalling the Romanesque buildings of the Hirsau group. Be that as it may, the sensation of vastness, of sheer spatial extension experienced at Constance is unprecedented.

Toward 1300, the mendicant orders began to forsake their vow of simplicity in favor of increasingly ambitious projects. Their buidings grew considerably in size, and their magnificent stained glass rivaled that of the great cathedrals.

This taste for the gigantic can be observed in two Erfurt structures — the Cathedral and Sankt Severin. Beginning in 1300, the Dominicans used octagonal supports. The vault arches spring from arcatures placed in the spandrels of the arcade; in this manner, the vault resembles a large fan opened above and across the nave. The edges of the supports and archivolts create clearly delineated boundaries of light and shadow.

The most beautiful early-fourteenth-century edifices are without question the churches of the Upper Rhine basin. First, there is the Franciscan church at Freiburg im Breisgau; its ceilinged nave was erected in the first quarter of the fourteenth century. Tall columns without capitals support arcades whose moldings stem directly from the shaft. Under each oculus lighting the nave, there are two arcades opening to the roof. Although this arrangement is not unlike a triforium, its spatial impression has little affinity with any contemporary French structure. In the nave of the Dominikanerkirche at Colmar (c. 1330), the space is further amplified by the virtual disappearance of the clerestory wall. This ceilinged pseudohall church is perhaps the most original creation in mendicant-order architecture. A comparison of Regensburg and Colmar will reveal the gradual movement toward unification of space. The new wall and support functions, combined with the elimination of arrangement by bays, bring us closer to what ultimately evolved into Late Gothic.

The mendicant orders were also largely responsible for developing and propagating a choir of increased length and height, broken only by tall lancet windows. The thirteenth and fourteenth centuries witnessed the construction of choirs more than five bays in length (at Mainz, Colmar, and Basel). The absence of carved decoration is compensated by the presence of both large paintings of narrative cycles and, as we have mentioned, immense surfaces of stained glass. The mendicant first placed new emphasis on windows, which explains the highly creative contours of their

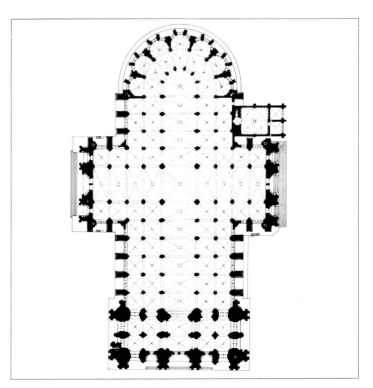

geometric tracery (Guebwiller, Vienna, etc.).

With its simple meeting-hall space designed for the spoken word, mendicant-order architecture presented an alternative to the triumphant hymn of the Gothic cathedral. These monuments are unquestionably the most explicit expression of the *Sondergotik* spirit (Gross, Gerstenberg).

NEW TRENDS AT THE END OF THE THIRTEENTH CENTURY

Out of the stylistic currents rushing in from the West, a phase of mature German Gothic that produced several noteworthy buildings arose. Lübeck played the major role in the expansion of *Backsteingotik* along the shores of the North Sea. In the westernmost reaches of the Empire, this was the task of the façade of Strasbourg Cathedral. Finally, the west tower of the parish church at Freiburg was destined to determine the design of structures in southern Germany during the Late Middle Ages.

The Marienkirche at Lübeck is not a cathedral, but a large parish church. One might be fooled by its dimensions. Actually, this church was a project by which the wealthy townspeople of this Hanseatic city hoped to compete with the immense cathedrals to the west. The structure of the Marienkirche shows that simplification of the Gothic cathedral style was the order of the day. To a certain extent, this was effected by the building material itself: brick is very amenable to large expanses of flat wall surface and does not lend itself easily to oversubtle modeling. However, the use of brick does not fully explain the architectonics of this church. The choir piers are compounded, whereas the great square piers of the nave seem better suited to the material.

The elevation of the nave at Lübeck comprises two stories of equal height: the arcade receives the clerestory windows directly (the lower part of the windows is blocked off by the side-aisle roof). Slender, barely visible colonnettes adjoining the pier respond to the vault ribs — their plasticity is inescapable. But the most fascinating aspect of the nave at Lübeck is that its especially rich polychromy functions architectonically as well. The intrados of the two superposed arcades in each bay is decorated with a different frieze. The plaster covering the walls simulates the bed joints of cut stone. Thus, the trend toward structuring of space is no less explicit here than in the French cathedrals (Gross).

The use of a particularly malleable substance — red sandstone — probably had a hand in the astounding virtuosity of the Strasbourg façade. Its construction (begun c. 1275) was based on drawings that we are fortunate enough to possess still: they surely constitute the most beautiful legacy of the Middle Ages. Aside from being a veritable catalogue of Gothic forms, they reveal the concept of a "double-shell" façade. In front of the wall stands a curtain of arcatures whose vertical sweep is an expression of Gothic in its purest state.

Strasbourg Cathedral — whose construction, incidentally, came under municipal control before the end of the century — clung to the idea of a

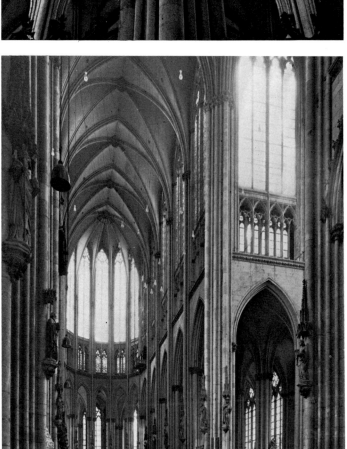

191. *Cologne, Cathedral, upper parts of the choir.*
192. *Cologne, Cathedral, choir and transept.*

harmonious façade. But just across the Rhine the parish church erected by the citizens of Freiburg was reviving the ancient concept of a façade with a tower planted on the axis of the nave. Begun in the mid-thirteenth century, the church acquired the shape of an octagon (c. 1300) pierced with tall, gabled windows. Its spire is a masterpiece of carving — the tower dematerializes as it rises.

It was not Strasbourg that yielded noteworthy imitations, but Freiburg. Its scheme can be found in the incomparable "technicity" of Esslingen, as well as at Ulm, Überlingen, and the spire of Strasbourg itself, constructed by Ulrich von Ensingen and Johann Hültz.

THE FIRST HALF OF THE FOURTEENTH CENTURY

Although, for political reasons, the first half of the century saw building activity especially in the southeastern regions (Swabia and Austria), Strasbourg and Cologne cathedrals still reigned as the greatest projects in the Empire. Work on the façade at Strasbourg continued, but with a marked reduction in the kind of creative energy that had produced the portal zone. However, the construction of Saint Catherine's Chapel was one of the most sophisticated moments in the history of the cathedral. The effect of Strasbourg was directly felt in Alsace and along the Upper Rhine, in such thoroughly original works as the nave at Nierderhaslach and the façades at Rouffach, Sélestat, and Reutlingen.

The architect Johann completed the choir at Cologne, and it was dedicated in 1322. He had begun work on the main façade in 1300 at the south side, following a layout that utilized a decidedly archaic scheme. Abutments subdivide the western elevation into five sections that correspond to the nave and four aisles. The two lower exterior stories allow the observer to "read" the interior elevation of arcade, triforium, and clerestory. This façade was not finished until the nineteenth century, in a great burst of nationalism. Its influence during the fourteenth century was restricted mainly to the Rhineland, at Oppenheim and Bacharach.

The south porch of the nave at Oppenheim (begun in 1317) may be considered its principal façade. By increasing the amount of tracery and placing rose windows in the openings, a window-within-a-window effect was obtained. The blind arcatures lining the spandrels of the walls give the impression that the arcades of the windows and walls lie on two separate planes. The really outstanding feature of this elevation is its tracery. From the viewpoint of stylistic evolution, Oppenheim, by "dissolving" the wall into geometric sections (Frankl), exploited the formal repertory invented at Cologne.

The Wernerkapelle at Bacharach (1293-1337) commands one of the most picturesque views of the Rhine. All it retained from its majestic neighbor across the river was the capacity to mount tracery with such finesse that it appeared metallic.

193. *Regensburg, Cathedral, apsidal view.*

194. *Regensburg, Cathedral, choir.*

195. Regensburg,
Dominikanerkirche, nave.

196. Erfurt, Cathedral and Sankt
Severin.

197. Erfurt, Sankt Severin, nave.

198. *Lübeck, Marienkirche and Rathaus.*

199. *Esslingen, Frauenkirche, interior.*

In 1335, the joint influence of Cologne Cathedral and Sainte-Chapelle in Paris led to the construction of the immense choir to the east of the octagon at Aachen. The intention of the canons was that this *capella vitrea* should accommodate the throngs of pilgrims who came to pay homage to the relics of Charlemagne. Like the palatial chapel of Saint Louis, the choir at Aachen is reduced to a framework enclosing sections of glass. In the tradition established at Saint-Chapelle and maintained in the thirteenth century at Cologne Cathedral, statues of the Virgin, Apostles, and the emperor are affixed to the interior piers.

When, in 1304, work on the choir at Vienna was initiated under the auspices of Albert I, the city had not yet attained the status of a diocese. The outright purchase of the land behind the old choir by the Viennese citizenry attests to the growth of their prosperity and their consciousness of it. This great cathedral repudiated the traditional French cathedral scheme (namely, a choir flanked by a lower ambulatory crowned with chapels) in favour of a choir type that was to meet with widespread success in Austria, the hall choir. Unlike its famous model — Heiligenkreuz, dedicated in 1295 — the choir at Vienna does not terminate at the east in a straight wall. Instead, the three "naves" are treated as three distinct elements, with the central apse protruding farther out than the two side apses. The Cistercians willingly adopted the hall choir in their churches as Zwettl (1343) and Kaisheim (1352). The architectonics of these two buildings are wholly original, but the hall choir at Verden (c. 1300) is an immediate derivative of Reims-Amiens.

In Westphalia, the architect of the Wiesenkirche at Soest produced a perfect *Halle*: the plan of both overall structure and individual bays is nearly square. The piers are composed of bundles of pear-shaped curves from which spring — uninterrupted by capitals — vault ribs of equal size. Unfinished until the fifteenth century, this building not only blends supporting and supported elements, but also eliminates the principal east-west axis, resulting in a beautifully unified, homogeneous space. Soest is the most successful specimen in the long line of German hall churches.

THE PARLER FAMILY

The term *parler* or *parlier* was used during the Middle Ages to designate the function of the assistant to the *magister operis* on the building site. In the fourteenth century, this term became a surname east of the Rhine, a fact that rather complicates identifications.

Sources indicate that the first member of the family was Heinrich I the Elder. Reared in Cologne, he emigrated to Schwäbisch Gmünd and there built the nave of the Heiligkreuzkirche. His three sons were Peter — the architect of Prague Cathedral — Michael I, and Johann I. Peter had two sons by his first marriage: Wentzel, who was probably the architect called to work at Vienna from 1400 to 1404, and Johann IV, creator of the choir at Kutna Hora (Kuttenberg) in Bohemia. From this point on, German

200. *Ulm, Cathedral, exterior.*
201. *Ulm, Cathedral, nave.*

202. *Ulm, Cathedral, vaults of the nave.*
203. *Ulm, Cathedral, side aisle.*

204. *Aachen, Cathedral, exterior.*
205. *Aachen, Cathedral, vaults of the choir.*

206. Vienna, Cathedral, plan.
207. Vienna, Cathedral.

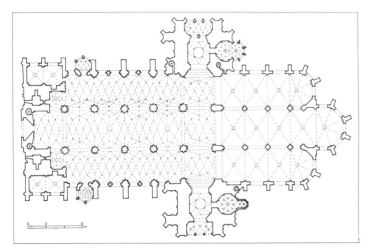

scholars distinguish a southern branch of the Parler family. This group includes Johann III, architect of the town of Freiburg im Breisgau (he worked at Basel as well), and his son Michael III, who was for a while master of works at Strasbourg.

Nothing would be more mistaken than to attribute to this architectural dynasty a coherent style with an evolution all its own. Without going so far as to speak of a distinct *Parlergotik* (Kletzl, Svoboda, Bachmann), one can nevertheless single out enough stylistic invariables in both architecture and sculpture to justify describing them as Parlerian. During the second half of the fourteenth century, Peter Parler used a new vocabulary to express the *Sondergotik* tendencies that had been developing since the mid-thirteenth century. In this sense, the architecture of Peter Parler constituted an irreversible stage in the evolution toward Late Gothic.

Like Freiburg and Ulm, Schwäbisch Gmünd is a parish church that proclaims an architectonic concept typical of the bourgeois spirit reigning in large cities within the Empire. Heinrich Parler the Elder, who began work on the church in the second decade of the fourteenth century, selected the *Halle* scheme, but one whose pier structure and general contours no longer bore the stamp of the great cathedrals. There are only simple round piers in the nave, a sign of conformity with the aesthetic of the mendicant orders. The façade, too, recalls the vision of the Cistercians and mendicant friars — a gabled wall with a large window adorned with magnificent tracery. Thus, the watchword here was simplification, but without the religious underpinnings. In its place, there arose a new ideology, a bourgeois humanism that was to lead directly to the upheavals at the end of the Middle Ages. The hall plan was also adopted for the choir (begun 1351), which is encircled with chapels separated by abutments. Along with Zwettl, it instituted a new concept of the choir. The Schwäbisch Gmünd architectural vision spread to other buildings, notably the Georgskirche at Nördlingen.

In 1356, at the age of twenty-three, Heinrich's son Peter was named architect of Prague Cathedral upon the death of Matthias of Arras. Up to that moment, this church had been erected according to the French cathedral plan, and Parler left the customary ambulatory and accompanying chapels untouched. However, it is interesting to note that Peter Parler introduced at Prague a Cologne influence alongside the Narbonne and Toulouse currents already transmitted to Prague by Matthias (for example, the decidedly ornamental treatment of the clerestory windows). On the other hand, the sacristy and chapel of Saint Wenceslas — north and south of the choir, respectively — present no indication of dependence on models. The square-field star vaults take on pendant bosses in the sacristy. It was at Prague that the fundamentals of Late Germanic Gothic took root: namely, the absence of capitals and the use of identically shaped components throughout the vaulting and piers regardless of functional disparity. The windows are few in number and

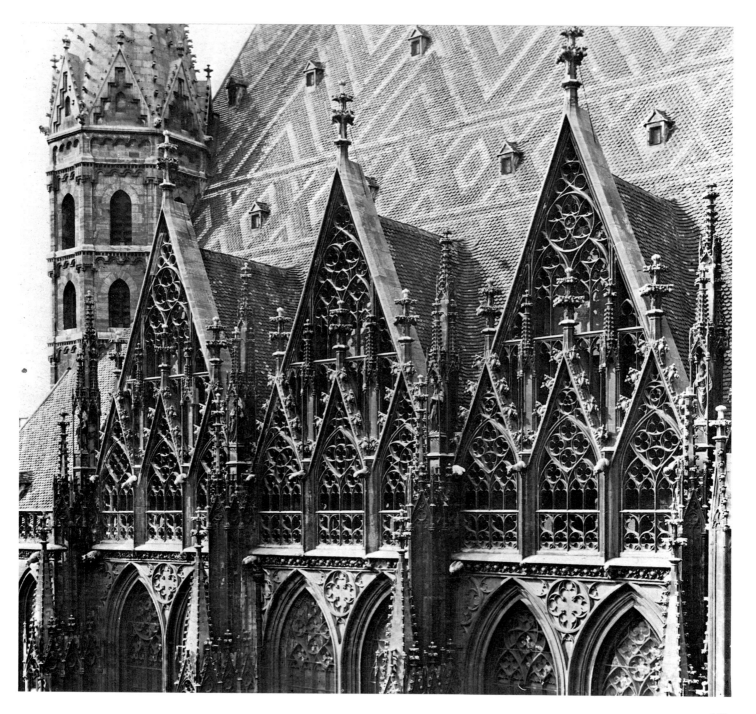

209. Heiligenkreuz, Abbey Church, choir.

limited in breadth. In short, this is an ornate, sophisticated style whose effect is entirely centered on the interior elevation.

The elimination of transverse arches in the choir allows the bays to interpenetrate and the vault ribs to intersect in such a way as to efface spatial limits. The triforium zone is articulated horizontally along the break created by the clerestory-window balustrade, and it seems to project into the interior space. In this manner, Peter Parler was able to underscore the ambiguity of this space, whose actual limits are difficult to determine.

Showered with honors from the emperor, Peter Parler also constructed All Saints' Chapel on the Hradčany (begun in 1366); the Charles Bridge across the Vltava (1357), with its impressive portal; and the choir at Kolin, begun in 1360. In his capacity as sculptor, he fashioned the tomb of Ottokar I (1377) and the stalls (demolished) of the cathedral.

It has not been determined whether or not Peter Parler was responsible for the Frauenkirche at Nuremberg. When the emperor called on the Swabian architect to replace the deceased French master, its foundation had already been laid by Charles IV on the site of the old Jewish ghetto and dedicated in 1358. Like Schwäbisch Gmünd, the Frauenkirche is a hall church, and certain elements (such as the cornice running continuously beneath both the interior and exterior sides of the windows) are typically Parlerian. The well-known sources of Parlerian art — Prussia, Cologne, Strasbourg, and, to a certain extent, England — did not completely dictate the Parlerian style. Parler used them as guides, refashioning them into a personal statement. His architectural language marked the definitive break with French Gothic, and it is especially ironic that this schism occurred in a building begun by a French architect.

BRICK ARCHITECTURE

The use of brick in Gothic construction was limited to two specific regions: Bavaria and the section of northern Germany bounded on the north by the lands along the North and Baltic seas (Friesland to eastern Prussia), on the west by the Netherlands, and on the southeast by Poland. This phenomenon also appeared in Denmark, Sweden, and Finland.

It was above all the great Baltic cities that witnessed the construction of gigantic parish churches during the thirteenth and fourteenth centuries. Several buildings in Lübeck, including the aforementioned Marienkirche, reveal the successive phases of brick architecture following the Romanesque era. One group of structures was particularly influenced by the nave elevation or choir plan of the Marienkirche: Sankt Nikolas at Stralsund, the Cistercian church at Doberan (the end of the thirteenth century), and the Cathedral of Schwerin (1327).

In many instances, the Franciscans and Dominicans had a hand in introducing Gothic into this region (for example, the adoption of the single nave or hall church in Neumark and Uckermark). The principle that dictated naves of equal height was especially popular throughout the inland districts of Pomerania and Mecklenburg (the Frauenkirche at Greifswald, begun in 1250), as well as in Stockholm (Riddaholm) and Lübeck itself (Sankt Jakob). The most noteworthy occurrence of the "hall choir" scheme can be found at Stettin (late fourteenth century).

Prussia played an innovative role in the development of *Backsteingotik*. The glazed, colored bricks and lovely star-vaults at Golub (palace chapel, c. 1300) and at Marienburg (1286) create a picturesque effect reminiscent of Eastern art.

However, thirteenth- and fourteenth-century brick architecture received its most original expression in the treatment of the façade. Preferred for large, uninterrupted wall surfaces, this substance is not amenable to the kind of carved decoration usually reserved for softer stone. By increasing the number of gables on the main and side façades, architects harmoniously integrated the church silhouette with the texture of urban architectural fabric. The façades of Chorin (1273-1335) and Sankt Katharina at Lübeck (Franciscan, 1280-1356) resemble vast tapestries "embroidered" with decorative motifs (blind arcades, rose windows, and the like). The revival of the so-called Lombardian arcature motifs points to a relationship with Lombardian architecture that should not be overlooked. The façade of the Frauenkirche at Neubrandenburg is covered with profuse, ornate tracery, as at Oppenheim or the east gable at Prenzlau. In fact, façades were, as a rule, gabled in the manner of Schwäbisch Gmünd or Salem in order to exploit fully the "pictorial" potential of the building material.

THE GENERATION OF 1400

A large number of architects born in the middle or second half of the fourteenth century are known to us both by name and by works. Included among these (followed by date of death) are Michael Knab (before 1418), Ulrich von Ensingen and Wenzel Roriczer (1419), Heinrich Brunsberg and Madern Gertener (1430), and Hans von Burghausen, better known by the name Stethaimer (1432). Unlike the decisive moment of the year 1000 or the generation of 1150, the period about 1400 did not yield a perfectly homogeneous building style. On the contrary, its interest derives precisely from its widely diverse tendencies, be they centered at Frankfurt, Landshut, Strasbourg, Milan, or Danzig.

Madern Gertener participated in the construction of Frankfurt Cathedral beginning in 1409: his originality was most forcefully expressed in architectural drawings and sculpture. His design of the tower of Sankt Bartholomäus at Frankfurt occupies a special niche in the architecture of the Holy Roman Empire. It betrays contact with the "courtly" style of the duchies of Burgundy and Berry, a kind of nostalgia for thirteenth-century French forms. As opposed to the spires at Ulm or

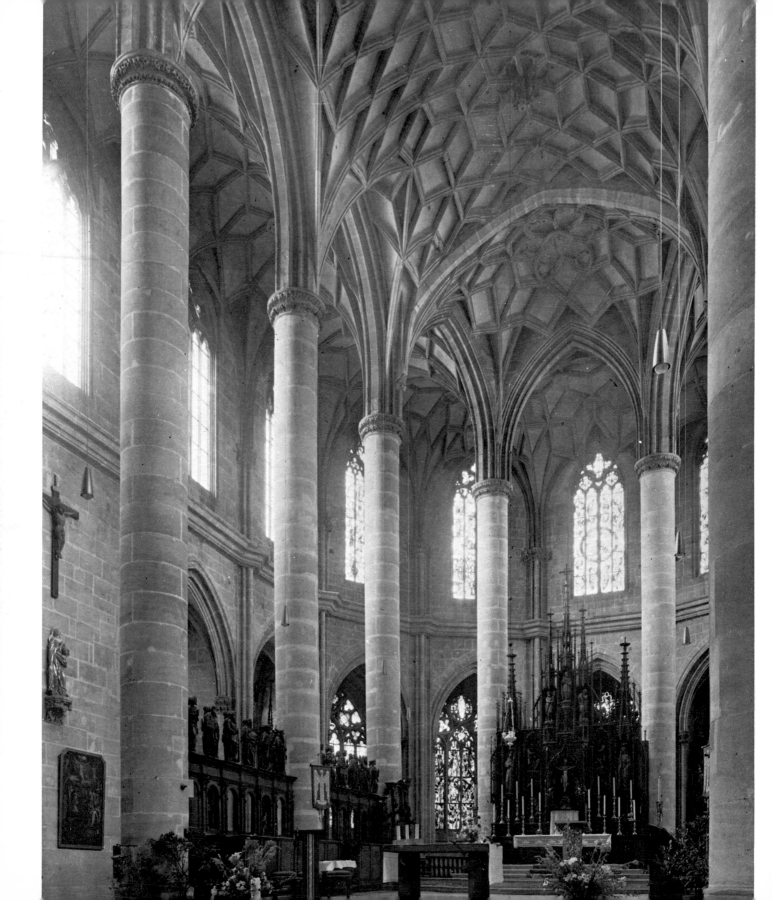

Strasbourg, this tower is crowned with a sort of ribbed dome. Upon the death of Ulrich von Ensingen in 1419, Madern (together with Jörg von Württemberg and Erhard Kindelin of Sélestat) was called on as a consultant for the continuing work on the spire at Strasbourg. The fact that certain of these architects were summoned to Chartres and Milan to give expert advice attests to the truly international scope of their fame.

The "decorated" style of the generation of 1400 may also be observed in the works of Michael Knab: the Spinnerin am Kreuz (a tower) at Wiener-Neustadt and Maria-am-Gestade at Vienna (begun 1394). He shared with Gertener a taste for the kind of sophistication that characterizes that offshoot of Louis IX's Sainte-Chapelle, the Cathedral of Vienna.

With the exception of a relatively brief assignment at Milan in 1391, Ulrich von Ensingen spent practically his entire life within the borders of his native Swabia. His is the most representative statement of what Pinder calls *Bürgergotik*, a stylistic throwback to thirteenth-century principles that flourished about 1400. In 1392, he began to restructure the nave at Ulm, replacing the hall-church configuration with a basilican plan. However, contrary to thirteenth-century architectural theory, this was combined with a single façade-tower positioned on the nave extension. The west entrance is covered with a porch formed by massive abutments. Work on the tower was continued by Ulrich's son-in-law, Hans Kun, but was not completed until 1890 following a plan of Matthäus Böblinger. This posthumous interpretation of Ulrich's plan (based on drawings of Ulm and London) drowned his rigorous architectural vision in a sea of decoration. As a matter of fact, it was the tower at Freiburg (begun in the thirteenth century) that inspired Ulrich's concept of the façade-tower as we see it at Ulm, Strasbourg (1399-1419), and Esslingen (begun in 1399).

A third personality whose life and works warrant consideration is Hans von Burghausen, known in contemporary writings as Stethaimer. He refashioned his immediate sources — Parlerian architecture in Swabia (Schwäbisch Gmünd) and Bohemia — into new elements that constituted a perfect expression of the final phase of Germanic Gothic. His building activity lasted between forty and fifty years and was centered mostly in the duchy of Bavaria.

His two churches at Landshut, Sankt Martin (begun in 1387) and the Spitalkirche (1407-61), proclaim the same architectural vision: a large, open space obtained by a hall-nave arrangement, and graceful, widely spaced piers supporting vaults that extend over the entire church, virtually eradicating bay compartmentalization.

Hans von Burghausen's quest to unify interior space as well as increase its height spurred him to push architectonic possibilities to their furthest limits. For example, the piers at Sankt Martin are 39 3/8 inches across and about 72 feet high. Begun in 1408, the choir of the Franzis-

kanerkirche in Salzburg combines the hall-church elevation with the idea of chapels bounded by abutments. Its plan reveals that the vault design plays an intrinsically formal role: the ribs, here transmuted into pure form, no longer answer specific structural demands.

The same preference for decoration is the hallmark of the style of Heinrich Brunsberg, who worked in Germanic Prussia before undertaking the reconstruction of Sankt Katharina at Brandenburg in 1401. To the west of the nave rises a gigantic, traceried window studded with gables, a design later utilized by Brunsberg for the town hall of Tangermünde (c. 1430). This desire to apply the same motifs to religious and civil buildings alike gave rise to harmonious urban skylines.

LATE GOTHIC

The architecture of the generation of 1400 has been referred to as a *weicher Stil* (a "soft" or "rounded" style), a critical term carried over from painting and sculpture. Ensingen's spires at Ulm and Strasbourg, planned with concave edges, certainly merit this label. But it is highly debatable that such is the case with the work of Stethaimer. By the same token, the expression *eckiger Stil* ("hard" or "angular" style) may legitimately describe a phase in the evolution of painting or sculpture, but it cannot fully account for the architecture of 1450-60. Concerned as it is only with form, this term has nothing to say about considerations of space. Again, we see that the wealth of this period lies in its diversity.

In many instances, structures built during the mid or late fifteenth century merely elaborated on lessons of previous generations. Erected according to a plan of Konrad Heinzelmann and continued by Konrad Roriczer, the hall choir of the Lorenzkirche at Nuremberg (1439-77) restates certain themes found in the Schwäbisch Gmünd hall choir a century before. The two stories of the elevation are demarcated by a balustrade-gallery that enhances the wall with exceptional plasticity. In Bavaria, a variety of brick architecture featuring a single-nave elevation with flanking chapels set closely together between interior abutments (the Wandpfeilerkirche) arose.

After working on the parish churches at Steyr (Austria) and at Donnersmark (Hungary), Hans Puchspaum succeeded his former superior at Vienna, Hans Prachatitz, to become master architect of the cathedral in 1446. Work on this structure (begun in the 1430s) shows the formation of Puchspaum's style, one that would prove crucial in the spread of Vienna's influence throughout central Europe. The north tower exemplifies his artistic vision: new vigor was imparted to Flamboyant forms by restructuring the tracery. A new relationship between the core of the building and the verticality of the arcatures and gables covering it emerged. The parish church at Annaberg is the consummate Germanic hall church. This newly founded town in Saxony had grown prosperous through silver mines. The octagonal piers of the Annenkirche are round-

214. *Landshut, Spitalkirche,*
interior.

215. *Ulm, Cathedral, detail*
of the spire.

216. Salzburg, Franziskanerkirche,
choir vault.

217. Nuremberg, Lorenzkirche,
interior.
218. Nuremberg, Sebalduskirche,
choir and ambulatory.

219. Annaberg, Annenkirche, plan
at the level of the chapel vaults
and plan at the level
of the principal vaults.

ed at the edges, and the vault ribs spring from twisting supports whose shape is echoed in the entire vault design. This torsion of the vaulting and hollowing of the supports set the interior space in motion, as it were. The architect's play with perspectives transforms the observer into an active participant in a dynamic architectural style.

Arnold von Westfalen, architect of Kurfürst in Saxony, is the perfect example of those fifteenth-century individuals who ventured into the realm of the seemingly impossible. Here was an indefatigable creator of unprecedented spatial arrangements, a peerless virtuoso in the art of fantastic vaulting. He was called to Meissen in 1470, built its town hall, castle, and cathedral, and died there in 1481. Though derived from French châteaux, the Albrechtsburg was laid out according to an innovative plan. Its exterior walls, which give the appearance of a closed volume, utterly belie the interior scheme: the masonry there is hollowed out by niches, a spatial fragmentation accentuated by the diverse contours of the vaults. There are prismoidal and spiral-shaped bases, and the diagonal arches spring from various points along the length of the pier, sometimes very near the base itself. Thus, the usual tension between supporting and supported elements has been eliminated, yielding a "moving" space. The spiral staircase has a dynamism all its own, one that elicits the torsion of its architectural components.

During the Gothic period, the cathedrals at Vienna, Cologne, Bern, and Strasbourg played a key role in the dissemination of great currents of architectural thought (witness the wealth of drawings preserved at the masons'lodge in Vienna). In addition, a large number of secondary projects were placed in the care of each principal lodge.

In 1459, at a stonecutters' convention in Regensburg, it was decided that the authority of the supremely powerful Strasbourg lodge held sway over other building projects. At that moment, activity had been either in progress (Bern, Vienna), completed (Strasbourg), or interrupted (Cologne, Prague). The degree of completion notwithstanding, architects felt the need to legislate and enforce universal regulations, as well as to pass on theoretical knowledge to future architects and associates. Matthäus Roriczer's *Puechlein von der Fialen Gerechtigkeit*, published in 1486, explains quite didactically the passage from plan to elevation. (We should add that the year 1486 also witnessed the publication of Vitruvius in Italy.) It is difficult to evaluate the actual degree of autonomy enjoyed by architects within the Empire, compared with the status of other municipal corporations. In certain cases, we know that cities exercised real financial and material control over construction. Such was the case of Strasbourg by the end of the thirteenth century. On the other hand, cathedral architects were apparently also sometimes responsible for civil building projects (Puchspaum, Brunsberg, and Arnold von Westfalen, among others). In any event, the privileged status of masonic lodges and their members was probably greatly exaggerated by Romantic interpretations.

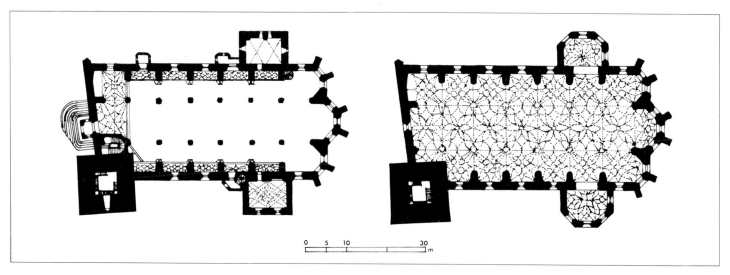

Chapter VI

GOTHIC IN ITALY AND THE IBERIAN PENINSULA

ITALY

Unlike England, the Italian peninsula did not show much interest in the twelfth-century structural and spatial efforts that led to the birth of Gothic art. The heavy cross-ribbed vaults of Lombardy, albeit remarkable in themselves, were not integrated into a formal or technical system conductive to the concept of Gothic space. True, there were isolated elements — intersecting arches on exterior walls (Monreale) or large circular apertures (Troia and Tuscania) — that might have inspired certain English, Norman, or French arrangements, such as the rose window in French churches between 1130 and 1140. Nevertheless, the weighty influence of Early Christian or classical models perpetuated old building traditions, thus impeding the evolution toward Gothic.

We will not recount here the first appearance of the new style in Cistercian buildings at the end of the twelfth century: these were Fossanova, near Rome, begun in 1187, and Casamari (1203-1207), where cross-ribbed vaulting was patterned after much older French Cistercian models. Built after 1219, the Church of Sant'Andrea at Vercelli was the first structure in which adoption of the French style proved to be problematic. Its plan is essentially traditional: the transept crossing is covered with a dome resting on pendentives (curved wall surface between the dome and supporting masonry), and the small windows are pierced in a continuous wall. But the pointed cross-ribbed vaults and the presence of tall colonnettes beneath the vaults and around the piers hark back to the Île-de-France. The elevation, which lacks both triforium and gallery, resembles Cistercian counterparts. However, it was the Franciscan and Dominican establishments — above all, the Basilica of San Francesco at Assisi — that were destined to be the more decisive factors in the development of Gothic architecture in Italy.

Begun in 1228 (two years after the death of Saint Francis), this church, though dedicated in 1253, was probably more or less finished by 1239. By virtue of its wealth of mural paintings and stained glass, as well as its extraordinary religious significance, San Francesco is one of the important sites of Christianity. The architectural style is so powerfully innovative that its prototype is unknown. Like pre-Romanesque or Romanesque episcopal or royal chapels, two stories comprise the elevation. The simple plan — single nave, protruding transept, a single apse to the east — is somewhat complicated by the more recent addition of side chapels and a kind of west transept, both in the lower church. In the upper church elevation, a tall base covered with painted mural decoration lies beneath a story of narrow, but elongated double-lancet windows recessed from the base plane, allowing a continuous passage to encircle the nave below the windows. This configuration, as well as the general plan of the church, has been likened to the Cathedral of Angers, whose reconstruction, begun in the mid-twelfth century, continued during the first third of the thirteenth century. However, the admirably coherent ef-

220. Fossanova, Abbey Church,
façade.
221. Casamari, Abbey Church,
interior.

222. Vercelli, Sant'Andrea,
interior.

fect of the nave at Assisi is a far cry from this presumed model. The square vault fields and bold accents of the tall, colonnetted wall supports create a rhythm quite consistent with the spirit of Gothic architecture. Furthermore, the form of the windows here corresponds to that typical of France. In short, nothing at San Francesco was dictated by Romanesque traditions. This, then, is a case of Gothic art adapted to particular circumstances: a church intended for preaching, with a unified, clearly distributed volume of wide, harmonious proportions, whose vaults are supported by massive, diagonal, square-shaped ribs. Due to later additions as well as to its inherently heavier, more squat proportions, the lower church does not produce the same captivating effect. Its general structure, however, is just as original as the upper sanctuary: it is supported by the interior abutments of the upper church, by huge exterior cylindrical abutments, and by low-lying flying-buttress piers that are only distantly related to the form and function of the French flying buttress of 1225-35.

San Francesco at Assisi was more than just a great creation of Franciscan architecture, designed to fit the needs of a particular order. Its wall space — so well-suited for fresco painting — its refusal to hollow out the wall as much as possible, and its logical structure all contributed toward making this church a model for the variant of Gothic peculiar to Italy. It has been suggested that the clerestory-level interior passage resembles Burgundian arrangements at Auxerre and at Notre-Dame at Dijon. This relationship can be seen even more clearly in Santa Chiara at Assisi, where the dissociation between the vaulting of the roof and the flatness of the wall is more clearly marked than at San Francesco.

The second great Franciscan church in Italy — a contemporary of the one at Assisi, but quite different in plan — is San Francesco at Bologna, founded in 1236, dedicated in 1250, and later repaired after a partial collapse. The plan is basilican, with side aisles and a choir whose ambulatory extends into nine radiating chapels. In accordance with a custom of the region of Emilia, the building material is brick, and the sexpartite vaulting in the nave is, for the thirteenth century, an obvious anachronism. The Cistercian influence is equally strong in the plan and elevation: diminutive windows are cut into the walls above a heavy, squat arcade. The undisputed beauty of the interior space comes from a clear distribution of volumes and supporting elements, whose red brick texture contrasts with the plastered surface of the walls and vault fields. This important edifice provided an example for religious architecture in Bologna for more than a century and a half.

It was the most important Dominican church of all — Santa Maria Novella at Florence — that proved to be the most successful and promising achievement of Italian Gothic during the middle and second half of the thirteenth century. This church was founded in 1279, and its plan was inspired by Cistercian abbeys that featured a rectilinear apse and

diagonally directed chapels opening onto an immense transept. Its ample proportions accentuate more the width of the bays than the height of the nave. The special quality of this church is due to its unified interior space: the side aisles open to the nave by a high arcade resting on slender piers engaged with half columns. The circular clerestory windows perforate uninterrupted expanses of bare wall surface. The clarity of its architectonic design is underscored by the polychromy of the diagonal ribs, transverse arches, and supports, all fashioned of *pietra serena*. In this manner, the open interior space, enclosed by flat walls, is boldly partitioned by means of a remarkable management of building material. The use of steeply curved vaults allowed the architects to solve the problem of equilibrium without having to rely on flying buttresses. Thus, nothing at Santa Maria Novella betrays contact with contemporary French architecture. It was here that Italian Gothic realized its first accomplished work of art. The exceptional status of the Dominican church at Florence quickly becomes obvious when it is compared to other examples of mendicant-order architecture during the second half of the thirteenth century: San Francesco at Cortona, San Francesco at Messina (after 1254), and San Lorenzo at Naples (the last being the most ''French'' by the disposition of its choir with ambulatory). These are churches with a single, immense, wood-ceilinged nave; vaulted roofing was reserved for the choir. The structure is simplified and the decoration is understated, factors that point to the original mendicant vow of poverty as well as the basically oral function of the sanctuary space. One trait does deserve special mention — side chapels were positioned between abutments flanking the nave. This very concept was spreading throughout southern France and Spain at the time and would continue to do so during the fourteenth century. The spirit of Gothic art breathes in the contours and proportions of the apertures — especially in the choirs lit by very tall windows — as well as in the concern for spatial unity.

However, certain outstanding thirteenth-century buildings do not fit neatly into these categories of Gothic architectural style. Initiated in 1250, construction of the Cathedral of Siena continued for more than 150 years as a result of considerable changes in the plans. Despite its vastness and height, it remains an essentially Romanesque structure: the horizontal polychromy of the bed joints and the volume of the piers cancel out all of the rhythmic effects typical of Gothic design. By its very plan (which includes a domed crossing tower), Siena shows itself to be more closely related to Romanesque prototypes in Tuscany (Pisa) or France (Poitou). The same anachronistic blending of elements characterizes another great Italian venture, the Basilica of Sant'Antonio at Padua (begun c. 1230). Although, like San Francesco at Bologna, it includes a choir with ambulatory and chapels, Sant'Antonio is much heavier in elevation. Its transept and nave are offshoots of Romanesque and Byzantine traditions. The exterior profile reveals the same peculiar

stylistic mixture. In fact, the only thirteenth-century Italian cathedral that might be considered typically Gothic is the Cathedral of Arezzo (choir erected between 1277 and 1289). True, the exterior wall decoration and the absence of flying buttresses and projecting abutments show a lack of response to the new trends, but, inside, the slenderized proportions, forceful and logical divisions, and distribution of light through double-lancet windows beneath tracery all conspire to produce an exceptional example of how Rayonnant Gothic was adapted to the Italian building techniques of lofty side aisles, domelike vaults (e.g. Santa Maria Novella at Florence), and columns engaged in piers. The fourteenth-century nave was built according to the same scale and design as the choir. During the Renaissance, the addition of rich decoration — wall paintings and vividly colored stained glass — brought the overall effect even closer to that of French interiors.

One other singular structure should be noted here: the Franciscan Church of San Fortunato at Todi, near Orvieto, built between 1292 and 1328. San Fortunato is a hall church; its lofty piers (a slender central core surrounded by colonnettes) support three naves of equal height. This arrangement cannot help but recall the late-twelfth-century Anjou type, especially the Cathedral of Poitiers. (For example, the simple convex profile of the ribs is reminiscent of Angevin practices at the beginning of the thirteenth century.) Interior braces were needed to reinforce this audaciously lightened structure. There is, however, one feature that indicates a kinship between the church at Todi and monastic architecture to the south. As in the aforementioned southern Italian buildings (San Lorenzo at Naples, for instance), side chapels are positioned between abutments along the sides of the nave. The choir opens onto a polygonal apse; a passage running along the base of its windows had already been utilized in San Francesco at Assisi. This complex eclecticism attests to the vacillation on the part of Gothic architects in Italy at the turn of the century, that is, on the eve of the great Florentine descendants of Santa Maria Novella.

We cannot take leave of thirteenth-century Italy without mentioning civil building projects. During this period, Italian city-states — to a greater extent than in countries to the west — created an architectural style whose luxury and quality of workmanship rivaled that of religious art. The demise of the Hohenstaufens (c. 1250) possibly provided the impetus for ''liberated'' local political forces to make a decisive move toward municipal splendor ''for the first time since antiquity'' (J. White). The growing independence and ambition of the cities were reflected in structures opened to the outside through ground-floor arcades and large two- or three-sectioned upper windows. Balconies and wide outdoor stairways contradict the militaristic appearance of previously fortified buildings; the only remaining traces of the old protective function are crenellated roofs and an occasional watchtower. Inside, the first floor

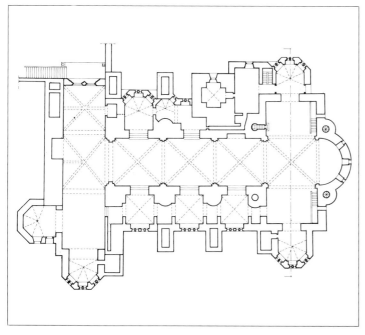

usually consists of a spacious hall that readily lends itself to painted decoration. Among these buildings are the Palazzo del Capitano del Popolo at Orvieto (after 1250), which was still partially based on a Romanesque design; the Palazzo Comunale at Piacenza, built after 1280; and, above all, the immense Palazzo dei Priori at Perugia, begun shortly after 1290 are continued into the fourteenth century. The rhythmic sequence of mullioned apertures beneath rose windows creates a harmonious composition that was to be exploited by municipal architecture as late as the Renaissance. Curiously, the Palazzo del Capitano (or Palazzo del Podestà) at Florence (now called the Bargello) falls well within this category, at least with respect to external form. Finally, the intersecting arcades in the upper story (loggia) of the Palazzo Papale at Viterbo (1266-67) bear witness to contacts with northern Rayonnant art.

ITALIAN GOTHIC DURING THE FOURTEENTH CENTURY

If we use Santa Maria Novella as a point of departure, a definition of Italian Gothic may be formulated. The innovative Florentine church incorporates northern Gothic elements and, unifying the naves by opening generously to the lateral areas, posits a new concept of space in terms of width. On the other hand, the choir — the central apse in particular — follows a different rhythm. The arrangement there of several tall windows placed side by side is analogous not to French High Gothic or Rayonnant design but to the Germanic *Hochchor*, as in the Dominican church at Regensburg (Gross). This Gothic variant (*Sondergotik*) would be more fully realized about 1300 with the great Franciscan Church of Santa Croce at Florence.

Although there is no decisive proof to support the hypothesis, this church may be the creation of the great Florentine sculptor Arnolfo di Cambio (died 1302), who was *capomastro* of the Duomo at Florence in 1300. In fact, Santa Croce is not totally dissimilar to the initial plans of the Duomo. The Franciscan church is an immense structure: the central nave is almost 66 feet wide (52 1/2 feet at Chartres) and matches the height of northern European cathedrals (almost 100 feet). With the exception of the apse and apsidal chapels, the roofing is wood. Like that of Santa Maria Novella, its plan was inspired by Cistercian design. The interior volumes, though arranged so as to interpenetrate, are nonetheless distinctly punctuated by polygonal piers, wall pilasters, and a corbel-supported balcony that demarcates the two stories of the elevation. The ten chapels (five on each side of the apse) afford ample wall surface for decoration. The vertical sweep of the lofty double-lancet apse windows distributes the light with a Gothic accent. Parallels with the apses at Saint-Nazaire at Carcassonne and San Francesco at Siena notwithstanding (Gross), Santa Croce remains a highly original expression of an autonomous style.

The claim that the plan of an initial work on Santa Croce may be at-

225. Bologna, San Francesco,
apsidal view.

tributed to Arnolfo di Cambio rests on the many similarities between this church and the first plan of the Cathedral of Florence (C. Boito, W. Paatz). The Duomo was begun in 1294, but thoroughly reworked between 1357 and 1366 by Francesco Talenti and other architects. The history of the cathedral's construction poses a good number of thorny problems, some of which have yet to be resolved. It appears that the plan of 1300 called for the eastern extremity to include a dome on an octagonal base opening to three apses. An enlarged version of this scheme was adopted in the fourteenth century, to which was later added Brunelleschi's magnificent fifteenth-century dome. Despite its nineteenth-century Neo-Gothic façade, the exterior reveals a polychromy of marbles and colored stones that blends harmoniously with the Romanesque Florentine style of the Baptistery (the latter is barely altered by the pointed casement arches topped with flat, triangular gables). The exterior abutments jut out only slightly and thus fit in well with the treatment of the surfaces. The calculated use of round arches and rectangular frames proclaims a Romanesque "rebirth", while the upper level's dome and tambour (a circular or polygonal wall below a dome) add nascent Renaissance elements. Volumes are broad and square in the nave, polygonal in the choir. The nave is composed of four bays whose pilastered polygonal piers support a tall, wide arcade, thereby permitting the same kind of spatial interpenetration as at Santa Croce. The elevation features the same corbeled balcony beneath the clerestory windows (they are round, like those in Santa Maria Novella). The large, steeply concave, cross-ribbed vaults adhere to a vaulting tradition that had already become firmly established in the thirteenth century. It is especially the colossal scale of all components that contributes to the church's impressive grandeur: the generous arcade, the forceful piers, and, above all, the vast east limb crowned with Brunelleschi's dome. Nothing in fourteenth-century northern European architecture, with its tightly woven spatial groupings, can match the Florentine Duomo. The relationship between window and surrounding surface gives the wall a clear advantage, precluding a skeletal structure. As a result, since exterior buttressing is not needed (except for wall abutments in the choir), the structural problem is greatly simplified. The aesthetic peculiar to Florence — one that was carefully plotted out at meetings of specialized commissions, the minutes of which survive — remained loyal to local traditions. It has been considered antithetical to the Gothic aesthetic (Dehio) and the first venture of the Renaissance that was gradually taking shape during the fourteenth century (C. Guasti, H. Saalman, White).

In Siena, the Tuscan rival of Florence, the Dominican and Franciscan churches are more representative of building trends than the Cathedral. Begun after 1309, San Domenico is an enormous brick structure whose rigorous square form renounces all architectural decoration. Although the rectangular chapels of the elongated transept parallel those of Santa

227. *Siena, Cathedral, plan.*
228. *Siena, Cathedral, interior.*

229. *Siena, Cathedral, detail of the façade.*

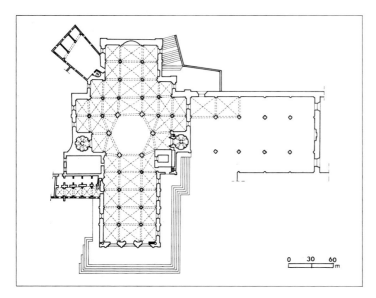

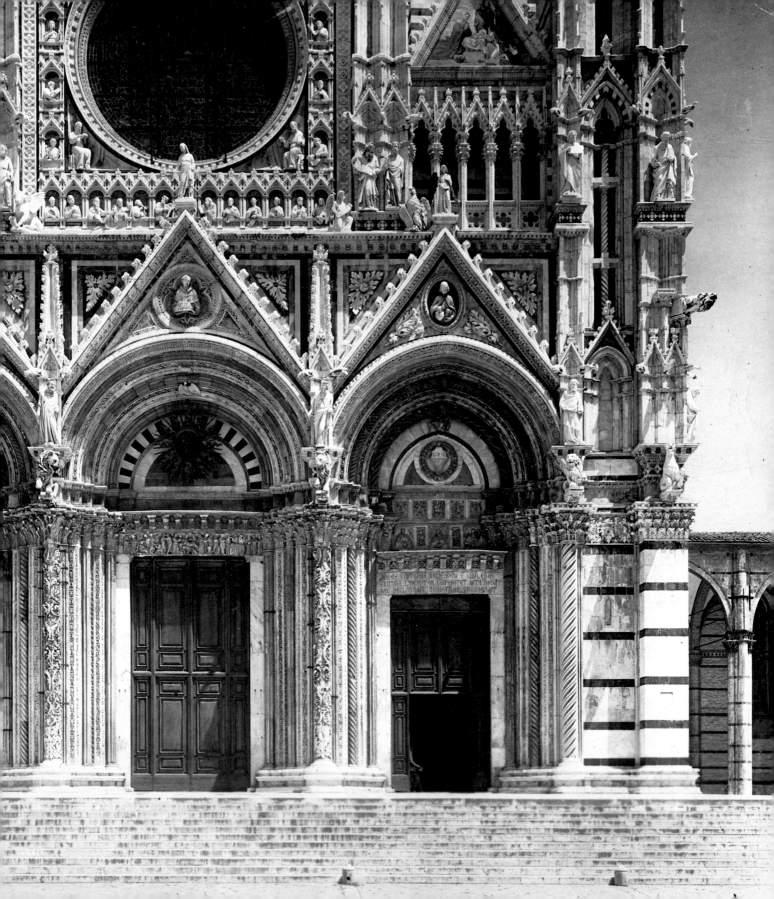

Croce in principle, the actual effect is considerably more severe. The other church, San Francesco, was begun in 1326 but modified when the height of the nave was increased in the fifteenth century. Its plan and elevation fall into the same category of Tuscan edifices as San Domenico, and the building material is again brick. However, the beautifully proportioned, wood-ceilinged space — that is, the subordination of the transept to the central nave volume — signals a mutation of the usual configuration. Moreover, the superior quality of the masonry and the tall, narrow, elegantly traceried windows (the great choir window in particular) disclose the influence of what might be called International instead of French Rayonnant.

Two other major projects were under construction in Siena during the fourteenth century: the Cathedral and the Palazzo Pubblico. In 1322, the momentous decision was made to enlarge the choir of the Cathedral the goal was doubtless to surpass the Cathedral of Orvieto and perhaps even the Cathedral of Florence. Following countless changes in the plans and the reuse of older portions of the design, work continued until 1359/60. The result of this confused construction was an outmoded style marked by incredible technical inconsistencies. The Cathedral of Siena has been called one of the most monumental failures in the history of Italian adaptation to Gothic architecture.

The Palazzo Pubblico, on the other hand, must be considered one of the most brilliantly successful ventures in civil architecture, perhaps in all medieval urban design. The entire *campo* (the semicircular public plaza) was "programmed" by municipal ordinances (1298) that regulated both the size and style of the houses. The palazzo itself was built in stages; between 1338 and 1348, it received the Torre del Mangia, the tallest and most graceful of all Italian municipal towers. Although scarcely homogeneous, the façade of the palazzo is dominated nonetheless by its admirably harmonious arrangement of stories, punctuated by triple Gothic windows. The exceptionally well-preserved interior reveals a complex grouping of meeting halls, vestibules, and passages; among their decorations are numbered some of the greatest masterpieces of medieval Italian painting. Since the architect is unknown, it is likely that this project was a collective effort, with contributions made by painters (Lippo Memmi), sculptors (Agostino di Giovanni), and an entire generation of Sienese architects.

Thus, fourteenth-century Tuscany witnessed the development of a truly original variety of Gothic. Though its preference for spacious volumes and immense expanses of plane surface distances it from the structural intricacies of Rayonnant art, this style nevertheless did borrow freely and creatively from northern European design, such as the form of windows and gables. Certain civil as well as religious buildings feature richly carved, polychromatic decoration, a distinctively Italian phenomenon in which the great masters of painting and sculpture gladly participated.

The master sculptor Arnolfo di Cambio drew the plans for the Cathedral of Florence and, in all likelihood, for Santa Croce as well. Giovanni Pisano provided the models for the façade of the Cathedral of Siena (completed c. 1360), and Giotto was responsible for the plans of the bell tower of the Duomo at Florence (begun in 1334).

The masterwork of this Italian-style "Decorated Gothic" is the façade of the Cathedral of Orvieto. Its reconstruction began in 1290, based on a design perfectly Romanesque in concept, but of exceptional height and width. In or before 1310, Lorenzo Maitani from Siena was called in as *universalis caput magister* to continue the work according to more modern techniques. But the real center of attention is the carved, polychromatic decoration of the façade and choir; it is one of the high points of medieval art. Maitani distributed typically Gothic decorative elements with a kind of academic dryness: molded abutments topped with tall pinnacles, sharply pointed gables atop both the portals and nave roofs, pointed-arched galleries, and a rose window set into a square frame. Nothing in the west wall ornamentation is structurally vital. It has instead the appearance of an ivory altarpiece made up of carved and painted panels. The same staggering effect occurs in the choir stalls and in the stained glass. Fashioned during the first half of the century, the decoration of Orvieto is an exemplary specimen of a Gothic ornamental zeal unmatched in workmanship and sumptuousness even by northern European art.

The plans for the bell tower of the Cathedral of Florence were originally drawn up in 1334 by Giotto. After his death in 1337, the work was taken on by Andrea Pisano and, after 1350, by Francesco Talenti. The lower story, its walls covered with sculpture and overlay, recalls the Arnolfian style of 1300. As the eye proceeds vertically, the stories increase in size: they are adorned with rows of statue niches and large double- or triple-lancet windows. These, in turn, are topped with purely decorative, flat gables that are carved into the wall surface itself, instead of being positioned in front of the wall. A spire that had been planned at the outset was never built. A traditional bell tower in the Florentine "Decorated Gothic" style, this structure is one of the most subtle creations in Italian Gothic art (Paatz). One other fourteenth-century project, albeit not as captivating, does figure among the Florentine masterpieces — the commercial loggia of Orsanmichele, where a picture of the Virgin had produced miracles in 1292. In 1337, construction began on a new hall, which, although later a church, did not cease to function as a storehouse for grain. Completed in 1360, it was decorated by such celebrated fifteenth-century masters as Ghiberti and Donatello. Gothic in both vault form and window design, this rectangular hall was, in essence, meant to serve as a carved, painted coffer, one produced in an entirely new manner (White).

There are two other famous municipal buildings in Florence that constitute a more important contribution of fourteenth-century architecture.

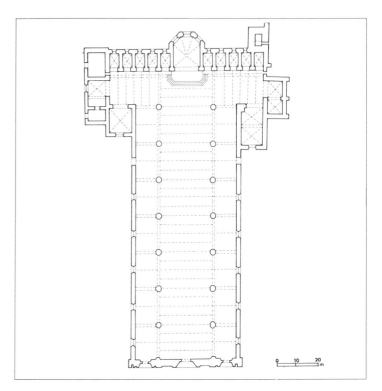

The first is the Palazzo Vecchio, rebuilt beginning in 1299 in an unpolished, Spartan style utterly bereft of the sophistication of the Palazzo Pubblico in Siena. The other is the Loggia della Signoria (or Loggia dei Lanzi), erected between 1376 and 1380, in which the lack of all characteristic Gothic motifs (pointed arches, gables, etc.) clearly illustrates the evolution of Florentine art toward Renaissance forms.

One city that played a major role in the rebirth of sculpture in the thirteenth century is Pisa. The most noteworthy structure here — after the impressive but somewhat monotonous Camposanto (begun in 1277) — is the little church or chapel of Santa Maria della Spina on the River Arno (modified after 1323). This is a wood-ceilinged hall whose arrangement of ground-floor windows and two-toned mural decoration betrays the influence of the traditional Pisan Romanesque Cathedral. On the roof, however, the unusual accumulation of gables and of pinnacles in the form of miniature sanctuaries housing statues is an expression of Gothic art at its most opulent. Although probably derived from northern Rayonnant models, the decoration at Pisa remained fundamentally sculptural, resembling the kind of ornamentation found in precious metalwork or on pulpits, rood screens, and reliquaries. This aesthetic points to the influence of the same dynamic sculptural activity in Tuscany that produced the façades of the cathedrals of Siena (Giovanni Pisano) and Orvieto (Lorenzo Maitani). Fourteenth-century monuments of great historical significance are less easily found in the region of Umbria. Begun in 1304, the monolithic San Domenico at Perugia outwardly appears to be but a continuation of thirteenth-century Dominican building traditions. However, the interior (greatly altered since the original construction) was a hall church made up of three equally tall naves, like the Dominican *Hallenkirchen* of Germany and the Rhineland. The effect is rather mixed, especially as seen from the outside. This great square block marked by heavy abutments never approaches the *élan* of Rayonnant architecture. We should not neglect city architecture, notably at Gubbio. Possibly the work of the architect Angelo da Orvieto, the Palazzo dei Consoli (after 1322) and the Palazzo Pretorio form a single complex of great beauty through a studied, coherent distribution of mass and façade. Its decoration, however, belongs stylistically to the thirteenth century.

A distinctive architectural phenomenon occurred in Naples and southern Italy during the period of Angevin rule. Buildings conceptually related to French trends were erected both by Charles I of Anjou and by his successor, Charles II. The first of these churches was San Lorenzo at Naples, to whose choir (1270-85?) was later added a wood-ceilinged nave. The early-fourteenth-century San Pietro a Maiella, with its rectilinear apse and unvaulted nave and transept, restates the Cistercian plan so typical throughout Italy. But the pure style of the molding (especially in the side-aisle vaults) and the form of the windows reveal dependence on French sources. The masterpiece of this trend is the little Neapolitan

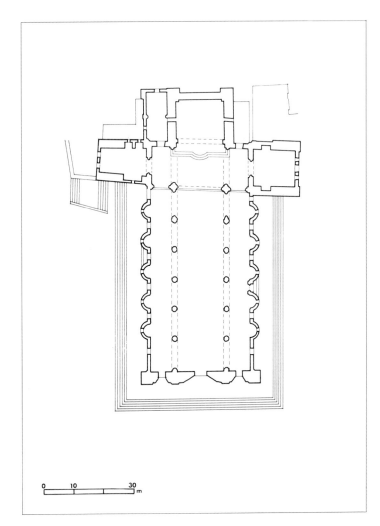

0   10   30
                m

church of the Order of Saint Clare, Santa Maria Donnaregina, founded in 1307 by Mary of Hungary, wife of Charles II of Anjou. Since the nave is surmounted by an immense gallery, the church actually consists of two distinct levels. The apse, with its five double-lancet windows, as well as its moldings and capital style, indicates the presence of northern Gothic, but there is also a hint of the Italianate and archaic, underscored by the lovely frescoes of Pietro Cavallini.

The most monumental Angevin structure in Naples is Santa Chiara, founded about 1310 for the Franciscan order by the wife of Robert I, Sancha of Mallorca. Flanked by deep chapels set between abutments, the large single nave is illuminated by tall, narrow clerestory windows cut into walls that are flat inside, punctuated by abutments outside. The nuns' choir is separate from the church and opens to the east and west by round windows as well as large lancets. This curious building is quite unlike any other, combining as it does French influences and the impressive spaciousness of Italian Franciscan churches. In addition, Santa Chiara is a royal burial site: the tomb of Robert of Anjou, among others, is located at the eastern extremity of the immense nave. Fourteenth-century Sicily, for its part, stuck fast to old Norman or even Muslim traditions and therefore remained largely untouched by Angevin art.

The situation was completely different in northern Italy — Lombardy in particular — where the type of artistic growth characteristic of the Tuscan republics and the Kingdom of Naples did not take place. Local despots quickly stifled the movement toward urban emancipation. Defensive military architecture was particularly well developed in this region: the walls of Montagnana, southwest of Padua, and those of Villafranca di Verona are among the most imposing and best preserved of the Middle Ages. In fact, cities often reserved their best efforts for such military installations. Certain strategic fortified castles — like the one built at Sirmione on Lake Garda by the Scaligeri — display a defensive complexity and stylistic quality that rival the most celebrated fourteenth-century castles in France and England. Another famous example of this feudalistic style is the castle built in 1340 by Aimon de Challant at Fenis, in the Val d'Aosta. An impressive defense system of towers and crenellated walls envelops the living quarters proper, where all was arranged and decorated to make the lord's life as agreeable as possible. At the end of the century — when Mehun-sur-Yèvre was being built for Jean de Berry and Pierrefonds for Louis d'Orléans — the castle at Verrès was being erected by Iblet de Challant. This is a masterpiece not only of defensive but also of artistic design, as seen in the luxurious courtyard and staircases.

Less intact, but no less impressive, are those castles constructed by nobles within the cities — buildings designed to serve as both fortresses and magnificent dwellings. These buildings include the Castelvecchio at Verona (the Scaligeri palace) on the banks of the Adige (c. 1355-70); the

238. Orvieto, Cathedral, interior.

Castle of the Visconti (Castello Visconteo) at Pavia (c. 1360-65); and the Castello Estense at Ferrara (c. 1370-1410). Split in two by a road with bridge access, each section of the castle at Verona has its own inner courtyard. Although its irregular plan and rather monotonous rows of interior halls may give this structure an archaic appearance, the number and dimensions of the windows looking out to the river place it closer to more recent castles. The Castello Visconteo, at Pavia, despite solid walls and strategically positioned corner towers, is practically a peacetime residence. Two stories of broad outer windows allow a great amount of light into the rooms. In the spacious rectangular courtyard, two levels of galleries lead off to the interior chambers, and the upper story is lined with wonderful arcatures, each comprising four openings. Nowhere else do the harsh imperatives of military defense find themselves so attenuated: all that remains is a mask of impressive grandeur. Built after a popular uprising in 1385, the Castello Estense, in Ferrara, retains the functionality of older fortified residences. However, its balanced plan of four towers at each corner of a square-shaped central courtyard, together with the interior scheme (much altered today), displays the same geometric regularity and concern for livability that Renaissance castles adopted as their own guiding principles.

The fourteenth century witnessed no truly significant examples of religious architecture in Piedmont, Lombardy, or Emilia. Only in the last years of the century did work begin on the Cathedral of Milan (1386) and on San Petronio at Bologna (1390). Certain churches, however, are not without interest: for example, the Cathedral of Asti and Santa Maria del Carmine at Pavia. The former was built between 1323 and 1348 and illustrates the innovative contacts between Italy and countries beyond the Alps. Its lofty side aisles recall such Germanic hall churches as Esslingen (White); its proportions are graceful; and the tall, narrow windows of the side aisles distribute light to the interior. On the other hand, the mass and structure of its pillars, the heavy vaulting, and the traditional arrangement of walls in the choir all betray the Romanesque sources of Lombardy. Begun only in 1370, Santa Maria del Carmine in Pavia, with its rectangular apse and oriented chapels, is based on an archaic plan of Cistercian origin. The combination of alternating piers, domelike square vaults, and oculi-shaped windows blends Tuscan and Lombardian elements. The extreme simplicity of the interior is matched by the façade, which, though lacking carved decoration, features a harmonious interplay of apertures and abutments (Romanini).

Also considered typical of this period are the multistoried, slenderly proportioned bell towers of San Gottardo at Milan and of the abbey church at Chiaravalle Milanese. What is interesting about these fourteenth-century structures is not their obedience to Gothic — their sources are almost exclusively Romanesque — but their link to the Early Renaissance tendencies of fifteenth-century Lombardian architecture. A lovely example of this regional continuity of form is the famous Certosa (Charterhouse) of Pavia, begun between 1396 and 1402 on the orders of Gian Galeazzo Visconti. In this structure, the transition from the Romanesque aesthetic to the Gothic spirit is especially self-evident (Ackermann).

Unlike the rest of northern Italy, Venice and the Veneto region displayed a dynamic, enterprising attitude during the Late Middle Ages, a spirit that continued unabated thereafter. Internal crises and the war against Genoa were succeeded by political and economic conditions favorable to artistic growth. Venice was not only freeing itself from Byzantine art but also exporting its own Gothic forms to such dependencies as Dalmatia. The best-known fourteenth-century Venetian edifices are Santi Giovanni e Paolo (work begun 1333) and Santa Maria Gloriosa dei Frari (begun c. 1330), the Dominican and the Franciscan church, respectively. The Dominican church, called San Zanipolo, famous for the statue of Colleoni in its square, is far from homogeneous: the façade and nave were built prior to the choir. The nave interior is quite impressive, its soaring round piers supporting domelike vaults. Despite the system of braces used to reinforce the springings of the arches and roofing, the overall effect of this huge, empty interior space is essentially quite Gothic. Even more striking is the choir (c. 1390 and early fifteenth century). The apse is opened by three tiers of windows that extend from just above the ground to the vaults. These are tall, narrow double lancets topped with multifoil rose windows; this is followed by yet another row of double windows; and the levels are divided by a network of braces. When one views this arrangement, his thoughts turn to both Santa Croce at Florence and to the Germanic *Hochchor* principle. Indeed, this arrangement may well be derived from northern Europe: there is a similar scheme (though less sophisticated, closer to the *Hochchor* models) in the Dominican church at Treviso, San Nicolò (begun c. 1303-1305). This structure was built only gradually, and its exterior retains traces of Romanesque plasticity. Needless to say, the simple effect and volumes of its choir are a far cry from the almost fantastic abundance of windows in the choir of the Dominican church at Venice. The Franciscan church, Santa Maria Gloriosa dei Frari, is basically the same type as Santi Giovanni e Paolo, but its elegantly proportioned cylindrical piers are more densely arranged than in the Dominican church. Although modified since the time of construction, the choir follows the same principle as San Zanipolo, with two levels of windows separated by braces and decorative tracery. The six oriented chapels feature miniature versions of the same composition: two double-lancet windows per chapel, each divided into four levels. As in the case of Late Rayonnant art in France and Germany, this style arrived at extremely subtle spatial solutions, but ones adapted to traditional plans and dependent on the technical and formal conditions peculiar to Italy.

240. *Naples, Santa Maria Donnaregina, detail of the interior.*
241. *Fenis, Castle.*
242. *Ferrara, Castello Estense.*

ITALIAN GOTHIC DURING THE FIFTEENTH CENTURY

The bulk of Italian architecture was unaffected by Gothic art during the fifteenth century. The rapid emergence of the Renaissance, already foreshadowed in the thirteenth century, formed the foundation of early-fourteenth-century Tuscan works. Either through a conscious return to Romanesque, Early Christian, or classical forms or through innovative ideas concerning arrangement, proportion, or decoration, Lombard and Florentine architecture managed to break loose from Gothic principles. Yet, even at this late date, certain isolated building sites, even entire regions, resisted the new stylistic currents. Such was the case of Venice — especially in regard to the Palazzo Ducale — as well as two important projects begun at the very end of the fourteenth century, the Cathedral of Milan and San Petronio at Bologna.

There are few medieval structures whose planning and construction are as thoroughly documented as the Cathedral of Milan (planned in 1386 and begun in 1387 under the direction of Simone da Orsenigo). From the outset, numerous experts were summoned for consultation: architects from Campione, Nicolas de Bonaventure from Paris, Antonio di Vincenzo from Bologna, the mathematician Gabriele Stornacolo, the German architect Hans Parler, and later Jean Mignot, another Frenchman. Only in 1401 did technical and, above all, aesthetic controversies subside. Better than any other medieval document, the minutes of these discussions attest to the opposing architectural theories or intellectual principles used to justify one decision or another. Questions of construction, though hotly debated, were nonetheless overshadowed by considerations of dimension, proportion, and even "space." The Parisian architect insisted on proven traditional Gothic schemes; Hans Parler proposed a structure of towering height; and the Italians favored the broad proportions of classical geometry. What ultimately emerged from this discussion was one of the most immense and original cathedrals in all Christendom, one that, in many respects, broke away from Italian traditions. Like the thirteenth-century Cologne Cathedral, the plan of the Cathedral of Milan seems to be an exercise in maximum size and complexity: double side aisles along the nave that are so spacious that it would be more correct to speak of five naves; side aisles in the protruding transept; and a polygonal choir with ambulatory. The proportions of the elevation are broad, allowing easy access from one area of the church to another. Owing to the relatively narrow windows and the dimming effect of stained glass, the intensity of illumination is reduced in the upper reaches of the cathedral. The powerful supports, not to mention their closely set rhythm and the profuse carved decoration above the capitals, run counter not only to the customary Italian tendency to reduce pier volume, but also to contemporary northern European Gothic trends (compare the Cathedral of Ulm). We are a long way indeed from the spatial principles of fifteenth-century Flamboyant art. On the other

XXI. Fossanova,
Abbey Church.

XXII. Assisi, San Francesco, interior of the upper church.

hand, the cathedral exterior offers the richest, most intricate example of Late Gothic style, perhaps the most exuberant and eclectic in all Europe. The ambulatory and side-aisle windows consist of up to twelve multiple lancets ingeniously grouped below wonderfully clever patterns of tracery. The wall decoration, literally covered with vertical tracery and topped with false-gabled balustrades, brings to mind the exaggerated Flamboyant ornamentation of England or Germany. The flying-buttress piers, partially covered with rectilinear motifs, are crowned with tall, sharply pointed pinnacles. The flying buttresses proper similarly adorned, climb to the upper walls, where there is an extraordinary pinnacled balustrade made up of gabled arcatures. Lastly, a polygonal tower over the transept crossing is topped with yet another spire. The planner undoubtedly sought to create the same formal maximum in the exterior as in the design of the interior and the general plan itself. Its appearance is sometimes likened to some eclectic Neo-Gothic masterpiece. The cathedral was not completed until 1858 at the height of the nineteenth-century revival of medieval archaeology. But even if the façade dates, in part, from the early nineteenth century, it is the spirit of the early fifteenth century that reigns in terms of overall effect. The main altar was dedicated in 1418, and construction nearly reached completion in 1572. During the seventeenth and eighteenth centuries, ongoing work perpetuated the Gothic tradition. As a result, certain details of ornamentation reveal a dryness comparable to the nave and façade of the Cathedral of Orléans, built in the Gothic style from the sixteenth to the nineteenth century.

A completely different situation exists at the other major fifteenth-century project, San Petronio at Bologna, begun in 1390 by Antonio di Vincenzo (one of the consultants for Milan Cathedral). The initial plans surpassed the Cathedral of Milan in length and height; even reduced to its present-day dimensions, the enormous edifice is the largest church in Bologna. There are three principal naves, a single apse, and side aisles lined with chapels. The immense central space is subdivided into six bays — each nearly 66 feet long — covered with steeply concave vaults, and oculi overlook the arcade. The form of the piers is clearly derived from the Duomo of Florence, while the simplicity of the general arrangement points to a thirteenth-century inspiration. The abundance of light at every level and the unified proportions of the interior space combine to make this church one of the most awe-inspiring, if not one of the most innovative, creations of Italian Gothic. We reiterate the fact that this is strictly an expression of the Gothic style peculiar to Italy, for San Petronio owes nothing to Flamboyant art of the Late Middle Ages. Begun at the western extremity — the central-portal decoration by Jacopo della Quercia dates from the first half of the fifteenth century — the church was finally completed in the mid-seventeenth century without major changes in the original design.

244. *Chiaravalle Milanese, Abbey,*
cloister and tower.

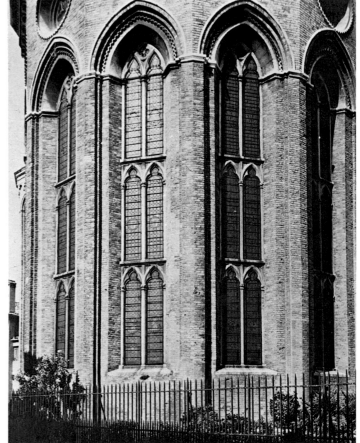

245. Venice, Santa Maria Gloriosa
dei Frari, exterior.
246. Venice, Santi Giovanni
e Paolo, apsidal view.

247. Venice, Santi Giovanni
e Paolo, exterior.

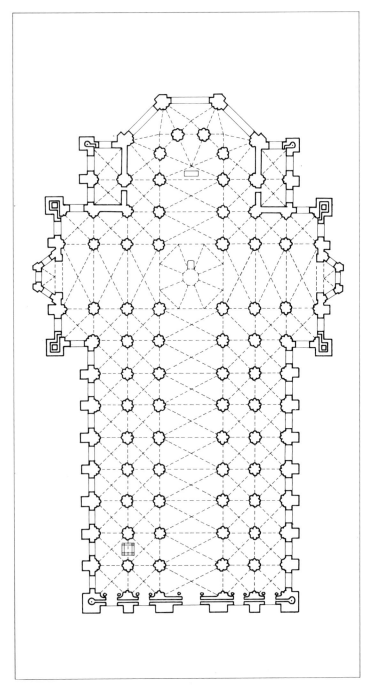

248. *Milan, Cathedral, plan.*

249. *Milan, Cathedral, apsidal view.*

Fifteenth-century architecture was indeed a complicated phenomenon. While great Gothic projects were under way in Milan and in Bologna and while Brunelleschi, in charge of the final stage of the Cathedral of Florence, was creating masterpieces of Renaissance art, Bernardo Rossellino was building the Cathedral of Pienza as part of an urban complex for Pope Pius II of the Piccolomini family (begun 1460). The great Florentine architect took the Germanic hall-church principle, together with polygonal choir and radiating chapels, and interpreted it according to his own personal style. The exceptional nature of this venture was probably a direct result of the pope himself: an admirer of the Cathedral of Strasbourg, he had spent long periods of time in Germanic countries as a papal legate.

The final chapter in the history of fifteenth-century Italian Gothic centers around Venice. After the death of Gian Galeazzo Visconti, Venice underwent a period of intense political and economic expansion. With the fall of the Byzantine Empire in 1453, responsibility for the eastern Mediterranean fell into the hands of the Venetian republic, now a major European power. A great many palaces were built for Venetian aristocrats of this era, several of which have survived: those mentioned most often are the Ca' d'Oro, built between 1421 and 1440 for Marco Contarini, and the Ca' Foscari, begun in 1452. Both exemplify the Venetian palace style: superimposed galleries open to the outside through arcades of multifoil tracery. The splendid intricacy of Late Gothic in Venice can best be seen in the Palazzo Ducale, the Doge's Palace, despite the fact that it was subjected to countless modifications during and after the Renaissance. Older buildings had previously occupied the site, including the fourteenth-century Sala del Gran Consiglio; certain alignments of the palace actually date from this era. Although some construction took place during the years 1400-1404, the palace received its present-day appearance from the plan of 1422, executed beginning in 1424 under the doge Francesco Foscari. At the heart of the design are two levels of arcades: the density of the second-story arches is twice that of the story below. The uppermost level consists of an expanse of unarticulated, multicolored wall surface perforated with large pointed windows. Technically speaking, this is the "underpinning" of an older structure, as well as an exercise in the harmonization of the façade. The wings turned toward the Piazzetta and the Grand Canal stand opposite those facing east, thereby forming a large, arcaded inner courtyard rectangular in shape. However, none of these elements are wholly original. The plan is an imitation of the central courtyard found in the castles of the nobility, while the elevation is but a refined adaptation of the private Venetian palace. Be that as it may, the characteristically Venetian forms of the Palazzo Ducale — sophisticated, yet simplified when observed as an organic whole — constitute an essentially Gothic contribution to medieval art. Moreover, this example illustrates a stylistic orientation

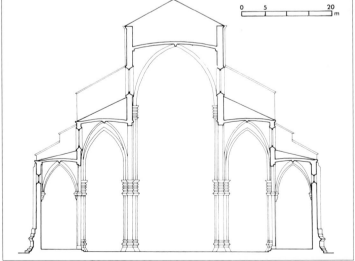

254. Zamora, Cathedral, interior.
255. Lérida, Old Cathedral, interior.

quite different from Tuscan or Emilian design or the Flamboyant eclecticism of the Cathedral of Milan (E. Arslan). To a certain extent, we might go so far as to compare Venetian Gothic to the equally innovative interpretations of Late Gothic in Spain and Portugal.

SPAIN

Both geographical and historical conditions fostered contact between France and the Iberian peninsula during the first years of the Reconquest. Thanks to Cistercian expansion and the pilgrimage route leading through France to Santiago de Compostela — the so-called *camino francés* — Romanesque architecture in northern Spain and Castile had, even before 1150, attained an extraordinary degree of development, as reflected in the quality and grandeur of their religious edifices. The success of Romanesque art in Spain was a potential obstacle in the path of the Gothic "invasion": indeed, in certain cases, it turned out to be just such an obstacle. Although most of the peninsula had been liberated by 1150, the deep-seated traces of the long Muslim occupation remained strong enough to affect the building techniques and decoration of Christian structures.

We have already had occasion to mention the fact that the rudiments of Gothic architecture were disseminated as the Cistercian order expanded during the second half of the twelfth century. Among these projects were Veruela, Poblet, Santas Creus, and Alcobaça in Portugal. The last of these, founded in 1152 and built between 1178 and 1223, is one of the most complete monastic complexes in western Europe. The principle of cross-ribbed vaulting was exploited in Spain at a fairly early date, even outside the framework of Cistercian architecture (Pórtico de la Gloria at Santiago de Compostela, and the cathedrals of Toro and Zamora). However, this practice in no way interfered with the profoundly Romanesque spirit that overshadowed the spatial effect of these structures. A much more coherent application of the Gothic system is to be found in two churches in Ávila, the Cathedral and San Vicente. Begun at the transept and apse during the first half of the century, the nave of San Vicente took on Cistercian-style diagonal ribs and galleries in the course of construction (Lambert, L. Torres Balbás). The date of this work has not been accurately determined. This is not the case with the Cathedral of Ávila, which had already been under construction for several decades at the time of the death of its architect, Furchel, in 1192. The double ambulatory and radiating chapels of the apse probably derive from Saint-Denis, but the exterior bears a closer resemblance to Pontigny II. There are also strong similarities between its elevation and the choir of Vézelay, that masterpiece of Burgundian Early Gothic. It is in fact possible that we are dealing with the same final decades of the twelfth century that witnessed the construction of Vézelay. However, certain doubts as to chronology remain to be resolved. In any event, the Cathedral of Ávila is

256. Burgos, Cathedral, Puerta
del Sarmental.
257. Burgos, Cathedral, interior.

the most accomplished twelfth-century Gothic work to be erected outside France.

According to Elie Lambert, one of the most penetrating specialists in Spanish Gothic art, certain changes in the political and cultural scene during the thirteenth century reoriented the direction hitherto followed by French influences. The victory of Las Navas de Tolosa (1212) brought about within less than half a century the liberation of nearly the entire peninsula. After the recapture of Seville in 1248, all that was left to the Muslims was the Kingdom of Granada, which they managed to retain until the end of the fifteenth century. The new power of individual states — Castile, Aragon, Portugal, and later the Kingdom of Mallorca — afforded Christian architects expanses of terrain still imbued with the memory of the Arab presence. The thirteenth century marked the birth of a truly Spanish architectural style.

This evolution consists of several distinct phases. The first covers the first quarter of the thirteenth century, during which time certain procedures or elements typical of Gothic architecture played an increasingly important role in the ongoing Romanesque movement. Projects already begun in the preceding century (the cathedrals of Toro, Zamora, Orense, and Ávila, as well as Cistercian establishments at Valbuena, Fitero, and Santas Creus) will be omitted from this category. However, we must include structures which, though heavily dependent on the past, were still only in the planning stage about the year 1200. Of particular interest are the cathedrals of Ciudad Rodrigo and Lérida. Ciudad Rodrigo acquired the status of a diocese in 1160, but the exact dates of the Cathedral, still under construction in 1230, are not known. Its plan, pier design, and spatial form all place it squarely in the Romanesque family of cathedrals, including Zamora. But this Cathedral — in particular, its octopartite vaulting with liernes and thinly molded ribs — also bear more clearly than anywhere else the same imprint of the Plantagenet style seen in the Cathedral of Poitiers. The old Cathedral of Lérida in Catalonia was not begun until 1203. This surprising complex includes a cloister west of an archaically designed church (abandoned for more than a century) that is obviously based on the Romanesque Cathedral of Tarragona. Even though its contours are pointed, its cross-ribbed vaulting coherent, and its light abundant, a heaviness of mass and a lack of dynamism in the proportions create an atmosphere at Lérida that is decidedly pre-Gothic.

The Cathedral of Cuenca, begun in 1199 or 1200 and completed after 1250, confronts the observer with quite a different phenomenon. The original exterior contours of the choir are today hidden by numerous additions made during the eighteenth century. But the elegant architectural style of the interior is filled with "modern" elements of French art. The alternating round piers in the choir respond to the rhythm of the sexpartite vaulting above. In the transept, the rose windows are above a tall blind arcade, and certain details, such as the tops of the abutments, are copied directly from that rather esoteric model, Saint-Yves at Braine. Everything seems to indicate that the first architect of Cuenca was a native of the Soissons or Laon region. The narrowly proportioned, but graceful nave arcade rests on piers articulated by colonnettes. At the clerestory level, the wall "doubles": the inner shell contains double lancets beneath an oculus, the outer one a simple but immense rose window. A gallery running along the base of the windows cuts across the piers, recalling similar passages found in late-twelfth- and thirteenth-century structures in Burgundy and Champagne. The latest innovations of French architecture likewise inspired the second architect of Cuenca, believed to have been of Norman origin. The crossing tower, a local tradition common to all important Spanish buildings, was not erected until the end of the thirteenth century.

The eastern end of a second Spanish cathedral, Sigüenza, reveals the same movement toward the adoption of the French or International Gothic style. Based on a traditional twelfth-century plan, the nave was reworked and vaulted just as a new transept and choir were being erected (the choir was modified at the end of the Middle Ages and again during the Renaissance). The dates established by Lambert for the Gothic phase of construction (second quarter of the thirteenth century) would account for the form of the clerestory windows in the transept—four lancets under three rose windows, a Rayonnant arrangement found at the cathedrals of Troyes and Amiens. This curious edifice thus "encases" backward Romanesque spatiality within the fashionable sophistication of the style of 1225-30. The same coexistence of conservative and innovative design can be observed at the ruins of the Convent of Santa María de la Huerta, between Sigüenza and Saragossa. Located on the Aragon border, this royal Castilian abbey retains vestiges of its church, cloister, and refectory (1215-23). True, the ample refectory windows and subtle molding of the interior and of the vaulting attest to a complete familiarity with post-Chartres French art. The sexpartite vaulting, however, is an anachronism, and it is still the sobriety of Cistercian architecture that strikes the dominant chord. Included in this group is the Cistercian convent at Burgos, Las Huelgas, which was, for a while, the burial site of the kings of Castile and thus enjoyed royal favor from the time of its founding in 1187. The rather harsh simplicity of its Romanesque monastic style is adapted to an Anjou-inspired vaulting system of great beauty and complexity. The chapter house (after 1225) is renowned for the daring virtuosity of its Gothic construction.

We must realize that neither the spatial design, structure, nor decoration of any of the aforementioned buildings offers definitive evidence of an architectural style peculiar to Spain. Indeed, none of them are a monument of major importance. On the other hand, the cathedrals of Toledo, Burgos, and León constitute a key group of structures. Burgos and Toledo were begun at approximately the same time—Burgos in 1223 or

1224, Toledo in 1224 or 1227. The former was built fairly rapidly and was dedicated in 1260; the latter remained unfinished until the end of the fifteenth century. Over the years, both have been altered to such a degree (for instance, by the addition of magnificent chapels) that an archaeologist's reconstruction is often needed in order to perceive their original forms.

In terms of both plan and elevation, the Cathedral of Toledo, with its double ambulatory and double side aisles of decreasing height, belongs to the Bourges family. However, a huge transept breaks the continuity of the nave, and the ambulatory vaulting bears a closer resemblance to that in the Cathedral of Le Mans. Moreover, the broad proportions of the church and the decorative abundance of windows produce an innovative effect in no way connected with French models. The oldest section of the cathedral is the choir, which is stylistically less ponderous than the nave. As at Bourges, round piers compounded with eight colonnettes demarcate spacious bays and support vaults that alternate (in the ambulatory) between diagonally ribbed oblong fields and triple-ribbed triangular fields. Of the fifteen original radiating chapels built during the thirteenth century, seven are still extant: they are relatively small and follow an unusual rhythm of alternating squares and semicircles. Again recalling Bourges, the windows of the inner ambulatory as well as the clerestory windows in the choir are situated above a very tall triforium. It is here especially that the Islamic (Mudejar) flavor of the Toledo style is most forcefully expressed. The trefoiled or quinquefoiled arcatures are grouped beneath other arches in accordance with traditional Islamic design. Likewise, the ambulatory rose windows are decorated with typically Moorish imaginativeness. The transept and nave of Toledo, with their massive, colonnetted piers, impose a certain structural heaviness. But the clerestory windows (four or six lancets below intricate tracery) and the triforium clearly belong to the phase corresponding to Rayonnant art of the mid and late thirteenth century. The rather awkward system of exterior abutment features flying buttresses "decomposed" into two levels, one for the nave, the other for the upper side aisle. Though perfectly logical, this scheme, technically speaking, contradicts northern French practices.

Among all thirteenth-century structures, the Cathedral of Toledo is perhaps the most ambitious in terms of plan and complexity; its French sources were interpreted, modified, and assimilated in such a way as to produce an innovative effect. Burgos, however, is more homogeneous and of greater architectonic significance. Its north flank resting on a steep hill, the cathedral exterior is dominated by its fifteenth-century east towers; by the *cimborio* (crossing tower rebuilt in the sixteenth century following its collapse); and by the lofty apsidal Capilla del Condestable, built after 1482 by Don Pedro Hernández de Velasco. This chapel, a masterpiece of Spanish Flamboyant art, will be examined at a later point. The choir plan of the thirteenth-century church is quite similar to the

259. León, Cathedral, plan
of the church and of adjoining
buildings.
260, 261. León, Cathedral, views
of the exterior and interior.

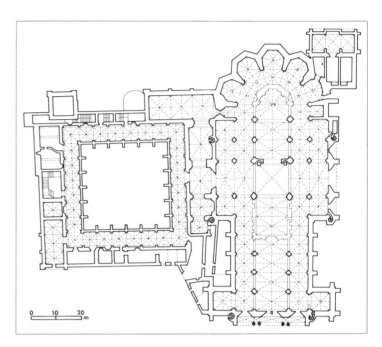

plan of the Cathedral of Coutances, but the construction of Coutances
evidently did not precede that of Burgos. The five-ribbed trapezoidal ambulatory bays and the liernes of the choir vault are particularly reminiscent of Coutances. This similarity ends in the elevation: the piers, as well
as certain details of design, are derived from Bourges. The really original
feature of Burgos is the immense triforium—multifoil arcades beneath
magnificent trefoiled and quatrefoiled tracery (except in the bays nearest
the crossing, which underwent reconstruction at the end of the fifteenth
century). To be sure, this triforium is not totally unrelated to that of
Bourges. But its exceptionally decorative effect places it closer to the
kind of uninhibited ornamentation found at Toledo. Again like Toledo,
the proportions of Burgos are broad, and the full windows afford ample
illumination. We are not that far removed from the Gothic style of Reims
and Paris during the 1240s, especially in the transept façades. In short,
the architects of Burgos, though evidently attuned to the evolution of
French architecture, still managed to stamp their creation with a style all
its own.

The Cathedral of León marks a watershed in Spanish architecture.
Contrary to the belief of certain historians, it appears that the construction of León was begun no earlier than 1254-55, just when Rayonnant
Gothic was at its zenith in France. Its plan is somewhat old-fashioned: it
falls into the Chartres line of descent, by way of the Cathedral of Reims
(begun 1211). The ambulatory with five polygonal chapels, the double
side aisles of the right portion of the choir, the nave elongating the entire
arrangement—all of these elements point to Reims. Furthermore, the
elevation echoes the three-storied superposition of arcade, triforium, and
a clerestory as tall as the arcade. Running along the base of the inner side-
aisle windows is a passage cut into the wall, a feature peculiar to
derivatives of Champagne art in general and Reims in particular. In certain respects, however, the Reims model was modernized: witness the
triforium openwork (as in post-1230 French Rayonnant churches) and, in
the apse, the clerestory double lancets beneath a rose window. In the
right-hand areas of the church, these windows are sexpartite, as at
Amiens after 1245. The overall spatial proportions are airy and graceful.
The colonnettes flanking the piers climb unbroken to the vaults, a verticality accentuated by the dense linear interplay of the numerous lancet
windows. León is surely one of the most accomplished of all Rayonnant
cathedrals. Outside, the double flying buttresses—the struts are straight,
not curved—exemplify the structural dynamism of the Gothic system.
But to what extent and by what specific means does León express the
kind of Spanish stylistic idiosyncrasies found at Toledo and Burgos? We
must acknowledge that this cathedral incorporates neither Moorish
(Mudejar) elements nor the old "resistant" Romanesque traditions.
Granted, certain forms, especially in the windows, do not perfectly
match those found in northern France. However, Lambert is doubtless

262. Barcelona, Monastery of Santa
Maria de Pedralbes, interior
of the church.

263. Barcelona, Cathedral,
axonometric section through
the apse.
264. Barcelona, Cathedral, interior.

correct in comparing León to Bayonne and in placing the two cathedrals in a kind of Franco-Hispanic architectural group that straddles the Pyrenees.

Lambert correctly notes that, though it is the most Gothic and the most "modern" example of thirteenth-century Spanish architecture, the Cathedral of León was not destined to influence subsequent generations. It was instead the less perfect model of Burgos that provided inspiration for further construction. Its progeny includes the Cathedral of Osma (begun c. 1236); the Cathedral of Castro Urdiales on the northern coast of the peninsula; the Abbey Church of Rueda in the Ebro Valley; and even churches built as late at 1300, such as San Gil at Burgos. That Burgos played this role is quite understandable: no area of Spain was sufficiently experienced or sophisticated to favor the development of Rayonnant architecture. What did exist there was the Romanesque tradition of heavy, broad proportions, the propensity toward decoration, the potential of Mudejar elements, and the rudiments of regional or national styles. The fourteenth century was a period of Spanish reaction against French Rayonnant art, whose purest and most beautiful representative was the Cathedral of León.

THE FOURTEENTH CENTURY

During the 1300s, the strongest national reaction occurred in Catalonia and the Balearic Islands—it was the result of certain political conditions. Beginning in the second half of the thirteenth century, Aragon extended its power to Catalonia and Valencia, controlled areas north of the Pyrenees (the Roussillon and Cerdagne regions, the town of Montpellier), and reconquered the Balearic Islands. The kings of Aragon would soon launch a campaign to conquer Sicily and Sardinia. A short-lived Kingdom of Mallorca, which extended into Aragon's French possessions, enjoyed a moment of brilliance from 1262 to 1394 but was soon swallowed up by Aragonese might. Along with the extraordinary maritime and commercial growth of Mallorca, we should also take note of similar developments in Catalonia and her chief city, Barcelona. These, then, were destined to be the most dynamic regions of construction in fourteenth-century Spain.

As for the provinces of Castile, the accelerated pace of construction during the glorious era of the thirteenth-century Reconquest had slowed to only a very few new projects. In terms of formal evolution, this kingdom was in a period of stagnation. For example, the nave of the Cathedral of Toledo, built during the late thirteenth and fourteenth centuries, reveals a structural heaviness that conflicts with the audacity of the church's eastern section. The choir of the Cathedral of Palencia, begun in 1321 according to a plan based on León, imitated the Burgos-style tall blind triforium, necessitating a reduction in the size of the clerestory windows. This was not the only case of a trend away from lightness through renewed emphasis on walls. However, at least

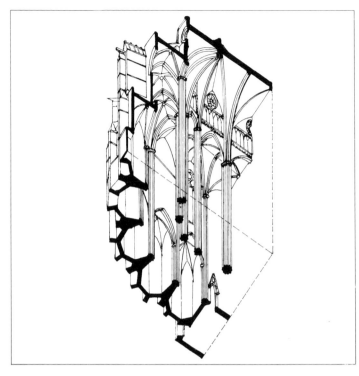

Palencia's exterior does achieve a certain lightness in its skillfully arranged flying buttresses. The same tendencies may be observed in the Old Cathedral of San Pedro at Vitoria (second half of the fourteenth century). Its three-storied elevation retains the blind triforium; the only lightened element is the elegant molding, probably derived directly from southern France. The mid-fourteenth-century Church of San Esteban at Burgos remained loyal to local traditions. Although work began on the great Monastery of Guadalupe about 1340, the church was not completed until the fifteenth century. At this time, the cloister and lavabo (ritual washbasin) were constructed; both are masterpieces of structure as well as of carved decoration. The triple-naved church features an innovative design: sober piers, sparingly decorated, support complex star-vaults interwoven with liernes and tiercerons. An integral part of Gothic structures in England from the thirteenth century on, this vaulting system met with great success in Gothic Spain as well, particularly in the *cimborio*, the ribbed dome atop the transept crossing. Its popularity was undoubtedly abetted by the intricately ribbed vaults already erected on Spanish soil by the Muslims. Built from 1316 to 1354, the chapter house at Burgos provides one of the earliest fourteenth-century specimens of this type of vaulting. Between 1312 and 1355, a star-vaulted dome was placed over the transept crossing of the Cathedral of Ávila. In the nave and apse of Guadalupe, this scheme is spread across all of the bays. Even the sumptuous Renaissance and Baroque decoration added during the fifteenth century could not spoil the Guadalupe vaults—they are among the finest examples of a Spanish preoccupation that reached its apogee at the end of the Middle Ages.

Let us now turn to Catalonia, the only region that managed to create an architecture of superior formal and structural quality. Gothic vaulting techniques made their way into twelfth-century Catalonia by way of the Cistercian churches at Santas Creus, Poblet, and Valbuena. These techniques were also exploited at the essentially Romanesque cathedrals of Tarragona and Lérida. During the middle of the thirteenth century, Franciscan and Dominican building activity generated a new wave of Gothic architecture in this area. According to certain writers (P. Lavedan), two Barcelona structures embody the quintessence of this mid-century style: the Dominican Church of Santa Catalina and the Franciscan Church of San Francisco. Both included a single nave covered with cross-ribbed vaults, with chapels situated between abutments on either side of the nave. Above the chapels, tall windows provided a great deal of illumination. Unfortunately, since both churches were demolished in the nineteenth century, their exact dates of construction are at best uncertain. We do know that work on Santa Catalina was in progress in 1268, and that San Francisco was not dedicated until 1297. The same type of single-nave church with chapels between abutments was also appearing in France—the Church of the Cordeliers at Toulouse (c. 1260-1340, but demolished in the nineteenth century) and new work on the Cathedral of Albi (begun in 1276)—as well as in Italy (San Francesco at Messina, after 1254). Thus, we are actually dealing with an international style that spread throughout the Mediterranean and was further developed in Catalonia and the Kingdom of Mallorca during the fourteenth century.

Though poorly preserved, the late-thirteenth-century Church of Santo Domingo at Gerona still stands. Though covered with a wood ceiling resting on diaphragm-shaped arches, the Chapel of Santa Agueda in the royal palace of Barcelona (1303-10) expresses the superior quality of Catalonian architecture by its elegant proportions, sophisticated contours, and double windows under tracery. This same period marked the beginning of the Cathedral of Saint-Bertrand-de-Comminges in the Pyrenees, a cathedral based on the same single-nave plan. This church, whose nave measures almost 50 feet across, holds an interesting place in the history of this structural type. Actually, the eastern section was originally an older Romanesque building that had been planned as a triple-naved church. The Gothic architect, while retaining the side walls, eliminated the interior piers in order to create a single, immense, vaulted space with deep lateral radiating chapels positioned between powerful abutments. As in the Church of the Carmelites at Toulouse and as in Santa Catalina at Barcelona, these chapels lie beneath clerestory windows.

Among Catalonian single-nave churches, the most noteworthy in terms of size is Santa María del Pino at Barcelona. Measuring about 54 feet across, the nave is flanked by chapels fully half as high as the nave, over which appear groups of four lancet windows arranged beneath tracery. Santa María del Pino illustrates, even more clearly than Saint-Bertrand-de-Comminges, both the structural and aesthetic advantages of this type of church. The single interior space is punctuated by chapel entrances and by colonnettes engaged in the walls supporting the vaults. Although brightly lighted through chapel and clerestory windows, the church's continuous walls are largely unaffected by the apertures—the accent is still on wall surface. Exterior abutments suffice to equalize the thrust of the nave. A smaller version of the same type, Santa María de Pedralbes (founded in 1326 at the gates of Barcelona), places even greater emphasis on the walls. Consider the absence of chapels in the three-storied apse, below rose windows and a clerestory. Yet, there is no feeling of heaviness—the thinness of the walls, their absence of structural functionality, echoes the principles of Rayonnant art. The exterior mass is geometric in its simplicity. Begun in 1329, the Church of Santos Justo y Pastor, also at Barcelona, is a kind of simplified Santa María del Pino. Beyond the Catalonian capital may be found the Franciscan church at Villafranca del Panadés and the Dominican church at Balaguer: both date from the first quarter of the fourteenth century and belong to the same structural category. Especially important is the great Franciscan church

at Palma de Mallorca, San Francisco. One of the oldest surviving edifices of this variety, it was begun about 1280, consecrated in 1317, and completed about 1349. Originally covered with wood on diaphragm-shaped arches, the nave was already vaulted by the fourteenth century. North of the Pyrenees, other members of this family were erected in the Roussillon and Cerdagne regions, then dependencies of the Kingdom of Mallorca. Although the Franciscan church at Perpignan is no longer extant, the same type may be found in the Franciscan churches in Puigcerdá and in Collioure, in San Jacobo at Palma de Mallorca, and in Santa María at Ciudadela (Menorca). The Cathedral of Perpignan, begun in 1324 by Sancho de Mallorca, may also be considered a part of this group. Among its outstanding features are a transept preceding the choir, and an apse flanked by two chapels that open to the transept.

M. Durliat has pointed out that the original plan called for a nave with side aisles, but, under the weight of local tradition, this was discarded in favor of a single nave about 59 feet wide. We will soon see that the same holds true for the Cathedral of Gerona. The nave at Perpignan opens to very tall chapels that leave just enough space along the massive walls for large oculi. The design of this church, though far from homogeneous, is nonetheless as striking as that used for the Barcelona structures. The quest for spatial unity at Perpignan is demonstrated by the clear divisions between chapels, which are lighted through tall but very narrow windows.

By means of a widespread, almost systematic application of the single-nave principle (with chapels between abutments), fourteenth-century Catalonia and southern France bordering the Pyrenees proclaimed their unequivocal opposition to the Rayonnant art of northern and central France. Even the multinaved churches built here during those years may be placed in the anti-Rayonnant camp, for they utilized the same building techniques and spatial design.

The year 1298 marked the beginning of the Gothic Cathedral of Barcelona under the direction of Jaime Fabre de Mallorca. The first ambulatory chapels were completed by 1317, but the remaining work required a much longer period of time. The nave and cloister were still being constructed in the middle of the fifteenth century, and the crossing tower was not added until the nineteenth century. Its choir plan closely resembles those of the cathedrals of Gerona (begun 1312) and Narbonne (begun 1286): the polygonal chapels opening to ambulatory and side aisles may even be considered a French plan derived from northern models. Especially logical is the fact that, by serving as interior abutments, the walls separating the chapels become fully integrated into the church structure. As for the elevation, the Catalonian cathedral rejects the Narbonne arrangement of triforium interposed between an arcade and clerestory of equal height. Instead, the arcade at Barcelona soars to so great a height that there is only enough room above the triforium for a

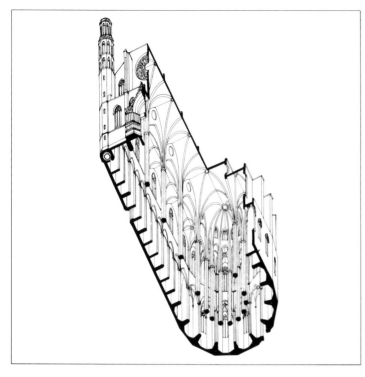

clerestory oculus. The ambulatory is lighted by elaborate windows above the chapel entrances, a feature that has prompted comparisons to Bourges. Thus each bay opens to three stories of windows; viewed from the outside, the three levels of the elevation are clearly delineated along the exterior wall. Forceful piers notwithstanding, the interior gives the impression of a single empty space sustained by supports of dizzying height. The nave consists of four immense square vaults flanked by side aisles as tall as those in the choir, but the nave side chapels (two per bay) are topped with galleries whose vaults reach the same height as those in the side aisles. More than just a beautiful arrangement that enhances the monumentality of the interior space, this scheme functions structurally as well—the chapels, galleries, and partitioning abutments give effective support to the interior mass. As a result, the span of the exterior flying buttresses could be reduced without jeopardizing the equilibrium of the structure. The Cathedral of Barcelona is a masterpiece of technical virtuosity in the service of a highly innovative spatial design. It seems to combine the Germanic hall-church principle with the classic French cathedral and, to a certain degree, with the Catalonian/southern French single-nave effect, the limits of which are well defined by continuous walls.

Everything we have just said about Barcelona may be applied to the Cathedral of Gerona, whose choir was built according to the same plan. There is, however, one important difference: the arcade, though quite elongated, is still sufficiently low to allow room for both clerestory windows and an openwork triforium. In addition, the ambulatory receives direct lighting from above the chapel entrances. Gerona, therefore, is somewhat less daring than Barcelona in proportion and distribution of windows. The nave at Gerona, one of the most startling works in medieval architecture, radically altered the overall effect of the church. In 1416—when only the choir had been built—the bishop of Gerona, Dalmau, called in twelve architects as consultants for the completion of the cathedral. The minutes of these advisory sessions, like those of Milan, have survived. In the end, the master architect Guillaume Boffy was authorized to adjoin to the triple-naved choir an aisleless nave about 75 feet wide and about 79 feet high. Between the supporting abutments lie two side chapels per bay, which are low enough to permit the same kind of clerestory windows and triforium (here unperforated) as in the choir. Since the nave is a good deal taller than the fourteenth-century choir, a large wall pierced by three rose windows was needed to unite the different levels of the two sections. Thus Gerona blends the two fundamental species of Catalonian architecture in a most original and spectacular manner.

According to Lavedan, the Cathedral of Palma de Mallorca and the Church of Santa María del Mar at Barcelona mark "the high point of Catalonian architecture." Begun in 1328, the Church (but not the out-

buildings) of Santa María was completed in 1383, designed and built to produce an admirably unified effect. There is no transept; the four large central bays are aligned with the choir; and, in addition to nine radiating chapels, each side-aisle compartment leads to three side chapels. The structural system is analogous to that of the choir in the Cathedral of Barcelona. Except for the apsidal semicircle, the nave is illuminated only through rose windows placed under the vaults. Fully developed windows light the tall side aisles without seriously interrupting the continuity of the wall surface. The chapels situated between the abutments are, on the exterior, enveloped within a single wall; the abutments themselves are wholly integrated into the church volume. Wall abutments are adequate to ensure the stability of the nave. The quest for interior spatial unity occasioned a reduction in the quantity and volume of the supports—octagonal piers about 59 feet high, crowned with simple octagonal capitals. To a greater degree than in the cathedral, Santa María produces the overwhelming impression of an immense void supported only by very slender piers. This is surely the purest, most coherent endeavor of its kind. Even the Cathedral of Palma de Mallorca, though based on the same structural design, cannot equal the perfection of Santa María del Mar.

The Cathedral of Palma de Mallorca, begun in the early fourteenth century (perhaps c. 1300), was under construction in 1306. After completion of the eastern limb in 1327, work resumed in the middle of the century in accordance with new, grandiose plans that would be fully—and arduously—realized only in the seventeenth century. In fact, this church is a mixture of several building programs. From the first plan comes a choir (no ambulatory) whose rectilinear apse is much lower than the nave. At the towering height of almost 145 feet, the nave itself is almost as tall as the choir of the Cathedral of Beauvais. Instead of a triforium, there are only very narrow, elongated arcade openings, a scheme repeated in the about-98-foot-high side aisles. Placed between interior abutments, the side chapels receive less light because of the forest of outer abutments that encircle the cathedral. The exterior of Palma is as thick with buttressing elements—piers, abutments, and flying buttresses—as the unencumbered exterior of Santa María del Mar is free of them. In any case, the "vertiginous" interior space supported by slender octagonal piers certainly fits in with the idea of Gothic architecture as a "fantastic" interpretation of space. Other contemporary Catalonian structures should be mentioned in passing: the Cathedral of Manresa, Santa María de Castellón at Ampurias, the Cathedral of Tortosa, Santa Eulalia at Palma, and the Cathedral of Huerta. Though interesting in themselves, these projects added little to the further development of the regional style.

We should underscore the importance of certain outbuildings—especially cloisters—lying in the shadow of fourteenth-century Spanish churches. All major cathedrals in Spain have a cloister: no other country can boast such quantity, variety, and opulence. We have already

mentioned the cloister at Guadalupe and its Moorish atmosphere. Others have survived at Burgos, Oviedo, and Pamplona. Although not completed until the fifteenth century, the cloister of the Cathedral of Barcelona is, stylistically speaking, perfectly matched to the church. Especially striking is the intricate traceried decoration resting on slender false-bedded colonnettes to be found in the Cathedral of Vich. The cloister sometimes consists of superimposed galleries, as at the Monastery of Santa María de Pedralbes on the outskirts of Barcelona.

In Catalonia and in the regions formerly ruled by the Kingdom of Mallorca, one can also find beautiful examples of civil and municipal buildings, royal and episcopal palaces, and commercial exchanges. Near the Cathedral of Barcelona stands a section of the royal palace, an immense hall called the Tinell (c. 1359-70) ceiled on diaphragm-shaped arches. At Perpignan, the royal palace of the Mallorcan monarchy was severely damaged by military occupation and later made part of seventeenth-century fortifications. Its recently restored central courtyard is a quadrilateral with corner towers and porches on each of two stories. In the tradition of palace construction, two superimposed chapels occupy the middle of the eastern side of the courtyard. This castle was begun in the thirteenth century and finished during the first half of the fourteenth. The royal palace of Almudaina at Palma de Mallorca, erected in an eleventh- and twelfth-century Muslim fortress, underwent modifications starting in 1305. Its delightful Chapel of Santa Ana in situated in the center of the complex, between two courtyards. The most extraordinary royal venture, however, is the castle of Bellver at the gates of Palma de Mallorca; its construction, begun about 1300, proceeded very rapidly. It is based on a circular plan: the round central courtyard is surrounded by a two-storied porch that features intersecting pointed arches at the upper level. The living quarters and service rooms leading off from this porch are lighted through lovely double windows. Three towers gird the circumference of the enclosure; a fourth, set at a distance from the residence as a donjon, is linked to the castle by a tall bridge. The outer defensive system of moats and towers has survived practically intact. Many have wondered about the possible origins of such a harmonious plan, comparable to the Renaissance castle of Charles V at Granada. However, round or polygonal castles did exist during the Middle Ages: witness Beynes, west of Paris. Another possible source is the castle of the Hohenstaufen ruler Frederick II, Castel del Monte in southern Italy.

Several municipal and commercial buildings of the period still stand in Barcelona: the city hall (Casa de la Ciudad), begun in 1369 as a meeting hall for the municipal council, and La Lonja (c. 1380-92), a kind of commercial exchange for merchants. All feature ceilings supported by round arches. Although the Casa de la Ciudad is made up of a single hall space, La Lonja consists of three such spaces. Like the great contemporary Catalonian churches, these structures are marked by simplicity, lightness

tending toward interior spatial unity, masterly craftsmanship, and carefully molded contours. We should not omit the vast covered docks (*atarazanas*) of Barcelona, designed to shelter the Catalonian fleet. The roofing of their spacious halls rests on transverse arches. Originally set up in the thirteenth century, then enlarged and rebuilt between 1378 and 1381, these docks were finally completed some years later.

THE FIFTEENTH AND SIXTEENTH CENTURIES

As we have seen, building activity in Spain maintained an intense pace throughout the formative and developmental years of Gothic architecture. The Late Middle Ages proved to be no less favorable to the continued evolution of this style on the Iberian peninsula. Although a great many internal conflicts pitted monarchs against nobles (or against each other), Spain managed to move toward unification under the Catholic Kings, Ferdinand and Isabella. The marriage of Ferdinand of Aragon and Isabella of Castile in 1469 took on political significance as they assumed power (1474 and 1479). The year 1492 marked the conquest of the Muslim Kingdom of Granada, and the Kingdom of Navarre was incorporated into Spain in 1512. Thanks to possessions in Sicily and southern Italy, as well as the adoption of an imperialistic policy upon the discovery of America, Spain soon became the preeminent European power. As Charles V, grandson of the Catholic Kings, ascended to the imperial throne in 1519, Spain was about to embark on a century of dominance in Europe. As a result, both civil and religious buildings dot the Iberian peninsula, a legacy of elegance that remained loyal to the Gothic style.

We will not go into the details of the continuing work on major projects begun in the preceding century, such as the cathedrals of Barcelona and Palma de Mallorca. After consultations with experts in 1401, a large single nave was added to the old choir of the Cathedral of Gerona. Unfinished until 1514, the nave of the Cathedral of Palencia reveals certain traits peculiar to the Late Middle Ages: simplified pier contours, deemphasis of the capital, increasingly complex vaulting with additional liernes and tiercerons in both nave and side aisles, and a richly decorated triforium. New cathedrals were begun at Oviedo and Pamplona; the later, started in 1392, was completed about 1500. Its fairly original plan includes a polygonal apse without axial chapel. Except for the star-vaulted apsidal semicircle, the elevation of Pamplona is quite uncomplicated: large expanses of wall fill the area between clerestory windows, and the side aisles open to a relatively low arcade.

All other endeavors of this period are eclipsed by the Cathedral of Seville, the largest in total area of all medieval churches. From the time of the Reconquest, the Cathedral had been situated in a large mosque, as is the one at Córdoba even today. In 1401, a decision was made to eliminate the mosque save for the tower called La Giralda. We know a great deal about the successive building programs and the architects that directed

273. Saragossa, Cathedral, vaults.
274. Saragossa, Cathedral, tower lantern.

them—Pedro García, Ysambert, Carlin, Juan Norman, and Pedro de Toledo. The choir was still unfinished in 1494, but the general dedication took place in 1519. Numerous sculptors and stained-glass craftsmen of Spanish, French, Flemish, and German origin were called in to decorate the church. By virtue of this diversity of foreign contributions, not to mention the *spiritus loci* of Moorish tradition, Seville may indeed be considered an "exotic" edifice. Cut by a transept, the nave is flanked on each side by two side aisles and a series of side chapels between abutments. Some of the numerous outbuildings (porches, sacristies, etc.) were constructed at the same time as the church, and others were added later. The lofty arcade rests on massive round piers, whose colonnettes and multiple projecting elements respond to the vault and arcade moldings. Above the arcade lies a balcony extending along the base of clerestory windows composed of four lancets beneath tracery; this richly decorated, Flamboyant balustrade reflects a taste for ornamentation typical of the Late Middle Ages in general and of this locality in particular. In fact, the balcony here functions as a kind of triforium, as it leads off in each bay to an exterior passage. The simple cross-ribbed vaults take on additional networks of ribs in the transept crossing and its neighboring vault fields. Created by Juan Gil de Hontañón in the early sixteenth century, this section of the vaulting is a masterpiece of Flamboyant design, an immense rose-shaped pattern of carved tracery covering vault fields and ribs alike. The tall, interpenetrating side aisles constitute vast spaces that complement the central area, and the overall effect is one of great fullness. The second side aisle opens to the outside through large windows, thereby distributing light throughout the interior. However, Seville remains faithful to the one invariable feature of Spanish Gothic architecture—the continuity of the wall. The interior structure is readable from the outside, where bold but nearly horizontal flying buttresses lean against the nave wall (shorter ones suport the side-aisle walls). A veritable forest of pinnacles surmounts the entire system of buttressing elements. The Cathedral of Seville is comparable to its near-contemporary at Milan, not in structure or interior spatial design, but in a mutual quest to surpass all previous endeavors in size and decorativeness.

Seville, however, was not the last Gothic cathedral to rise on Spanish soil. The one at Astorga, begun in 1477, was still under construction in 1559. Its traditional scheme of tall side aisles along a nave, flying buttresses, and star-vaulting also includes a magnificently decorated apse. The preference for Gothic persisted well beyond 1500. In 1497, work on the new Cathedral of Palencia—begun by a certain Francisco of Cologne—came under the direction of Rodrigo Gil de Hontañón. Here, prolific vault ornamentation is blended with certain features of northern European Late Gothic, such as the elimination of capitals below vault springings and the replacement of colonnettes by angular moldings. The new Cathedral of Salamanca was begun in 1513 under the direction of

Juan Gil de Hontañón. With the exception of the two classical façade domes and the transept crossing, this structure is Gothic in design and execution. Together with broad, spacious side aisles, the soaring height of the Cathedral not only creates an effect of impressive monumentality, but also endows the interior with harmonious proportions and ornamental richness. The piers and flying buttresses lining the gradated exterior mass are totally in keeping with the "national" flavor of preceding centuries. In 1526, the Cathedral of Segovia began to take shape under the same Juan Gil de Hontañón, who died shortly thereafter; it was completed in 1617, during the heyday of Flamboyant art. With its arcade, balcony, and clerestory, it is structurally analogous to Salamanca. The first stones of the choir were laid in 1562, a year that also witnessed the initial work on the Escorial. Although the structure of Segovia is strictly Gothic, it is interesting to note the use of round arches in the windows and the absence of Flamboyant tracery.

The dynamism of Spanish architecture during the fifteenth and sixteenth centuries was truly exceptional. This era also produced countless transept crossings crowned with richly decorated *cimborios*. The most celebrated of these is unquestionably the star-vaulted *cimborio* of the Cathedral of Burgos (1540-68), which lies atop a tambour covered with sculptures. In the Cathedral of Saragossa (1505-20), a sumptuous crossing tower is highlighted with a Mudejar-inspired network of ribs.

Alongside the *cimborios* should be placed the usually centrally planned funereal or votive chapels that were erected near main church buildings. Two of these chapels deserve special consideration. The Chapel of Álvaro de la Luna (1430-40) of the Cathedral of Toledo is probably the work of Hanequin de Bruxelles, a Flemish architect who grafted Flamboyant decoration to traditional Mudejar elements. The square plan is intersected at the corners by triangular vaults, yielding an octagonally shaped roof. Located in the apse of the Cathedral of Burgos, the Chapel of the Condestable Hernández de Velasco was possibly designed in 1492, but in any case remained incomplete until 1532. Even more grandiose than the Toledo chapel, its shape was transformed when a large octagon was added to the thirteenth-century structure. That this was the work of Simon of Cologne is borne out by the presence of elements clearly derived from the Rhineland and Flanders. Heraldic motifs dominate the luxurious decoration, which also reveals certain Renaissance traits.

The Church of San Juan de los Reyes at Toledo was erected in commemoration of the Battle of Toro (1476), a confrontation that opened the way for the conquest of Granada. By the time the city of Granada was captured in 1492, construction of the church (except for the choir) was already well under way. That this is a Franciscan edifice can be deduced from the traditional single nave lined with chapels between abutments. A magnificent *cimborio* rises above the transept crossing; and the intricately traceried vaults—except for those in the apse—mark a departure from

275. Burgos, Cathedral, Capilla
del Condestable.
276. Barcelona, Casa de la Ciudad,
detail.

277. Barcelona, La Lonja, interior.
278. Palma de Mallorca, La Lonja,
exterior.

the usual eight-ribbed star pattern. Here, as well as in the cloister and
convent halls, we are dealing with veritable *Netzgewölben* of northern
European Late Gothic. The carved decoration recalls the profuse style
peculiar to Toledo. Like the votive church at Batalha in Portugal, San
Juan de los Reyes exemplifies the new direction taken by the Christian
church at the end of the Middle Ages. There was no longer any trace of
Franciscan simplicity and poverty. Indeed, the mystical ideal symbolized
by thirteenth-century Gothic architecture was now displaced by a taste
for showy display geared toward overwhelming the observer. This
technical and artistic virtuosity, more befitting Renaissance than
medieval aesthetics, also characterizes the church of the Dominican convent at Ávila, Santo Tomás. Established in 1479 by a royal treasurer, it is
the burial site of the Infante Don Juan. The French church of Brou,
near Bourg-en-Bresse, also falls into this architectural category.

Since this phase of the evolution occurred during the reign of the
Catholic Kings, it has often been called Isabellan style after Isabella of
Castile, who ruled with her husband. Under the auspices of the Church
and of various municipalities, international contact was forested by the
contributions of architects from Flanders, France, and Germany. The
Frenchman Juan Guas was the chief architect of San Juan de los Reyes at
Toledo; the sculptor Gil Siloe of Antwerp also worked at Burgos; and
Simon of Cologne likewise brought his talents to Spain. Despite the
weight of Mudejar tradition and the fact that the plans were executed by
Spanish workmen, Burgundy, Flanders, and Normandy still managed to
leave their mark on Spain and Portugal. The most representative
specimens of this new stylistic modality are the remarkable Isabellan
façades: the Monastery of Santa Cruz at Segovia (1494) and, in
Valladolid, the College of San Gregorio (1487-96) and the Convent of
San Pablo (c. 1505). Resembling gigantic altarpieces, these works display
a degree of plastic creativity unmatched in France or Flanders. But we
should not lose sight of the fact that these façades were determined by
the same aesthetic responsible for the decoration of contemporary *cimborios* and commemorative chapels. The same abundance of ornamentation, often Mudejar-inspired, dominates the upper gallery of the cloister
of San Gregorio at Valladolid. As was often the case throughout
fifteenth-century Spain, France, Flanders, and central Europe, the columns and colonnettes here are twisted.

During the last years of the Middle Ages, both public and private civil
architecture continued to prosper, especially in Catalonia. The most
outstanding of these buildings within Barcelona is the Parliament
building or Generalidad (1416-25): a staircase adorns its luxurious courtyard, while the upper patio features finely worked arcades resting on
slender colonnettes. The molded and sculpted decoration of the façade
exploits to the fullest the resources of Flamboyant curvilinear tracery and
naturalistically carved figures or foliage. The other major civil edifice is

279. Alcobaça, Monastery of Santa
Maria, interior of the church.
280. Alcobaça, Monastery of Santa
Maria, cloister.

La Lonja, or the commodities exchange, at Palma de Mallorca. Created by the architect Guillermo Sagrera, it was begun in the early fifteenth century and completed in 1451. Instead of a tripled-nave space, the great rectangular hall may be considered a single volume supported along its center by six twisting piers that have neither bases nor capitals. This spatial unity is further ensured by the fact that the entire roof lies at the same level. Highlighted by cornices at mid-elevation and slender abutments, the sober exterior is enlivened by doors and windows filled with Flamboyant tracery. La Lonja at Valencia (1490-98), though similar in terms of interior effect—there are eight twisting piers in the great hall—is enveloped in a more complex exterior that lacks the stylistic rigor of the exchange at Palma de Mallorca.

At Valladolid and Salamanca, in western Spain, the fifteenth and sixteenth centuries saw the construction of ecclesiastical and university college buildings. We have already alluded to the Dominican College of San Gregorio at Valladolid (1488-96), whose façade, the most opulent creation in Isabellan architecture, is emblazoned with coats of arms above a triple ogee. The twisting columns supporting the porches of the cloister recall the piers in the Valencia and Palma exchanges. Begun in 1415, the construction of the University of Salamanca, slowly paced, was not concluded until the middle of the sixteenth century, subjected as it was to frequent modification. The city of Salamanca was rapidly becoming a center of Renaissance humanism, a development indicated by the mixture of Italianate and Gothic elements on the main entrance to the university. In addition, the great courtyard of the Escuelas Menores (c. 1500-33) is in the form of a cloister: its arcaded enclosure remained loyal to Mudejar and Gothic influences.

As in France, Flanders, and Germany, the early sixteenth century did not bring any significant stylistic changes to Spain. Founded in 1504, the funereal chapel of the Gothic Kings stands in the shadow of the mosque of Granada, itself later rebuilt according to sixteenth-century artistic standards. The richly carved Isabellan portal of the chapel opens to an interior whose effect is sober, the intricate starvaults overhead notwithstanding. So prolific was Christian building activity at Segovia, Plasencia, Saragossa, and the newly conquered cities of Málaga and Granada, that this period may truly be called the Golden Age of Spanish architecture. Even though certain forms peculiar to the Italian Renaissance did begin to appear with greater frequency—grotesqued pilasters, Corinthian capitals, classical entablatures, and humanist iconography—the structure of religious edifices, the proportions of their interior and exterior volumes, remained medieval in spirit. The new cathedrals of Saragossa (1490-1550) and Segovia (begun in 1525 by Juan Gil de Hontañón) and the two Andalusian cathedrals of Guadix and Granada—all are medieval in plan, but Renaissance or Baroque in decoration. In other words, they are traditional structures wrapped in a

skin of modern ornamentation. Although begun in 1510, the better part
of the Cathedral of Guadix took shape during the seventeenth and eighteenth centuries. Its space and proportions are offshoots of medieval
design, and the vaults (except for the "classical" dome atop the transept
crossing) are covered with Gothic tracery. Begun in 1523, the Cathedral
of Granada—situated next to the medieval tomb of the Catholic Kings,
the Capilla Real (1504-21)—imitated the plan of the Cathedral of Seville
and of thirteenth-century buildings. The *capilla mayor*, or choir, soars to a
height of almost 148 feet; it is Gothic in structure but decorated in the
Baroque manner. Unfinished until 1703, work on the central building
bears witness to the hardiness of the medieval system.

The Middle Ages did not prove to be as resistant when it came to civil
architecture. Such royal buildings of Charles V and Philip II as the palace
at Granada and the Escorial were heavily influenced by the Italian
aesthetic. In any event, the fifteenth and sixteenth centuries constituted
a period of magnificent construction by nobles and municipalities alike.
Included among the innumerable private dwellings are two palaces at
Salamanca, the Casa de las Conchas (1512) and the Casa de Álvarez
Abarca (after 1491). Though dependent on Moorish tradition, their
façades also reveal the "naturalism" peculiar to Late Gothic, a tendency
not unrelated to the exoticism of Portuguese art.

PORTUGAL

Gothic architecture entered Portugal by way of the Cistercians, whose
abbey at Alcobaça was founded in 1152 or 1159, under construction by
1178, and dedicated in 1223. Patterned after Burgundian models, it remains one of the best preserved and most impressive of Cistercian
monasteries. Historical events brought about numerous changes in the
monastery. It became a royal burial site under Peter I and was the final
resting place of Inés de Castro. But the abbey church was left untouched,
soaring to a height unprecedented in Early Gothic art. In this respect,
Alcobaça was far ahead of other thirteenth-century Portuguese structures. For instance, the Cathedral of Évora, though built after 1250, still
utilized Romanesque building techniques: the nave, covered with pointed
barrel vaults, is buttressed by the side-aisle galleries.

As in Spain and the rest of Europe, the fourteenth century was a
period of accelerated activity on the part of the Dominicans, Franciscans,
and the Order of Saint Clare. One of the oldest buildings from this
period is Santa Clara at Coimbra, begun at the end of the thirteenth century. The two most important churches in Portugal, those of the
Dominicans and Franciscans at Lisbon, were almost completely destroyed
by the 1755 earthquake. Santa Clara at Santarém, with its simply molded
naves, is remarkable for its graceful proportions and sober effect.
However, the fourteenth century's undisputed masterpiece is the
Dominican Church of Santa Maria de Vitória at Batalha. The victory

commemorated by this church—the Battle of Aljubarrota (1385)—set in motion the re-establishment of Portuguese independence and the ascendance of the Aviz dynasty. Begun in 1388 by a Portuguese architect, Alfonso Domingues, Batalha was a royal edifice, the burial site of John I and his successors.

It appears that the conventual church was originally planned according to the hall-church principle, that is, three naves of equal height. But in the second quarter of the fifteenth century, the second architect, Onguete or Huguet, raised the level of the central nave, which not only permitted direct lighting, but also gave the structure an impressive verticality. One of the original aspects of this church is the rigorous Dominican-style sobriety of the molding and decoration. The fifteenth-century addition of exterior funereal chapels and three cloisters make Batalha the most representative work in Portuguese Gothic architecture, and one of the most inspired of the entire Middle Ages. The chapel of its founder, John I, completed in 1434, is a large square beneath a lantern tower supported by columns. Shortly afterward, his successor, Edward, chose the eastern end of the church as the site for an immense, luxuriously decorated funereal rotunda surrounded by apsidal chapels. In the last years of the fifteenth century, Manuel the Great resumed work on this project in the superabundant Manueline style that bears his name, but soon abandoned it in order to build the Convent of Belém. The rotunda was never completed, and therefore it bears the name Capellas Imparfaitas.

The Abbey of the Hieronymites at Belém, erected near the port entrance that saw ships set sail for the New World, stands on the site of a chapel founded in 1460 by Henry the Navigator. Construction began in 1502 and continued until 1572. We are fairly certain that, until 1517, work on the church was guided by Boytac, an architect who had already made contributions to Batalha and Coimbra. Needless to say, Belém is a Manueline masterpiece. But this style is more than just the Portuguese counterpart of Spanish Isabellan or a variant of the last phase of Flamboyant art. Its profusion of ornamental motifs also points to a tendency toward the exotic, an evolution stimulated by discoveries in America and the subsequent establishment of a Portuguese colonial empire in the mid-fifteenth century. It is interesting to note that the Mudejar elements so prevalent in Spain were to play virtually no part in Portuguese Gothic art. The Manueline style preferred to concentrate on highly elaborate naturalistic motifs—shellfish, plants, vines, and fantastic fauna. The prodigious creativity of this decoration surpassed even the excesses of Late Gothic in France, Flanders, and Germany. After 1520, especially after the arrival of the Spanish architect Joao de Castillo at Belém, the Portuguese aesthetic became blended with the ornamental Italianate style to the point that Manueline art lost its separate identity within a few decades.

To what extent was late-fifteenth- and early-sixteenth-century Manueline art dominated by the personality of Boytac (or Boitac), the first architect of Belém, who was possibly of French origin? From the structural point of view, he had little to add to previous efforts. Begun at the eastern extremity (later modified), the Church of Belém is a hall church composed of three equally tall naves; their intricately ribbed vaults are supported by slender polygonal piers. The unusually opulent cloister in the Abbey of the Hieronymites makes use of Gothic structural techniques—for instance, the flattened arches peculiar to International Gothic of 1500. After 1550, a third architect, Diego de Torralva, rebuilt the choir of the Church of Belém in the Italian manner. Along with this masterwork of Manueline style, we must not omit the decoration on the Church and Convent of Christ at Tomar (by Joao de Castillo) and the famous tower at the entrance of Belém, erected opposite the monastery between 1515 and 1520. The significance of Portuguese architecture of about 1500 does not derive from its influence—which was, in fact, quite limited—but from its intrinsic features. Its innovativeness notwithstanding, this style has been categorized with other variants considered part of the Late Gothic or, as it is sometimes called, Baroque phase. It is decoration, not structure or spatial concept, that lies at the heart of Portuguese Late Gothic. In terms of historical or spiritual meaning, it set itself apart from the architectural mainstream, evolving as an offshoot of Gothic that specialized in picturesque decorativeness and formal virtuosity.

284. *Batalha, Santa Maria de Vitória, exterior.*
285. *Belém (Lisbon), Abbey of the Hieronymites, cloister.*

286. *Belém (Lisbon), Tower of Belém.*

FRENCH ARCHITECTURE IN THE LATE MIDDLE AGES

In seems only right to conclude a study of Gothic architecture by considering its status in France during the Late Middle Ages. After all, this is where Gothic was born and the point from which it was disseminated throughout the West. The great models of previous generations—especially those of the thirteenth century—gave rise to a formal continuity that can be more clearly observed in France than in countries that had only passively received the Gothic aesthetic. Consequently, France provides a more readable framework of successive stylistic phases, of technical and formal evolutionary patterns, than any other region in Europe. For example, it is important to note that the great Parisian Church of Saint-Eustache, designed in the sixteenth century, was modeled after the twelfth-century plan of Notre-Dame at Paris, and that the Cathedral of Orléans, destroyed by fire in 1568 during the wars of religion, was gradually rebuilt in accordance with Gothic tradition until 1829. Finally, civil and public architecture, which played so crucial a role in the overall evolution of function and form after the late 1200s, has yet to receive adequate consideration.

Born in the mid-thirteenth century at the Cathedral of Troyes and the Abbey Church of Saint-Denis, French Rayonnant architecture attained a high degree of formal and technical sophistication between 1240 and 1265 in Sainte-Chapelle and in Saint-Urbain at Troyes. Although it subsequently spread beyond the *domaine royal* into northern and southern France, it also catalyzed the English, Germanic, Italian, and Spanish "resistance movements" already discussed above. In a way, the years 1270-80 marked a similar reaction in southern France as well. However, we should remember that, during the last quarter of the thirteenth century and the first half of the fourteenth, post-Rayonnant architecture grew almost academic in its invariability. Dehio calls this the era of Dogmatic Gothic.

The thirteenth century saw the continuation of projects begun during the years 1240-60: the apse of Notre-Dame at Paris was being rebuilt, as was the Cathedral of Beauvais after the collapse of the apse vaulting in 1284. The ongoing work at the cathedrals of Jean Deschamps, Clermont-Ferrand and Limoges, remained stylistically faithful to the original plans. This was also the case of the Cathedral of Évreux (begun c. 1260, choir completed c. 1320, then modified), as well as the cathedrals of Narbonne (choir 1272-1332), Toulouse (1282 to the mid-fourteenth century), Rodez (begun 1276-77), and Bordeaux (choir c. 1280-1332). A certain number of new buildings begun about 1300 added little to either the structural principles or formal characteristics of thirteenth-century Rayonnant art: witness the Abbey Church of Évron, at the edge of Brittany and Normandy. Other rebuilding efforts attest to the academic conservatism of Gothic at this time: the choir of the Abbey Church of La Trinité at Vendôme (begun 1306); the choir of the Cathedral of Nevers (begun 1308); and the Abbey Church of Saint-Ouen at Rouen (begun 1318). Essentially traditional in plan, these structures include numerous side chapels that help broaden the nave. The three-storied elevation was usually retained, with a maximum hollowing out of the wall from floor to vault. Moreover, the perforated triforium grew quite tall and was often integrated into the clerestory windows. However, the overall effect is quite different from that experienced in thirteenth-century churches. For one thing, vividly colored stained glass was replaced almost everywhere with panes of glass in *grisaille*; sections that were to remain colored took on glass of a lighter, discontinuous hue. The resulting flood of bright illumination is augmented by a less towering elevation that brings the light source closer to the ground. Formal enrichment is especially evident in the varied and sophisticated perforation of tracery, either openwork or against the walls. In other words, the immense, impressive, "fantastic" interior space so dear to the architects of High Gothic structures now gave way to transparency, to the "dematerialization" of volumes through light. Outside, ornamental gables, tracery, and rose windows, covering façade and wall alike, blended harmoniously with the decorative window partitions. Strictly speaking, none of these forms were wholly original; they were all invented about 1250 in the Île-de-France. But this style took a finite repertory of forms and systematically produced an infinite number of variations.

The less ambitious, less grandiose mendicant-order structures were, of course, still being built, but only a few northern French specimens have survived. Their general contours remain quite refined even in the case of those churches built in the so-called Severe Style of the fifteenth century (the Church of Saint-Satur on the Loire, Saint-Pourçain-sur-Sioule in the Auvergne, Redon in Brittany, and the Old Cathedral of Uzeste in the Gironde). To the south, architecture in Languedoc and French Catalonia is distinguishable by the use of brick, the traditional emphasis on wall surface, and a preference for the single-nave plan. Next, a simplified version of the northern French cathedral appeared rather frequently in eastern France and the Rhône Valley. In this third type of church, the absence of an ambulatory allows the apse to take on windows that begin near the floor, climbing upward to fill the entire elevation with glass. We have already seen that this *Hochchor* principle yielded marvelous results during the thirteenth century: for instance, the Cathedral of Toul, begun in 1221 but not completed until the fifteenth century. It was a scheme often exploited by the Dominicans in Germanic countries as well as in Italy and France, as at Saint-Maximin in the Var district. In addition, it was adapted to smaller churches, such as Saint-Urbain at Troyes and Saint-Thibaut, and produced fourteenth-century examples at Vermenton, Mussy-sur-Seine, and the charming Church of Tour-en-Bessin in Normandy.

As of 1340, building activity slowed down considerably and nearly

287. *Vendôme, Abbey Church of La Trinité, choir.*

288. *Rouen, Saint-Ouen, choir.*

came to a halt during the darkest decades of the Hundred Years War. A great many projects were abandoned until the fifteenth century. Perhaps this is the reason why, when compared to the dynamic evolution of Germanic, Italian, and Spanish architecture, fourteenth-century Rayonnant strikes us as being static and traditional. But this decline in France should not be exaggerated. In the area of castles and palaces erected for the nobility, construction not only continued, but also did so with distinction. As a matter of fact, it was during this period—not the thirteenth century—that the château took its rightful place of honor in art history. The previously all-important defensive function of the castle now donned an outer layer of luxury and pomp. The Château-Gaillard, Coucy, and the bastions of Carcassonne are masterpieces of military art; their design reappeared in such fourteenth- and fifteenth-century fortresses as Murols, Vincennes, and Sully-sur-Loire. At the same time, residences were being built on the order of those in Italy, in which defense was relegated to a secondary consideration. Chief among these is the one located in the city that was ceded to the papacy—the Palais des Papes at Avignon. Built in a series of increasingly ambitious campaigns under Benedict XII, Clement VI, and their successors, this stronghold consists of a complex network of meeting rooms, chapels, and apartments grouped around inner courtyards. Whether it be the audience room or the Chapel of Clement VI, interior volumes are spacious and filled with paintings. Numerous other residence castles were established by the papacy: those in the *domaine royal*, now demolished or poorly preserved, rivaled the Avignon residence in aesthetic splendor. Although the Louvre of Charles V is no longer extant, we know that it was studded with a wealth of sculptures and paintings. All that remains of the residences of Jean de Berry are the great hall of his château at Bourges and the ruins at Mehun-sur-Yèvre. But we are familiar with the latter's fantastically decorated towers and turrets from early-fifteenth-century illuminated manuscripts (e.g. *Les Très Riches Heures du Duc de Berry*). The great hall of what is today the Palais de Justice at Poitiers (1384-86) illustrates the care with which contours and decorations were arranged in the dwellings of the nobility. The fortified castles of the generation of 1400 mark a new stage in this movement toward opulence. The château built for Louis d'Orléans, Pierrefonds, was reconstructed somewhat excessively by Viollet-le-Duc. Aside from ingenious military installations, it also features living quarters in the donjon and reception rooms, servants' quarters, and a chapel around the perimeter of the Courtyard. As at La Ferté-Milon—a castle built at the same time for the same nobleman—sculptures were placed in exterior niches as a sign of the building's political significance. In short, fourteenth-century castles were shedding their defensive armor and becoming increasingly residential, as indicated by the use of immense windows to provide as much illumination as possible. The models cited above inspired similar ventures at Saumur and at

Tarascon, the latter rebuilt for René d'Anjou. The introduction and subsequent spread of firearms during the fifteenth century reoriented the fortified castle in the direction of the bastioned fortress. After adapting to these new exigencies of combat, the castle as dual-purpose fortress-residence eventually disappeared.

Urban construction in France and Flanders experienced the same surge of development that was occurring in Italy and Spain. City residences were built for nobles (the château of the dukes of Brittany at Nantes), wealthy merchants and professionals (the famous house of Jacques Coeur at Bourges, 1443-51), and bishops or abbots (the Parisian *hôtels* of the abbots of Cluny and the archbishops of Sens). New emphasis was placed on carved exterior decoration, frames around windows and doors, and dormer windows adorned with openwork gables. However, at least in France, little value was given to orderly alignments, well-balanced masses, or plans aimed at creating agreeable perspectives. In most cases, the façade is asymmetrical, and openings are arranged to suit both the interior scheme and the irregularities of the urban landscape. Among the most important of these are the municipal buildings erected in northern French and Flemish towns during the Late Middle Ages. Communities incorporated into free cities now felt the need to display their wealth and civic pride in the form of city halls and commercial structures that would rival religious buildings in size and opulence. The municipal tower became, literally and figuratively, the high point of the town. Although the oldest Flemish municipal buildings date as far back as the thirteenth century, the most luxurious specimens were built during the fourteenth, fifteenth, and sixteenth centuries. The tower at Bruges, though begun in the late thirteenth century, was enlarged and decorated in the fourteenth, while its city hall (1376-1420) served as a prototype for an entire group of similar fifteenth- and sixteenth-century buildings. Of those at Ghent, Louvain, and Brussels, it is especially the last that, despite restoration, suggests most accurately the urban atmosphere of the Late Middle Ages.

It is customary to affix the label Flamboyant to the last medieval phase as soon as decorative elements—above all, window tracery— became the center of attention. From the same analytical approach emerges the conclusion that the most revealing aspect of the style is the use of the ogee, with its curves and countercurves. The ogee is a natural descendant of Rayonnant contours: it was frequently used during the fourteenth century in both England (Lady Chapel at Ely Cathedral, c. 1340) and France (palace at Poitiers, 1380-84). By the early fifteenth century, the ogee, though grown more complex, retained the general Rayonnant outlines. These nonessential elements have always been assigned a key role in the definition of Flamboyant; perhaps it is because they give the style its quality of movement or motion. This same dynamism can be seen in pier torsion or in networks of vertical moldings that sprout from pier to vault without being interrupted by capitals (Saint-Séverin at Paris after 1489).

This emphasis on the dynamic has been called a Baroque phenomenon, an interpretation that, historically speaking, sees Baroque as the immediate successor to Rayonnant Mannerism.

Another set of frequently proposed observations concerns the realism of late-medieval decoration. Actually, the architectural application of foliage copied from nature or of animals intertwined with decorative elements already existed in the thirteenth century and continued to appear in various forms throughout the Gothic era. During the fifteenth century, however, the trend toward realism crystallized into even more specific forms (fruits, such vegetables as kale, tree branches, etc.), and the representations of monstrous creatures acquired a frenzied appearance. Portraits of donors or patrons that were painted on portals (as at the Charterhouse of Champmol at Dijon, c. 1400) show new concern for a faithful rendering of particular human features. In the *hôtel* of Jacques Coeur, busts gaze at the observer from the sills of false windows. The realism of fifteenth-century painting and sculpture is echoed in their architectural framework.

These are, however, only superficial matters. Of greater import are questions of architectonics—form and function. A great many Gothic techniques that had originally played a structural role now lost their functionality. For example, the gable, previously used to weight the extrados of arches, evolved unchecked into a purely decorative openwork motif, taking on horizontal fillets. Granted, the Rayonnant period has seen the gable "lightened" through subdivision, but the fifteenth century witnessed its metamorphosis into almost perverse fantasy (consider the façade of Saint-Maclou at Rouen and Notre-Dame at Louviers). The articulation of interior piers underwent the same kind of transformation. In the early days of Gothic architecture, colonnettes engaged in the pier gave additional support to arches and vaults. In the thirteenth and fourteenth centuries, this function became more readable even as it grew more illusory. The Flamboyant style then freely—sometimes irrationally—arranged the vertical elements of pier molding around the base: moldings could now be twisted about the pier, or removed from the surface altogether. Vaults were subjected to a similar process. We have already examined how, especially in thirteenth-century England, ribs were no longer arranged to ease the structural difficulties of vaulting or to create a spatial rhythm. In the fifteenth century, Germanic net-vaults began to appear in France as flat, highly ornate star-vaults with pendant bosses: consider the Chapelle du Saint-Esprit at Rue, begun 1480 or Caudebec-en-Caux. To look at these vaults, one would think that the architects, in their quest for pure ornamentality, tried at all costs to avoid the slightest hint of functionalism. It was not uncommon for vault components to become blended into the masonry, thus creating a formal contrast between the articulated roofing and the unarticulated support. For such scholars as Focillon, this antifunctionalism is one of the hallmarks of Baroque.

Flamboyant art proposed a variety of solutions to the problems of volume and space. One of the most beautiful of these arrangements was to unify interior space according to the hall-church principle, using naves of equal or near-equal height. Though rare in French-speaking regions, this scheme did appear in the north and east, especially in Champagne churches with low vaulting. But the heart of France preferred a different structural path: the side aisles and lower story were used as a base for a taller nave of clearly defined proportions and spatial limits. At times the triforium was eliminated to create a bare wall surface between the arcade and the clerestory, resulting in a two-storied elevation. This was far from an inferior solution. At the royal Church of Notre-Dame at Cléry (1429-83), the bold lines of arcade and clerestory alike lend an authority to the interior volumes that is echoed in several late-fifteenth-century Parisian churches—Saint-Gervais (1494-1508), Saint-Étienne-du-Mont (after 1494), and, in Lorraine, Saint-Nicolas-de-Port, built between 1514 and 1541. A typical example of the short elevation is the Collegiate Church (now the Cathedral) of Moulins, begun in 1468 for the dukes of Bourbon. In Normandy, the traditional elevation was retained, including a tall triforium fused into the dividing elements or apertures of the upper windows. Such is the case of the great Norman masterpiece Saint-Maclou at Rouen (1436-1520), Caudebec-en-Caux (after 1406), and the impressive choir in the Abbey Church of Mont-Saint-Michel, begun in 1446.

Situated at the summit of an enormous rock, the astounding Mont-Saint-Michel dwarfs the surrounding eleventh-, thirteenth-, and fourteenth-century monastic buildings. Outside, a forceful arrangement of numerous flying buttresses brings to mind the spatial effect experienced at thirteenth-century cathedrals. Outstanding though this monument may be, it does not stand alone, for this was the era of resumed projects, of renewed construction following the Hundred Years War. Among these must be included the Cathedral of Nantes (begun in 1434), Saint-Pol-de-Léon (begun in 1429), and Saint-Vulfran at Abbeville (after 1488). Certain regions displayed extraordinary vigor; one might say that Normandy and Champagne took on an entirely new architectural tenor between the mid-fourteenth and the mid-sixteenth century. Once-abandoned churches were now completed in accordance with the dictates of the new style: rich screens of decoration were applied as façades to older naves (the cathedrals of Rouen, Évreux, Tours, and Toul). The south transept of the Cathedral of Sens, the transept of the unfinished Cathedral of Beauvais, and the west façade of the Cathedral of Troyes were some of the projects under the guidance of Martin Chambiges (architect of the Old City Hall of Paris) from 1494 until well into the sixteenth century. The first signs of the Italian Renaissance appeared in his work after 1510.

By this time, Italianate decoration was already making its way into France via Normandy, Lyons, and the southern part of the country. But French religious architecture held fast to Gothic principles of plan, eleva-

296. Rue, Chapelle du Saint-Esprit, vaults.

297. Saint-Nicolas-de-Port, Church, nave.

298. Mont-Saint-Michel, general view.

298. Mont-Saint-Michel, general view.

299. Mont-Saint-Michel, Abbey Church, choir.

299. Mont-Saint-Michel, Abbey Church, choir.

tion, and spatial configuration during most of the sixteenth century. A noteworthy example is the funereal church at Brou, near Bourg-en-Bresse (1513-32). The tombs of Philibert of Savoy and Margaret of Austria are children of the northern Renaissance, but the structure that houses them is a pure expression of Flamboyant Gothic.

In France, as in Germany or in Spain, this stubborn resistance to new aesthetic trends shows the remarkable vitality of Gothic architecture during the Late Middle Ages. Building activity was given new impetus by perfected techniques of construction and by innovative methods of working stone. Although we have used the term *realism* in our discussion of this style, we must also appreciate its capacity to suggest the fantastic, the irrational, even the unreal. The stylistic means may have differed from those used in the thirteenth century, but the goal remained the same: to create temples whose mystical essence would set them apart from the dwellings of humankind. With this principle as its unshakable foundation, Gothic architecture spawned technical, spatial, and formal innovations with a vigor unknown to preceding and subsequent generations alike. For at no other time did religious architecture serve to such a degree as the aesthetic and material focal point of society.

SELECTED BIBLIOGRAPHY

MANUALS AND GENERAL WORKS

AUBERT M., SCHMOLL GEN. EISENWERTH J.A., HOFSTÄTTER H.H., *Le gothique à son apogée*, Paris, 1964 (It. ed. *Il trionfo del gotico*, Milan, 1964).

BIAOSTOCKI J., *Spätmittelalter und Beginnende Neuzeit* (Propyläen Kunstgeschichte), Berlin, 1972.

BOCK H., *Der decorated Style*, Heidelberg, 1962.

BRANNER R., *Gothic architecture*, New York, 1961 (It. ed. *L'architettura gotica*, Milan, 1963).

BRAUNFELS W., *Abendländische Klosterbaukunst*, Cologne, 1969.

BRUTAILS J.A., *Précis d'archéologie du moyen-âge*, 3d ed., Toulouse, 1936.

CHOISY A., *Histoire de l'architecture*, vol. II, Paris, 1899.

CLASEN K.H., *Baukunst des Mittelalters*, vol. II: *Die gotische Baukunst*, Wildpark / Potsdam, 1930.

DEHIO G., VON BEZOLD G., *Die kirchliche Baukunst des Abendlandes, historisch und systematisch dargestellt*, 2 vols. text and 5 vols. plates, Stuttgart / Hildesheim, 1892-1901. Reissued, Hildesheim, 1969.

DEUCHLER F., *Gotik*, Stuttgart, 1970.

DIMIER A., *Recueil de plans d'églises cisterciennes*, Grignan / Paris, 1949. *Supplément*, Grignan / Paris, 1967.

FISCHER F.W., TIMMERS J.J.M., SCHMOLL J.A., *Spätgotik. Zwischen Mystik und Reformation*, Zürich, 1971.

FOCILLON H., *Art d'occident, le moyen-âge roman et gothique*, Paris, 1938.

FOCILLON H., *The Art of the West in the Middle Ages*, vol. II, Gothic Art, London, 1963 (It. ed. *L'arte dell'Occidente*, Turin, 1965).

FRANKL P., *Baukunst des Mittelalters. Die frühmittelalterliche und romanische Baukunst*, Wildpark / Potsdam, 1926.

FRANKL P., *Gothic architecture* (Pelican History of Art), Harmondsworth, 1962.

FRANZ H.G., *Spätromanik und Frühgotik*, Baden-Baden / Halle, 1969.

FRISCH T.G., *Gothic art, 1140-1450: sources and documents*, Englewood Cliffs / Hemel Hemstead, 1971.

GÖTZ W., *Zentralbau und Zentralbautendenz in der gotischen Architektur*, Berlin, 1968.

GROSS W., *Gotik und Spätgotik. Ein Umschaubildsachbuch*, Frankfurt, 1969.

HARVEY J.H., *The gothic world, 1100-1600. A survey of architecture and art*, London / New York / Toronto, 1950.

KARLINGER H., *Die Kunst der Gotik* (Propyläen Kunstgeschichte), Berlin, 1927.

KING T.H., *The study-book of mediaeval Architecture and Art*, London, 1868, 4 vols.

KINGSLEY-PORTER A., *Mediaeval Architecture, its origins and development*, vol. II, New York, 1909.

KUBACH H.E., *Architettura romanica*, Milan, 1972.

LAMBERT E., *L'architecture des templiers*, Paris, 1955.

MARTINDALE A., *Gothic Art from the Twelfth to the Fifteenth Centuries*, New York, 1967.

PIJOÁN J., *Arte gótico de la Europa occidental, siglos XIII, XIV y XV*, Madrid, 1971.

ROSE H. *Die Baukunst der Zisterzienser*, Munich, 1916.

SALET F., *L'art gothique*, Paris, 1963.

VON SIMSON O., *Das Mittelalter II. Das hohe Mittelalter* (Propyläen Kunstgeschichte), Berlin, 1972.

TECHNICAL AND FORMAL PROBLEMS

ABRAHAM P., *Viollet-le-Duc et le rationalisme médiéval*, Paris, 1934.

AUBERT M., *La construction au moyen-âge*, in "Bulletin Monumental," CXVIII, 1960, pp. 241-259, and CXIX, 1961, pp. 7-42, 81-120, 181-209, 297-323.

BALTRUŠAITIS J., *Le problème de l'ogive et l'Arménie*, Paris, 1936.

BEHLING L., *Gestalt und Geschichte des Masswerks*, Halle, 1944.

BILSON J., *The Beginnings of Gothic Architecture: Norman Vaulting in England*, in "Journal of the Royal Institute of British Architects," VI, 1899, pp. 259-269, 289-319.

BILSON J., *Les origines de l'architecture gothique, les premières croisées d'ogives en Angleterre*, in "Revue de l'art chrétien," vol. 12, 1901, pp. 365-393, 463-480.

BONY J., *La technique normande du mur épais à l'époque romane*, in "Bulletin Monumental," 1939, pp. 153-188.

BUCHER F., *Design in Gothic Architecture. A preliminary assessment*, in "Journal of the Society of Architectural Historians," vol. 27, 1968, pp. 49-71.

CAUMONT A., DE, *Courts d'antiquités monumentales*, Paris, 1830-1841.

CAUMONT A., DE, *Abécédaire ou rudiments d'archéologie*, Caen, 1859.

DEHIO G., *Untersuchungen über das gleichseitige Dreieck also Norm gotischer Bauproportionen*, Stuttgart, 1894.

FITCHEN J., *The construction of Gothic cathedrals: a study of mediaeval vault erection*, Oxford, 1961.

FOCILLON H., *Le problème de l'ogive*, in "Recherche," no. 1, 1939, pp. 5-28.

FRANKL P., *The Secret of Mediaeval Masons*, in "Art Bulletin," XXVII, 1945.

FRANKL P., *The "crazy" vaults of Lincoln Cathedral*, in "Art Bulletin," XXXV, 1953, pp. 95-107.

GALL E., *Niederrheinische und normännische Architektur im Zeitalter der Frühgotik*, Berlin, 1915, 2 vols.

HELIOT P., *Les origines et les débuts de l'abside vitrée du XI au XIII siècle*, in "Wallraf Richartz Jahrbuch," vol. 30, 1968, pp. 89-127.

KINGSLEY-PORTER A., *Construction of gothic and lombard vaults*, New Haven, 1911.

KUBACH H. E., *Das Triforium. Ein Beitrag zur kunstgeschichtlichen Raumkunde Europas im Mittelalter*, in "Zeitschrift für Kunstgeschichte," vol. 5, 1936, 275 ff.

KUBLER G., *A late Gothic Computation of Rib Vault Thrusts*, in "Gazette des Beaux-Arts," XXVI, 1944, pp. 135-148.

LAMBERT E., *La croisée d'ogives dans l'architecture islamique*, in "Recherche," I, 1939, pp. 57-71.

LUNDBERG E., *Arkitecturens Formsprak*, vol. IV, Stockholm, 1950.

REINHARDT H., *Die Entwicklung der gotischen Travée*, in "Gedenkschrift Ernst Gall," 1965, pp. 123-142.

SAINT-PAUL A., *Viollet-le-Duc, ses travaux d'art et son système archéologique*, Paris, 1881.

UEBERWASSER W., *Spätgotische Baugeometrie*, in "Jahresbericht der öffentlichen Kunstsammlung Basilea," new series 25-27, 1928-1930, pp. 79-122.

UEBERWASSER W., *Nach rechten Mass*, in "Jahrbuch der Preussischen Kunstsammlungen," LVI, 1935, pp. 250-272.

VELTE M., *Die Anwendung der Quadratur und Triangulatur bei Grund- und Aufrissgestaltung der gotischen Kirchen* (Basler Studien zur Kunstgeschichte), Basel, 1951.

VIOLLET-LE-DUC E., *Dictionnaire raisonné de l'architecture française du XI au XVI siècle*, Paris, 1858-1868, 10 vols.

VIOLLET-LE-DUC E., *Entretiens sur l'architecture*, Paris, 1863-1879, 3 vols.

WARD C., *Medieval Church Vaulting*, London, 1915.

WILLIS R., *Architectured Nomenclature of the Middle Ages*, Cambridge, 1844.

DOCTRINES AND INTERPRETATIONS

BANDMANN G., *Mittelalterliche Architektur als Bedeutungsträger*, Berlin, 1951.

BRANNER R., *Gothic architecture 1160-1180 and its Romanesque sources*, in "Studies in Western Art" (XXth Intern. Congr. Hist. Art), New York, 1961, vol. I, pp. 92-104.

BRUYNE E., de, *Etudes d'esthétique médiévale*, Bruges, 1946.

DEHIO G., *Die Anfänge des gotischen Baustils*, in "Repertorium für Kunstwissenschaft," 1896, pp. 169-185.

DVORÁK M., *Idealismus und Naturalismus in der gotischen Skulptur und Malerei*, Munich/Berlin, 1918.

ENLART C., *Origine anglaise du style gothique flamboyant*, in "Bulletin

Monumental," vol. 70, 1906, pp. 38-81, and vol. 74, 1910, pp. 125-147.

FRANKL P., *Der Beginn der Gotik und das allgemeine Problem des Stilbeginns*, in "Festschrift Heinrich Wölfflin," Munich, 1924, p. 107 ff.

FRANKL P., *The Gothic: literary sources and interpretations through eight centuries*, Princeton, 1960.

GALL. E., *Neue Beiträge zur Geschichte vom "Werden der Gotik,"* in "Monatshefte für Kunstwissenschaft," IV, 1911, pp. 309-323.

GRODECKI L., *Le vitrail et l'architecture au XII et au XIII siècles*, in "Gazette des Beaux-Arts," 2, 1949, pp. 5-24.

GROSS W., *Die Hochgotik im deutschen Kirchenbau*, in "Marburger Jahrbuch für Kunstwissenschaft," 7, 1933, pp. 290-346.

GROSS W., *Die abendländische Architektur um 1300*, Stuttgart, 1948.

GROSS W., *Zur Bedeutung des Räumlichen in der mittelalterlichen Architektur*, in "Beiträge zur Kunst des Mittelalters," Berlin, 1950, p. 84 ff.

JANTZEN H., *Über den gotischen Kirchenraum*, Freiburg-im-Breisgau, 1927.

JANTZEN H., *Über den gotischen Kirchenraum und andere Aufsätze*, Berlin, 1951.

JANTZEN H., *Die Gotik des Abendlandes, Idea und Wandel*, Cologne, 1962.

LÓPEZ R. S., *Economie et architecture médiévale*, in "Annales d'Histoire économique et sociale," 1952, October-December.

MERTENS F., *Die Baukunst des Mittelalters, Geschichte der Studien über diesen Gegenstand, Berlin, 1850.*

PANOFSKY E., *Gothic architecture and scholasticism*, Latrobe, 1951.

SAUER J., *Die Symbolik des Kirchengebäudes und seiner Ausstattung in der Auffassung des Mittelalters*, Freiburg-im-Breisgau, 1st ed. 1902, 2nd ed. 1924.

SEDLMAYR H., *Die Entstehung der Kathedrale*, Zürich, 1950.

VON SIMSON O., *The gothic cathedral, origins of gothic architecture and the medieval concept of order*, London, 1956.

WORRINGER W., *Formprobleme der Gotik*, Munich, 1911.

ARCHITECTS

AUBERT M., *Pierre de Montreuil*, in "Festschrift K. M. Swoboda," Vienna/Wiesbaden, 1959, pp. 19-21.

BOOZ P., *Der Baumeister der Gotik* (Kunstwissenschaftliche Studien), Berlin, 1956.

BOWIE T., *The sketchbook of Villard de Honnecourt*, Bloomington/London, 1959.

BRANNER R., *Villard de Honnecourt, Reims and the origin of Gothic architectural drawing*, in "Gazette des Beaux-Arts," LXI, 1963, pp. 129-146.

COLOMBIER P., du, *Les chantiers des cathédrales*, Paris, 1973.

GIMPEL J., *Les bâtisseurs de cathédrales*, Paris, 1958.

GRAF H., *Opus francigenum*, Stuttgart, 1878.

HAHNLOSER H.R., *Villard de Honnecourt, Kritische Gesamtausgabe des Bauhüttenbusches ms fr. 19093 der Pariser Nationalbibliothek*, 1st ed. Vienna, 1935, 2nd ed. Graz, 1972.

HARVEY J.H., *Henry Yevele, c. 1320 to 1400. The life of an English architect*, London, 1944.

HARVEY J.H., *The master builders; architecture in the Middle Ages*,

New York, 1971.

HARVEY J.H., *The medieval architect*, London, 1972.

HARVEY J.H., OSWALD A., *English medieval architects. A biographical dictionary down to 1550*, London, 1954.

KLETZL O., *Planfragmente aus der deutschen Dombauhütte von Prag in Stuttgart und Ulm*, Stuttgart, 1939.

KLETZL O., *Peter Parler, der Dombaumeister zu Prag*, Leipzig, 1940.

KNOOP D., JONES G.P., *The Mediaeval Mason. An Economic History of Stone Building in the Later Middle Ages and Early Modern Times*, Manchester/New York, 1967.

KOEPF H., *Die gotischen Planrisse der Wiener Sammlungen*, Vienna / Cologne / Graz, 1969.

MORTET V., DESCHAMPS P., *Recueil de textes relatifs à l'histoire de l'architecture et à la condition des architectes en France an moyen-âge, XII-XIII siècles*, Paris, 1911-1929, 2 vols.

SIEBENHÜNER R., *Deutsche Künstler am Mailänder Dom*, Monaco, 1944 (It. ed. *Il Duomo di Milano e gli artisti tedeschi*, Milan, 1945).

SWOBODA K.M., *Peter Parler, der Bankünstler und Bildhauer*, Vienna, 1940.

FRANCE (excluding Alsace)

ADENAUER H., *Die Kathedrale von Laon*, Düsseldorf, 1934.

ANFRAY M., *La cathédrale de Nevers et les églises gothiques du Nivernais, Paris, 1964.*

AUBERT M., *L'architecture cistercienne en France*, Paris, 1943, 2 vols.

AUBERT M., *Notre Dame de Paris, sa place dans l'histoire de l'architec-*

ture du XIIème au XIVème siècle, Paris, 1909.

AUBERT M., Monographie de la cathédrale de Senlis, Senlis, 1910.

AUBERT M., VERRIER J., L'architecture française à l'époque gothique, Paris, 1943.

BARNES C.F., The Cathedral of Chartres and the architect of Soissons, in "Journal of the Society of Architectural Historians," XXII, 1963, pp. 63-74.

BAUDOT A., DE, PERRAULT-DABOT A., Les cathédrales de France, Paris, n.d., 2 vols.

BEGULE L., Monographie de la cathédrale de Lyon, Lyons, 1880.

BILSON J., Les voûtes d'ogives de Morienval, in "Bulletin Monumental," LXXII, 1908, pp. 484-510.

BONNENFANT G., Notre-Dame d'Evreux, Paris, 1939.

BONY J., La collégiale de Mantes, in "Congrès archéologique Paris-Mantes," CIV, 1946, pp. 163-220.

BONY J., The resistance to Chartres in early thirteenth century architecture, in "Journal of the British Archeological Association," XX-XXI, 1957-1958, pp. 35-52.

BONY J., MEYER P., Cathédrales gothiques en France, Paris, 1954.

BRANNER R., Burgundian Gothic Architecture, London, 1960.

BRANNER R., La cathédrale de Bourges et sa place dans l'architecture gothique, Paris / Bourges, 1962.

BRANNER R., Le maître de la cathédrale de Beauvais, in "Art de France," II, 1962, pp. 78-92.

BRANNER R., Paris and the origins of rayonnant Gothic architecture down to 1240, in "Art Bulletin," XLIV, 1962, pp. 39-51.

BRANNER R., St. Louis and the court style in Gothic achitecture, London, 1965.

BRANNER R., Chartres Cathedral, New York, 1969.

BULTEAU A., Monographie de la cathédrale de Chartres, 2nd ed., Chartres, 1887-1892, 3 vols.

CROSBY S. McK., L'abbaye royale de Saint-Denis, Paris, 1953.

CROSBY S. McK., Abbot Suger's Saint-Denis, the New Gothic, in "Studies in Western Art" (XXth Intern. Congr. Hist. Art), New York, 1961, vol. I, pp. 85-91.

CROSBY S. McK., The inside of St.-Denis' west facade, in "Gedenkschrift Ernst Gall," Munich/Berlin, 1965, pp. 59-86.

CUZACQ R., La cathédrale gothique de Bayonne, Mont-de-Marsan, 1965.

DURAND G., Monographie de l'église Notre Dame, cathédrale d'Amiens, Amiens/Paris, 1901-1903, 3 vols.

DURAND P., LASSUS J.B.A., Monographie de la cathédrale de Chartres, Paris, 1867.

ENLART C., Manuel d'archéologie française. Architecture religieuse, Paris, 1919, 2 vols.

FONTAINE G., Pontigny, Paris, 1928.

GALL E., Die gotische Baukunst in Frankreich und Deutschland, vol. I: Die Vorstufen in Nordfrankreich von der Mitte des elften bis gegen Ende des zwölften Jahrhunderts, Leipzig, 1925.

GARDELLES J., La cathédrale Saint-André de Bordeaux. Sa place dans l'évolution de l'architecture et de la sculpture, Bordeaux, 1963.

GAUCHERY R., GAUCHERY-GRODECKI C., Saint-Etienne de Bourges, Paris, 1959.

GOUT P., Le Mont-Saint-Michel, histoire de l'abbaye et de la ville, étude archéologique et architecturale des monuments, Paris, 1910.

GRODECKI L., Chronologie de la cathédrale de Chartres, in "Bulletin Monumental," CXVI, 1958, pp. 91-119.

HACKER-SUCK I., La Sainte-Chapelle et les chapelles palatines du Moyen-Age en France, in "Cahiers Archéologiques," XII, 1962, pp. 217-257.

HAMANN-MAC LEAN R., Zur Baugeschichte der Kathedrale von Reims, in "Gedenkschrift Ernst Gall," 1965, pp. 195-234.

HÉLIOT P., La basilique de Saint-Quentin et l'architecture du Moyen-Age, Paris, 1967.

HOUVET E., La cathédrale de Chartres, Chartres [1919-1921], 7 vols.

JANTZEN H., Kunst der Gotik. Klassische Kathedralen Frankreichs. Chartres, Reims, Amiens, Hamburg, 1957.

KUNZE H., Das Fassadenproblem der französischen Früh-und Hochgothik, Leipzig, 1912.

KURMANN P., La cathédrale Saint-Etienne de Meaux. Etudes architecturales, Geneva/Paris, 1971.

LAMBERT E., L'église des Jacobins de Toulouse et l'architecture dominicaine en France, in "Bulletin Monumental," CIV, 1946, pp. 141-186.

LAMBERT L., Caen roman et gothique. Ses abbayes et son château, Caen, 1935.

LASTEYRIE R., DE, L'architecture religieuse en France à l'époque gothique, Paris, 1926-1927, 2 vols.

LEDRU A., La cathédrale Saint-Julien du Mans, ses évêques, son architecture, son mobilier, Mamers, 1900.

LEFEVRE-PONTALIS E., L'architecture religieuse dans l'ancien diocèse de Soissons au XIème et au XIIème siècle, Paris, 1894, 3 vols.

MÂLE E., L'architecture gothique du Midi de la France, in "Revue des Deux-Mondes," 15 February 1926, pp. 826-857.

MÂLE E., La cathédrale d'Albi, Paris, 1950.

MUSSAT A., Le style gothique de l'Ouest de la France (XIIème-XIIIème siècles), Paris, 1963.

PANOFSKY E., Abbot Suger. On the abbey church of St.-Denis and its art treasures, Princeton, 1946.

REINHARDT H., La cathédrale de Reims. Son histoire, son architecture, sa sculpture, ses vitraux, Paris, 1963.

REY R., L'art gothique du Midi de la France, Paris, 1934.

RUPRICH-ROBERT V., L'architecture normande aux XIème et XIIème siècles en Normandie et en Angleterre, Paris, 1884-1889, 2 vols.

SALET F., La Madeleine de Vézelay, Melun, 1948.

SALET F., La cathédrale du Mans, in "Congrès Archéologique Maine," 1961, CXXIX, pp. 18-58.

SANFAÇON R., L'architecture flamboyante en France, Laval, 1971.

SCHÜRENBERG L., Die kirchliche Baukunst Frankreichs zwischen 1270 und 1380, Berlin, 1934.

SEYMOUR C. JR., Notre-Dame de Noyon in the twelfth century, a study in the early development of gothic architecture, New Haven, 1939.

VAN DER MEER F., Cathédrales méconnues de France, Brussels/Paris, 1968.

VAN DER MEULEN J., Histoire de la construction de la cathédrale Notre-Dame de Chartres après 1194, in "Bulletin de la Société Archéologique d'Eure-et-Loir," 18, 1965, pp. 5-126.

Series: Petites Monographies des Grands Edifices de France, Paris, 1906-1960.

THE LOW COUNTRIES, LORRAINE, AND SWITZERLAND

BACH E., BLONDELL L., BOVY A., *La cathédrale de Lausanne*, Basel, 1944.

BAUM J., CREUTZ M., *Belgische Kunstdenkmäler*, vol. I: *Vom 9. bis Ende des 15. Jhs.*, Munich, 1923.

BLOESCH H., STEINMANN M., *Das Berner Münster*, Bern, 1938.

La cathédrale de Lausanne, collected works, Bern, 1975.

La cathédrale de Metz, collected works published under the direction of M. AUBERT, Paris, 1931.

GANTNER J., *Histoire de l'art en Suisse*, vol. II: *Epoque gothique*, Neuchâtel, 1956.

LEURS C., *Een en ander betreffende de ontwikkeling van de Kerkelijke gothiek in de Nederlanden*, in "Genetse Bijdr.," 9, 1943, p. 137 ff.

LEURS C., *De geschiedenis der bouwkunst in Vlanderen van de Xde to het einde der XVIII de eeuw.*, Antwerp, 1946.

VERMEULEN F., *Handbook tot de Geschiedenis der Nederlandsche Bouwkunst*, The Hague, 1923, 2 vols.

VIELES A., *Les compagnes de construction de la cathédrale de Toul*, in "Bulletin Monumental," 130, 1972, pp. 179-189 and 133, 1975, pp. 233-241.

WARICHEZ J., *La cathédrale de Tournai*, Brussels, 1935.

GERMANIC COUNTRIES

BEYER V., HAEUSSER J.R., LUDMANN J.D., RECHT R., *La cathédrale de Strasbourg*, Strasbourg, 1974.

BICKEL I., *Die Bedeutung der süddeutschen Zisterzienserbauten für den Stilwandel im 12. Jh. von der Spätromanik zur Gotik*, Munich, 1956.

BOCK H., *Der Beginn spätgotischer Architektur in Prag (Peter Parler) und die Beziehungen zu England*, in "Wallraf Richartz Jahrbuch," XXIII, 1961, pp. 191-210.

BRÄUTIGAM G., *Gmünd-Prag-Nürnberg. Die Nürnberger Frauenkirche und der Prager Parlerstil vor 1360*, in "Jahrbuch der Berliner Museen," 3, 1961, pp. 58-75.

BUCHOWIECKI W., *Die gotischen Kirchen Österreichs*, Vienna, 1952.

BURMEISTER W., *Norddeutsche Backsteindome*, Berlin, 1938.

CLASEN K.H., *Deutsche Gewölbe der Spätgotik*, Berlin, 1958.

DONIN R.K., *Die Bettelordenskirchen in Österreich. Zur Entwicklung der österreichischen Gothik*, Baden (Vienna), 1935.

DÖRRENBERG I., *Das zisterzienser Kloster Maulbronn*, Würzburg, 1937.

EYDOUX H.P., *L'architecture des églises cisterciennes d'Allemagne*, Paris, 1952.

FATH M., *Die Baukunst der frühen Gotik im Mittelrheingebiet*, in "Mainzer Zeitschrift," 63-64, 1968-1969, pp. 1-38 and 65, 1970, pp. 43-92.

FINK E., *Die gotischen Hallenkirchen in Westfalen*, Emsdetten, 1934.

FISCHER F.W., *Die spätgotische Kirchenbaukunst am Mittelrhein*, Heidelberg, 1962.

FLEMMING J., LEHMANN E., SCHUBERT E., *Dom und Domschatz zu Halberstadt*, Vienna/Cologne, 1974.

FREY D., *Die Denkmale des Stiftes Heiligenkreuz* in "Österreichische Kunstopographic," XIX, 1926.

GERSTENBERG K., *Deutsche Sondergotik. Eine Untersuchung über das Wesen des späten Mittelalters*, Darmstadt, 1969.

HAMANN R., KÄSTNER W., *Die Elisabethkirche zu Marburg*, Marburg, 1929.

HEMPEL E., *Geschichte der deutschen Baukunst* (Deutsche Kunstgeschichte), Munich, 1949.

KONOW H., *Die Baukunst der Bettelorden am Oberrhein* (Forschungen zur Geschichte Kunst am Oberrhein), Berlin, 1954.

KRAUTHEIMER R., *Die Kirchen der Bettelorden in Deutschland* (Deutsche Beiträge zur Kunstwissenschaft), Cologne, 1925.

KUNST H.J., *Der Domchor zu Köln und die Hochgotische Kirchenarchitektur in Norddeutschland*, in "Niederdeutsche Beiträge zur Kunstgeschichte," 8, 1969, pp. 9-40.

KUNST H.J., *Die Entstehung des Hallenumgangchors. Der Dom zu Werden an der Aller und seine Stellung in der gotischen Architektur*, in "Marburger Jahrbuch für Kunstwissenschaft," 18, 1969, pp. 1-104.

KUNZE H., *Der Stand unseres Wissens um die Baugeschichte des Strassburger Münsters*, in "Elsass-Lothringen Jahrbuch," XVIII, 1939, pp. 63-115.

MEYER-BARKAUSEN W., *Das grosse Jahrhundert kölnischer Kirchenbaukunst 1150 bis 1250*, Cologne, 1952.

MRUSEK H.J., *Drei deutsche Dome (Quedlinburg, Magdeburg, Halberstadt)*, Dresden, 1963.

OTTE H., *Handbuch der kirchlichen Kunst, Archäologie des deutschen Mittelalters*, 5th ed. Leipzig, 1883-1884.

PAATZ W., *Die Marien Kirche in Lübeck*, Burg, 1926.

RECHT R., *L'Alsace gothique de 1300 à 1365. Etude d'architecture religieuse*, Colmar, 1974.

REINHARDT H., *La cathédrale de Strasbourg*, Paris, 1972.

RINGSHAUSEN G., *Die spätgotische Architektur in Deutschland unter besonderer Berücksichtigung ihrer Beziehungen zu Burgund im Anfang des 15. Jahrhunderts*, in "Zeitschrift des deutschen Vereins für Kunstwissenschaft," XVII, 1-4, 1973, pp. 63-78.

SCHMOLL GEN. EISENWERTH J.A., *Das Kloster Chor und die askanische Architektur in der Mark Brandenburg, 1260-1320*, Berlin, 1961.

SCHOTES P., *Spätgotische Einstützenkirchen und zweischiffige Hallenkirchen im Rheinland*, Aachen, 1970.

STIEHL O., *Das deutsche Rathaus im Mittelalter*, Leipzig, 1905.

THÜMMLER H., *Mittelalterliche Baukunst im Weserraum*, in "Kunst und Kultur im Weserraum, 800-1600" (Exposition Corvey, 1966).

THURM S., *Norddeutscher Backsteinbau, gotischen Backsteinhallenkirchen mit dreiapsidialem Chorschluss*, Berlin, 1935.

ZASKE N., *Gotische Backsteinkirchen Norddeutschlands zwischen Elbe und Oder*, Leipzig, 1968.

ZYKAN J., *Die Stephankirche in Wien*, Vienna, 1962.

Collections: *Deutsche Bauten*, Burg bei Madgeburg, 1920-1939.

ENGLAND

BILSON J., *Durham cathedral: the chronology of its vaults*, in "Archaeological Journal," LXXXIX, 1922, pp. 101-160.

BOASE T.S.R., *English art, 1100-1216* (The Oxford History of English Art), Oxford, 1953.

BOCK H., *Der Decorated Style, Untersuchungen zur englischen Kathedralarchitektur der 1. Hälfte des 14. Jhs.*, Heidelberg, 1962.

BOND F., *Gothic architecture in England. An analysis of the origin and development of English church architecture from the Norman conquest to the dissolution of the monasteries*, London, 1905.

BOND F., *An Introduction to English Church Architecture from the 11th to the 16th century*, London, 1914.

BONY J., *French Influences on the Origins of Gothic Architecture*, in "Journal of the Warburg and Courtauld Institutes," XII, 1949, pp. 1-15.

BRANNER R., *Westminster Abbey and the French Court Style*, in "Journal of the Society of Architectural Historians," XXIII, 1964, pp. 3-18.

BRIEGER P., *English Art, 1216-1307* (The Oxford History of English Art), Oxford, 1957.

BROWN R.A., COLVIN H.M., TAYLOR A.J., *The history of king's works*, London, 1963, 3 vols.

CLIFTON-TAYLOR A., *The cathedrals of England*, New York, 1970.

COOK G.H., *The story of Gloucester Cathedral*, London, 1952.

COOK G.H., *The English medieval parish church*, London, 1954.

COOK G.H., *English collegiate churches of the Middle Ages*, London, 1959.

COOK G.H., *Medieval chantries and chantries chapels*, London, 1963.

EVANS J., *English art, 1307-1461* (The Oxford History of English Art), Oxford, 1949.

FLETCHER B., *A History of Architecture*, New York, 1950.

GARDNER S., *A guide to English Gothic architecture*, Cambridge, 1922.

HARVEY J.H., *Gothic England, a survey of national culture, 1300-1500*, London, 1947.

HARVEY J.H., FELTON H., *The English cathedrals*, London, 1950.

HAYTER W., *William of Wykeham, Patron of the Arts*, London, 1970.

MARTIN A.R., *Franciscan architecture in England*, Manchester, 1937.

MOORE C.H., *Medieval Church Architecture in England*, New York, 1912.

POWER C.E., *English medieval architecture*, London, 1923, 3 vols.

SALZMAN L.F., *Building in England down to 1540. A Documentary History*, Oxford, 1952.

VALE E., *Cambridge and its colleges*, London, 1959.

WEBB G.F., *Gothic architecture in England*, London, 1951.

WEBB G.F., *Architecture in Britain: The Middle Ages* (The Pelican History of Art), Harmondsworth, 1956.

ITALY

ARGAN G.C., *L'architettura italiana del Duecento e Trecento*, Florence, 1937.

ARSLAN E., *Venezia gotica. L'architettura civile gotica veneziana*, Milan, 1970.

BARTALINI A., *L'architettura civile del medioevo in Pisa*, Pisa, 1937.

BERTAUX E., *L'art dans l'Italie méridionale*, Paris, 1904.

BESCAPÉ G., MEZZANOTTE P., *Il Duomo di Milano*, Milan, 1965.

BIEBRACH K., *Die holzgedeckten Franziskaner- und Dominikanerkirchen in Umbrien und Toskana* (Beiträge zur Bauwissenschaft), Berlin, 1908.

BONELLI R., *Il Duomo di Orvieto e l'architettura italiana del Duecento e Trecento*, Città di Castello, 1952.

BRAUNFELS W., *Mittelalterliche Stadtbaukunst in der Toskana*, Berlin, 1953.

CARLI E., *Il Duomo di Orvieto*, Rome, 1965.

CASSI RAMELLI A., *Luca Beltrami e il Duomo di Milano*, Milan, 1965.

CHIERICI G., *Il palazzo italiano, dal secolo XI al secolo XIX*, Milan, 1952-1957, 3 vols.

DECKER H., *Gotik in Italien*, Vienna, 1964.

DELLWING H., *Studien zur Baukunst der Bettelorden im Veneto. Die Gotik der monumentalen Gewölbebasiliken*, Munich, 1970.

ENLART C., *Origines françaises de l'architecture gothique en Italie*, Paris, 1894.

FIORENSA A., *Il gotico catalano in Sardegna*, in "Bollettino del Centro di Studi per la storia dell'Architettura," 17, 1961, pp. 81-116.

FRACCARO DE LONGHI L., *L'architettura delle chiese cistercensi italiane*, Milan, 1958.

FRANKLIN J.W., *The cathedrals of Italy*, London, 1958.

HERTEIN E., *Die Basilika San Francesco in Assisi. Gestalt, Bedeutung, Herkunft*, Munich, 1964.

KLEINSCHMIDT B., *Die Basilika S. Francesco in Assisi*, 3rd ed., Berlin, 1915-1938.

KRÖNIG W., *Hallenkirchen in Mittelitalien*, in "Kunstgeschichtliches Jahrbuch der Bibliotheka Hertziana," 2, 1938, p. 1 ff.

Il nostro Duomo, collected works, Milan, 1960.

MORETTI I., STOPANI R., *Chiese gotiche nel contado fiorentino*, Florence, 1969.

MORETTI M., *L'architettura medioevale in Abruzzo (dal VI al XVI secolo)*, Rome [1971].

PAATZ W., *Werden und Wesen der Trecento Architektur in Toskana. Die grossen Meister als Schöpfer einer neuen Baukunst: Die Meister von S. Maria Novella; Niccolo Pisano; Giovanni Pisano; Arnolfo di Cam-bio und Giotto*, Burg, 1937.

PAATZ W., PAATZ E., *Die Kirchen von Florenz. Ein kunstgeschichtliches Handbuch*, Frankfurt, 1940-1954, 6 vols.

Il palazzo ducale di Venezia, collected works, Turin, 1971.

PAUL J., *Der Palazzo Vecchio in Florenz, Ursprung und Bedeutung seiner Form*, Florence, 1969.

RODOLICO F., MARCHINI G., *I Palazzi del popolo nei communi toscani del medio evo*, Florence, 1962.

ROMANINI A.M., *Le Chiese a sala nell'architettura "gotica" lombarda*, in "Arte Lombarda," 3, 1958, p. 48 ff.

ROMANINI A.M., *L'architettura gotica in Lombardia*, Rome, 1965.

SALMI M., *L'architettura nell'Aretino: il periodo gotico*, in "Atti del XII congresso di storia dell'architettura, Arezzo, 10-15 September, 1961. L'architettura nell'Aretino," Rome, 1969, pp. 69-103.

SCHÖNE W., *Studien zur Oberkirche von Assisi*, in "Festschrift Kurt Bauch," 1957, pp. 50-116.

SUPINO J.B., *L'architettura sacra in Bologna nei secoli XIII e XIV*, Bologna, 1909.

TOESCA P., *Storia dell'arte italiana*, vol. II: *Il Trecento*, Turin, 1951.

WAGNER-RIEGER R., *Die italienische Baukunst zu Beginn der Gotik*, Graz / Cologne, 1956-1957.

WAGNER-RIEGER R., *Zur Typologie italienischer Bettelordenskirchen*, in "Römische Mitteilungen," II, 1957-1958, pp. 266-298.

WAGNER-RIEGER R., *S. Lorenzo Maggiore in Neapel und die süditalienische Architektur unter den ersten Königen aus dem Hause Anjou*, in "Miscellanea Bibliothecae Herzianae zu Ehren von Leo

Bruhns, Franz Graf Wolff Metternich, Ludwig Schudt,'' Munich, 1961, pp. 31-143.

WHITE J., *Art and Architecture in Italy, 1250-1400* (The Pelican History of Art), Hardmondsworth, 1966.

SPAIN AND PORTUGAL

ANGULO IÑIGUEZ D., *Arquitectura mudéjar sevillana de los siglos XIII, XIV, y XV*, Seville, 1922.

JOSÉ MARÍA DE AZCÁRATE RISTORI, *El protogótico hispánico* (Real Academia de Bellas Artes de San Fernando), Madrid, 1974.

BASSEGODA Y AMIGÓ B., *La catedral de Barcelona*, Barcelona, n.d.

BASSEGODA Y AMIGÓ B., *La catedral de Gerona*, Barcelona, 1889.

BASSEGODA Y AMIGÓ B., *Santa María de la Mar*, Barcelona, 1925.

BLANCH M., *L'art gothique en Espagne*, Barcelona, 1972.

CHAMAÑO MARTÍNEZ J.M., *Contribución al estudio del Gótico en Galicia (Diócesis de Santiago)*, Valladolid, 1962.

CHICÓ M.T., *Arquitectura gòtica em Portugal*, Sul, 1954.

CHUECA GOITIA F., *Historia de la arquitectura espanola, Edad antigua y edad media*, Madrid, 1965, 2 vols.

CONTRERAS LOZOYA J., *Historia del arte hispánico*, vol. II, Barcelona, 1934.

DURLIAT M., *L'art dans le royaume de Majorque. Les débuts de l'art gothique en Roussillon, en Cerdagne et aux Baléares*, Toulouse, 1962.

DURLIAT M., *L'architecture espagnole*, Toulouse, 1966.

ELÍAS F., *La catedral de Barcelona*, Barcelona, 1926.

GÓMEZ-MORENO M., *El primer monasterio español de cistercienses: Moreruela*, in "Boletín de la Sociedad española de excursiones," XIV, 1906, pp. 97-105.

GÓMEZ-MORENO M., *La catedral de Sevilla*, in "Boletín de la Real Academia de la Historia," XCII, 1928.

GUDIOL Y RICHART J., *La catedral de Toledo*, Madrid, 1948.

HARVEY J.H., *The cathedrals of Spain*, London, 1957.

HAUPT A., *Die Baukunst der Renaissance in Portugal*, Frankfurt, 1890.

HERSEY C.K., *The Salmantine Lanterns: their origin and development*, Cambridge, Mass., 1937.

LAMBERT E., *L'architecture bourguignonne et la cathédrale d'Avila*, in "Bulletin Monumental," 83, 1924, pp. 263-292.

LAMBERT E., *L'art gothique en Espagne aux XIIème et XIIIème siècles*, Paris, 1931.

LAMBERT E., *L'art gothique à Séville après la reconquête*, in "Revue archéologique," 1932, pp. 155-165.

LAMBERT E., *L'art portugais*, Paris, 1948.

LAMBERT E., *L'église du monastère dominicain de Batalha et l'architecture cistercienne*, in "Mélanges d'études portugaises, offerts à G. Le Gentil," Lisbon, 1949, pp. 243-256.

LAMBERT E., *La catedral de Pamplona*, in "Principe de Viana," XII, 1951.

LAMPÉREZ Y ROMEA V., *Historia de la arquitectura cristiana española en la edad media*, Barcelona / Madrid, 1908-1909, 2 vols.

LAMPÉREZ Y ROMEA V., *Catedral de Burgos*, in "Las obras maestras de la arquitectura y de la deco-ración en España," I, Madrid, 1912.

LAVEDAN P., *L'architecture gothique religieuse en Catalogne, Valence et Baléares*, Paris, 1935.

LAVEDAN P., *L'église Sainte-Marie-de-la-Mer à Barcelone*, in "Congrès Archéologique. Catalogne," CXVII, 1959, pp. 75-83.

RUBIO Y BELLVER J., *La catedral de Mallorca*, Barcelona, 1922.

SERRA I RÀFOLS E., *La nau de la Sen de Girona*, in "Miscellània Puig i Cadafalch," vol. I, Barcelona, 1947-1951, pp. 185-204.

STREET G.E., *Some account of gothic architecture in Spain*, London/Toronto, 1924.

TORRES BALBÁS L., *Arquitectura gótica* (Ars Hispaniae), Madrid, 1952.

VILLACAMPA C.G., *La capilla del condestable, de la catedral de Burgos*, in "Archivio español de arte y arqueología," IV, 1928, pp. 25-44.

WATSON W.C., *Portuguese Architecture*, London, 1908.

Collections, *Arte em Portugal*, Oporto, 1928-1967.

NORDIC AND EASTERN COUNTRIES

ALNAES A., ELIASSEN G., LUND R., PEDERSEN A., PLATOU O., *Norwegian architecture throughout the ages*, Oslo, 1950.

BOETHIUS G., ROMDAHL A.L., *Uppsala domkyrka 1258 till 1435*, Upsala, 1935.

CLASEN K.H., *Die mittelalterliche Kunst im Gebiete der Deutschordensstaaten Preussen*, Königsberg, 1927.

CURMAN S., *Sveriges Kyrkor*, Stockholm, 1912-1920.

ENLART C., *L'art gothique et la Renaissance en Chypre*, Paris, 1899, 2 vols.

FISCHER G., *Domkirken in Trondheim*, Trondheim, 1965.

GALL E., *Danzig und das Land an der Weichsel*, Munich, 1953.

GEREVICH L., *Mitteleuropäische Bauhütten und die Spätgotik*, in "Acta historiae artium," V, 1958, pp. 241-282.

KUTAL A., *L'art gothique en Bohême*, Prague, 1972.

LIBAL D., *Gotická architektura v Cechách a na Morave*, Prague, 1948.

LINDBLOM A., *Sveriges Konsthistorica fran Forntid till Nutid*, vol. I, Stockholm, 1944.

MADSEN H., *Kirkekunst i Danmark*, Odense, 1965, 3 vols.

MARÖSI E., *Stiltendenzen und Zentren der Spätgotischen Architektur in Ungarn*, in "Jahrbuch des Kunsthistorischen Institutes der Universität Graf," 6, 1971, pp. 1-38.

MENCL V., *Ceská architektura doby Lucemburské*, Prague, 1948.

MENCL V., *Die Aufgabe der Donauländer in der Reform der gotischen Architektur des 14. und 15. Jh.*, in "Acta historiae artium," 13, 1967, pp. 51-59.

MIOBEDZKI A., *Zarys dziejów architektury w Polsce, Wydanie drugie poprawione i uzupelnione*, Warsaw, 1968.

ROOSVAL J., *Die Kirchen Gotlands. Ein Beitrag zur mittelalterlichen Kunstgeschichte Schwedens*, Leipzig, 1911.

SWIECHOWSKI Z., *Regiony w póznogotychkiejarchitekturze polski*, in "Pózny gotyk," 1965, p. 113 ff.

SWOBODA K.M., *Gotik in Böhmen*, Munich, 1969.

ZACHWATOWICZ J., *Architecktura polska*, Warsaw, 1966.